AMC'S COMPLETE GUIDE TO TRAIL BUILDING AND MAINTENANCE

PROVEN TECHNIQUES • SAFETY GUIDELINES • EQUIPMENT TIPS

FIFTH EDITION

EDITED BY RYAN HARVEY

T0302676

AMC SKILLS SERIES

Appalachian Mountain Club Books
Boston, Massachusetts

AMC is a nonprofit organization, and sales of AMC Books fund our mission of protecting the Northeast outdoors. If you appreciate our efforts and would like to become a member or make a donation to AMC, visit outdoors.org, call 800-372-1758, or contact us at Appalachian Mountain Club, 10 City Square, Boston, MA 02129.

outdoors.org/books-maps

Distributed by National Book Network.

Front cover photograph of the Bay Circuit Trail by Paula Champagne © Appalachian Mountain Club
Back cover photograph of Crawford Path by Paula Champagne © Appalachian Mountain Club
Photograph of Andrew Norkin by Heather Wyman
Photograph of Robert Proudman courtesy of the Appalachian Trail Conservancy
All other photographs © Appalachian Mountain Club unless otherwise noted
Cover design by Katie Metz
Interior design by Abigail Coyle
Illustrations by Aaron North © Appalachian Mountain Club

Library of Congress Cataloging-in-Publication Data

Names: Harvey, Ryan, editor. | Appalachian Mountain Club. issuing body.
Title: AMC's complete guide to trail building and maintenance / edited by Ryan Harvey.
Other titles: Complete guide to trail building and maintenance
Description: Fifth edition. | Boston, Massachusetts : Appalachian Mountain Club Books, 2021. | Includes bibliographical references and index.
Identifiers: LCCN 2021008216 (print) | LCCN 2021008217 (ebook) | ISBN 9781628421040 (trade paperback) | ISBN 9781628421057 (epub) | ISBN 9781628421064 (mobi)
Subjects: LCSH: Trails--Design and construction. | Trails--Maintenance and repair.
Classification: LCC TE304 .D46 2021 (print) | LCC TE304 (ebook) | DDC 634.9/3--dc23
LC record available at https://lccn.loc.gov/2021008216
LC ebook record available at https://lccn.loc.gov/2021008217

The paper used in this publication meets the minimum requirements of the American National Standard for Information Sciences-Permanence of Paper for Printed Library Materials, ANSI Z39.48-1984. ∞

Interior pages and cover are printed on responsibly harvested paper stock certified by The Forest Stewardship Council®, an independent auditor of responsible forestry practices.
Printed in the United States of America, using vegetable-based inks.

7 6 5 4 3 2 1 21 22 23 24 25 26 27

In Memory of Andrew Norkin
1963–2021
AMC White Mountain Trails Manager and
Director of Trails & Recreation Management 1999–2021

Robert David Proudman
1948–2018
Trail builder, steward, and advocate

CONTENTS

FOREWORD

This newly revised fifth edition parallels the 200th anniversary of Crawford Path, the oldest continually maintained hiking trail in the United States. Ethan Allen Crawford first cut this 8½-mile trail in 1819 and subsequently used it for foot travel and horse packing up through the southern Presidential Range to the summit of Mount Washington, beginning at the notch that now honors his name: Crawford Notch. One may wonder if the Crawford family ever envisioned that this trail would continue on for another 200 years. Did they imagine that it would be one of the premier hiking trails in North America? Much of the route remains in the same location due to work performed on it through the decades.

With this trail bicentennial and the fifth edition of *AMC's Complete Guide to Trail Building and Maintenance* it appears there is another outdoor recreation boom. Unprecedented numbers of hikers, backpackers, and outdoor recreationists frequent local and state parks, national forests, and national parks across the country. Therefore, more and more people are tromping the trails therein. This presents land managers and trail organizations the challenge of accommodating this increased traffic while stewarding the ecological integrity of the lands these trails thread their way through. It is a good challenge in that more people are getting exercise in fresh air and exploring the landscape, but this comes at the expense of resource degradation and the diminished opportunity for experiencing the sense of wildness and solitude that one may seek in the backcountry.

Throughout the recent decades, specialization in trail work has given rise to trail professionals, a career niche within the natural resource and contractor communities. Some age-old woods/trails skills have become more refined, and other skills remain practically unaltered. Trails are being integrated into regional and community planning. The question is how do we, as trail stewards and professionals, adapt to this surge of use while keeping the ecological integrity and character of the land that these trails explore? How do we maintain opportunities to experience a sense of wildness? As trail workers and stewards, we directly shape and influence this ongoing dialogue with the structures we build and the ethics we promote. Therefore, the members of the trail community have an important responsibility.

More than 100 years ago, many trails in the northeastern United States were laid out for use by a select group of individuals, especially affluent travelers who had time to recreate. Most trails were constructed as a way to get quickly from point A to point B so people could reach the summit of a mountain via the most straightforward route, usually directly up the "fall line" or along river corridors. During the heyday of trail construction, newly formed trail clubs and inns employed crews to maintain their interest areas, which saw few visitors until the modern era. The trails withstood limited travel, but many decades of use and erosion greatly changed their character and durability; today, trail maintainers face the significant task of combating the cumulative effects. Some trails have been nearly eroded away (especially steep trails with poor soil), leaving an unsightly scar on the landscape with sometimes little option for rehabilitation.

By planning, constructing, and rehabilitating networks of trails through the years, maintainers have learned to approach new trail design with a more complete understanding of the impact on future resources as well as the experience offered to users. Trail professionals today know that a thorough and comprehensive plan is essential for a route that will withstand the rigors of erosion and user traffic for many years.

One imminent issue that has permeated most disciplines and institutions is the threat of climate change, and trail building and maintenance is no exception. This threat may not directly change the nature of trail-building techniques, but it puts increased emphasis on planning and good-quality construction in relation to increasingly severe weather events. Climate change underlines the fundamental importance of good integrated design and strong construction with the view of longevity and resilience.

This book will cover the tools, layout, and techniques used to build, maintain, and rehabilitate trails while minimizing erosion and resource degradation. Trail sustainability can be achieved while protecting trail environs, ensuring ecosystem integrity and durabilty in the face of increasingly severe weather patterns and significant hiker traffic. The beginning chapters walk the reader through the planning and design phase; the central chapters offer detailed, practical guidelines for tools, safety protocols, general trail construction methodologies, and structures for a variety of terrains and materials, with edited and updated information throughout. New chapters in this fifth edition address accessible and universal trail design and trail crew leadership. New and expanded resource information is also included. For those interested in building, relocating, or rejuvenating a trail or trail structure, this book provides essential guidelines for each project phase.

Even though a lot has changed since the cutting of Crawford Path, one aspect remains timeless: the hard work of trail building and maintenance. One can safely surmise that the spirit of adventure and love of these wild places was shared 200 years ago as Ethan Crawford hacked his way through the dense krummholz, breaking above treeline and threading himself along the ridge, leading the way for millions to follow. In this spirit we can celebrate in the timeless, tough, and satisfying labor of trail work!

ACKNOWLEDGMENTS

AMC's Trails Department manages over 1,800 miles of trails in the Northeast. They work with countless land managers across ten states, support thousands of trails volunteers, and tackle basic maintenance needs to technical trail projects on public lands. It is the collective expertise of the current staff that have built on the 100 years of AMC trail stewardship that makes this text a success.

Ryan Harvey would like to thank Bethann Weick, who reviewed much of the edited and revised content with precision and care. Thanks to colleagues and mentors both current and former, within the trails and forest management community from whom I learned much along the way.

The following AMC Trails Department staff contributed to review of content for the fifth edition: Andrew Norkin, Alex DeLucia, Amanda Peterson, Zack Urgese, Joe Roman, Kate Johnson, Christine Viola, Bridget Likely, and Aaron North. Photo collection and new photos for the fifth edition were provided by Joe Roman, Zack Urgese, Kate Johnson, and Ryan Harvey. Thank you to Aaron North for creating the new illustrations.

CHAPTER 1

TRAIL FORMATS AND ANATOMY

AT-A-GLANCE

Before you embark on a trail project, familiarity with trail design and its components is essential.

- ➔ **Understand different trail formats and designs:** Learn the kinds of trails and their ideal uses.
- ➔ **Understand basic trail anatomy:** Familiarize yourself with the parts of the trail to determine which ones you will need.

➔ TRAIL FORMATS

The general trail format will most likely be determined by the initial scope of the proposed project and therefore its use. Three major formats can be combined to compose a trail system.

The loop (see figure 1.1) is popular for day-use trails because it enables easy access and parking. Hikers do not have to return on the same trail, thus maximizing interest and satisfaction.

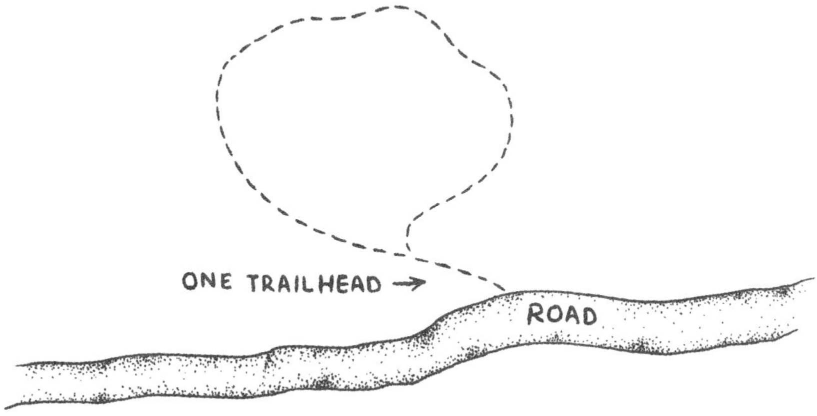

Figure 1.1. A loop design starts and ends at the same location.

The horseshoe (see figure 1.2), which sports two separate trailheads, can be especially valuable in areas where public transportation is available. It can also be used as an alternative to auto travel on roads where distances between terminuses are not too great. Ski touring trail development in the Mount Washington Valley of New Hampshire has trailheads at inns and restaurants in the valley that are connected by trails in the horseshoe format.

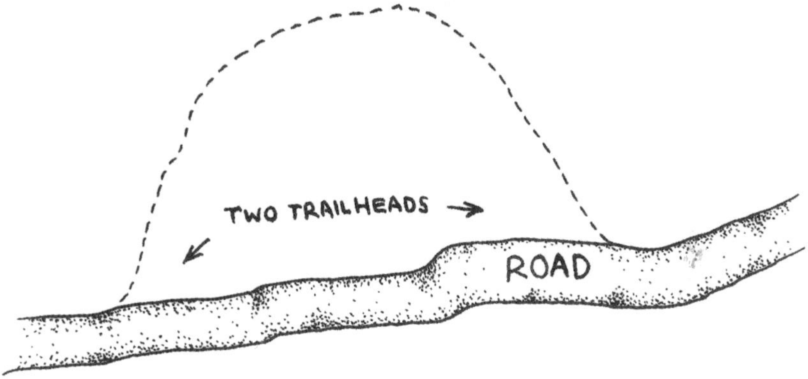

Figure 1.2. A horseshoe design requires a shuttle or road walk.

The line format, also known as "out and back" (see figure 1.3), is the simplest and most common format for trails. It connects two points—the roadside trailhead and the destination. Good examples are fire wardens' trails to lookout towers on mountain summits. Long-distance trails, such as the Appalachian Trail and Pacific Crest Trail, are prime examples of trails in the line format. Line-style trails with high scenic value are augmented with side paths, alternate routes, and connectors to form trail systems.

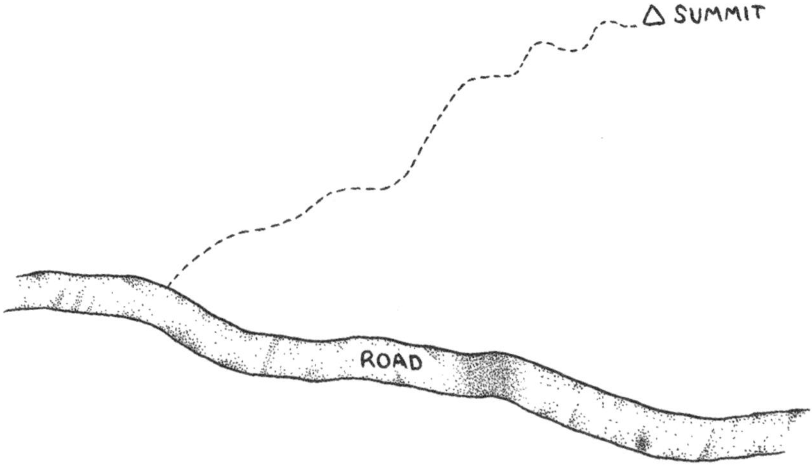

Figure 1.3. An "out and back" trail is an efficient way to get from point A to B.

A trail system (see figure 1.4) combines formats to satisfy diverse recreation needs. Careful design will provide trails for various users with different expectations. Multiday backpackers, day hikers, and others all can be served by a well-designed system.

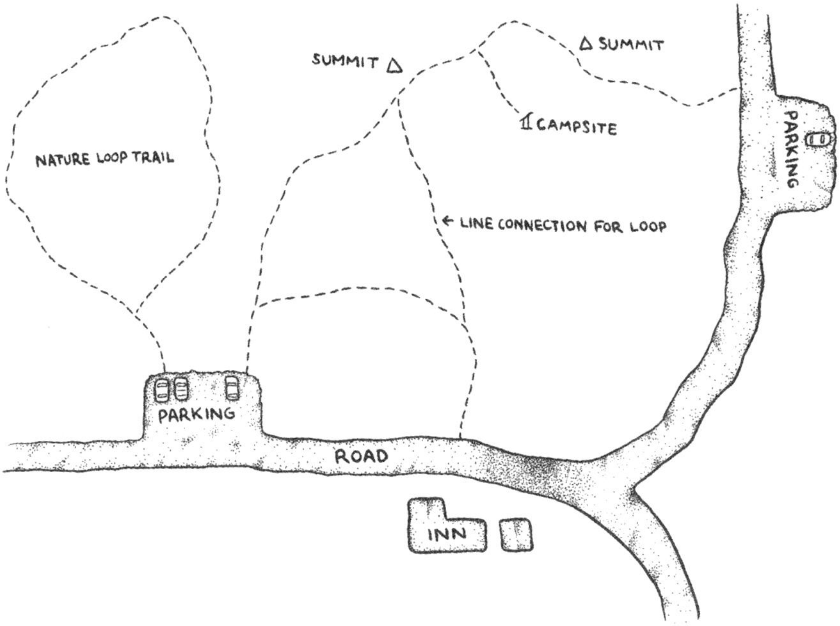

Figure 1.4. A trail system combines out and back, loop, and horseshoe designs.

➔ UNDERSTANDING TRAIL ANATOMY

Before getting started on a trail project, it is important to understand the components of a sustainable trail system because these components should complement each other as a hiker experiences a trail.

All trails have *termini*: the *trailhead*, or start of the trail (usually at roadside), and the destination, which could be a mountain summit, waterfall, historic site, or other notable feature. Destinations along any single trail in a system can also include other paths and possible campsites or overnight facilities.

The trail *treadway*, or trail tread, is the surface upon which the hiker makes direct contact with the ground (see figure 1.5). The treadway is the most important component of any foot trail. All improvements to a natural surface treadway are made to conserve soil resources while protecting surrounding vegetation and bodies of water. These improvements (which often also make hiking easier) usually involve tread hardening and soil stabilization to prevent the trail from shifting, eroding, or becoming muddy. Popular routes in sensitive areas, such as slopes and wet terrain, will inevitably be damaged; therefore, effective maintenance of the treadway may require reconstruction and rehabilitation of the original soil profile.

Figure 1.5. The treadway is what users make direct contact with and can consist of different soils, rock, wood, and so on.

The *trail clearing limit* is the area around the treadway that is cleared for passage of hikers (see figure 1.6). The trail clearing width is usually 4 to 6 feet wide, and the trail clearing height is usually 8 to 12 feet, depending on intended use and landowner/agency management directives. If a trail has other uses besides hiking, such as cross-country skiing or mountain biking, the corridor will be wider.

Within the trail clearing limit, the treadway is the traveled path, and the adjacent area on the slope comprises the *backslope* and *downslope*. The backslope is above the treadway and the downslope is below. Both features are important to consider when dealing with clearing limits for the trail and tread stability.

The *buffer zone*, or *protective zone*, is the space on each side of the trail clearing (see figure 1.7). Buffer zones diminish the impact of activities detrimental to the hiking experience, such as residential development, mining, or logging. While hikers may still hear, see, or even smell such activities, the buffer does provide some

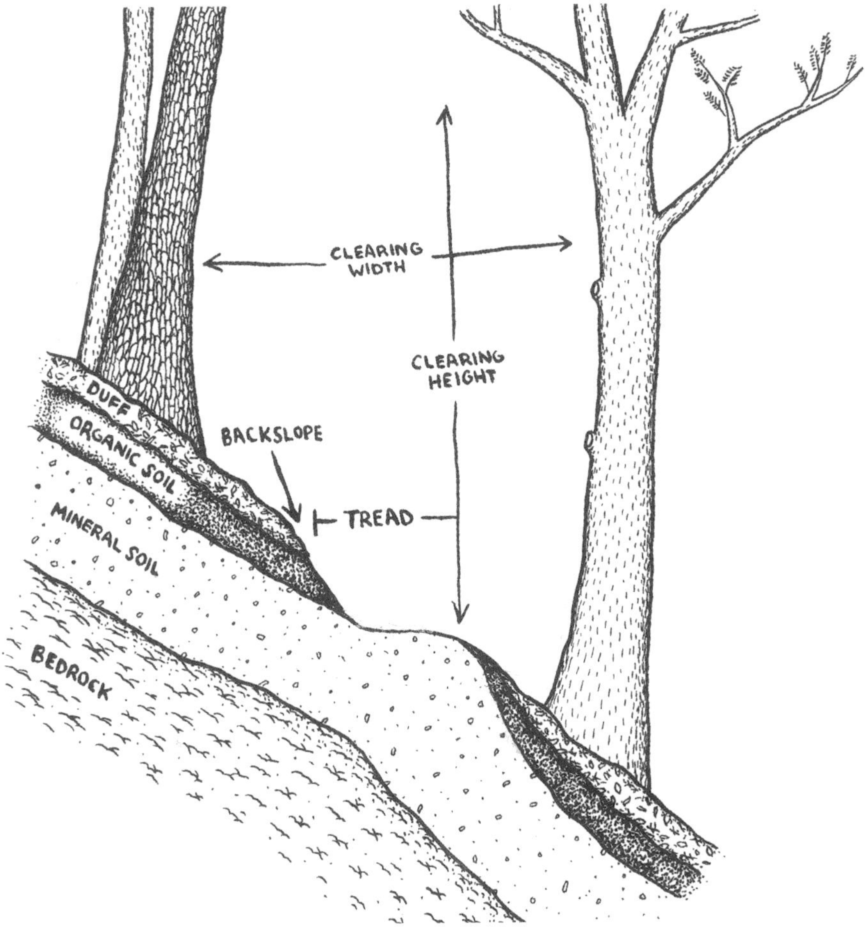

Figure 1.6. Many hiking trails have a 4-by-8-foot clearing limit, although these dimensions can vary.

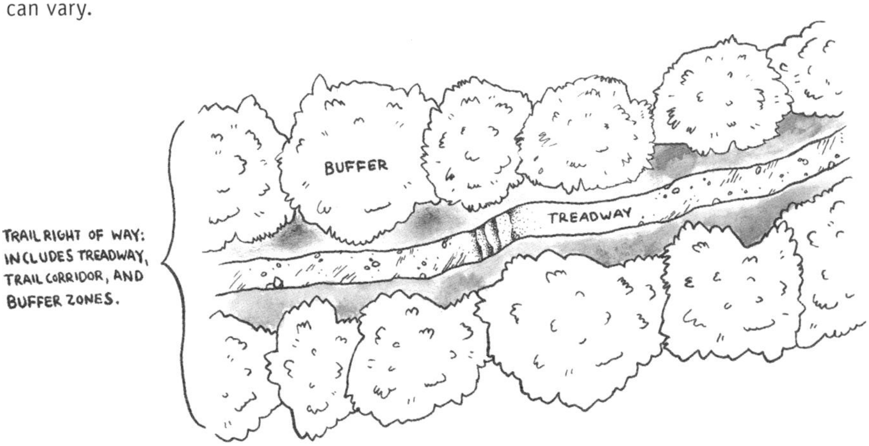

Figure 1.7. Buffer zones help insulate the user within the trail corridor. The trail corridor is the space between buffer zones and includes the treadway.

1

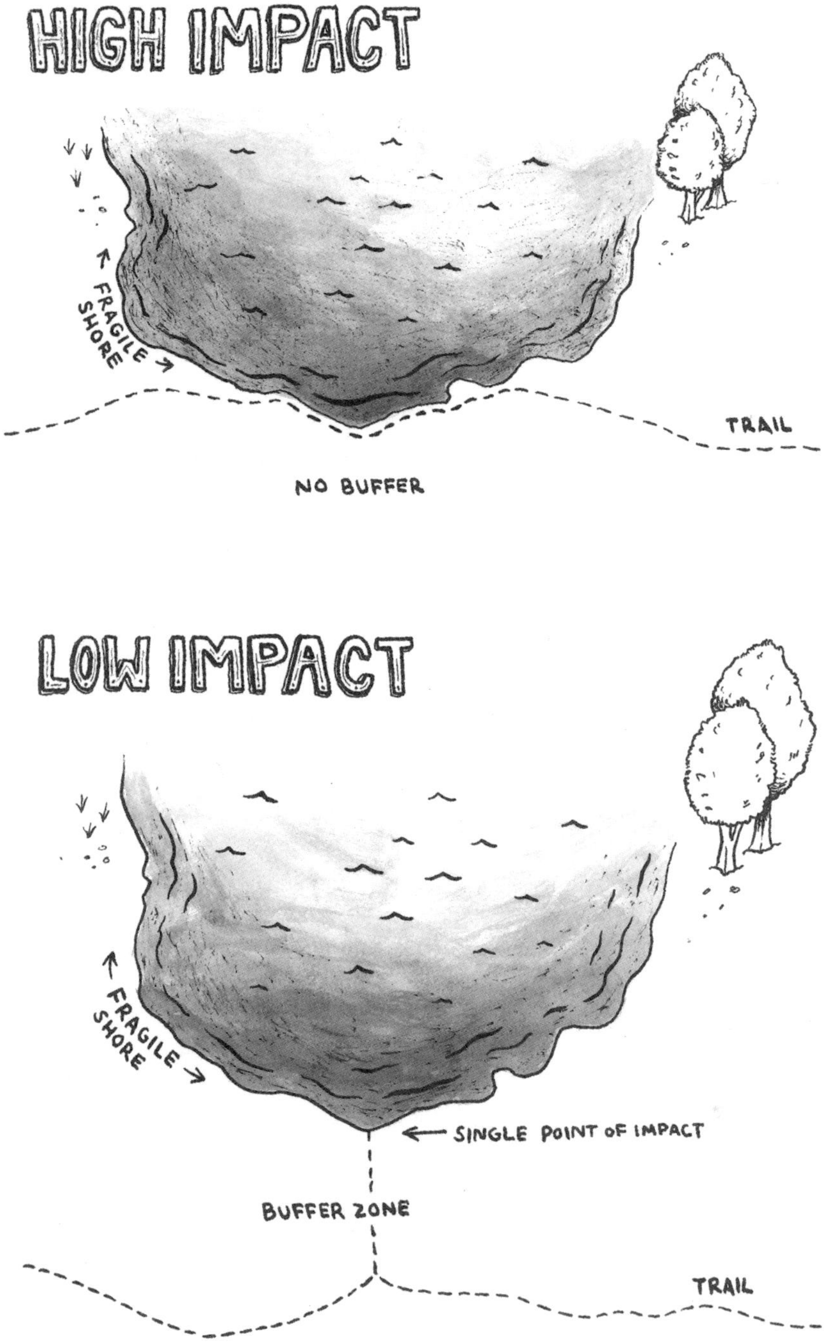

Figure 1.8. Buffer zones help protect sensitive areas from user impacts.

degree of mitigation. Buffers are also used to protect particularly fragile areas from hikers. Trail layout around sensitive plant communities, riparian areas, and exemplary ecological communities should include buffers to protect these sites from becoming disturbed by trail traffic (see figure 1.8).

The *trail corridor* includes the treadway, clearing limit, buffer zones, and all the lands that make up the environment surrounding the trail (see figure 1.7). The U.S. Forest Service has called it the "zone of travel influence." This area is the most likely to be affected by trail traffic and to have an impact on the hiker's experience.

In particularly important trail systems, such as the Appalachian Trail and other routes governed by legislative authority within the National Trails System, the trail corridor takes on added importance. Legislation passed by the United States Congress requires that the corridor of the Appalachian Trail be protected from developments that would be detrimental to its natural quality. Virtually the entire Appalachian Trail and its zone of influence are protected by a corridor averaging 1,000 feet. However, in open forests, on lakeshores, and above treeline the delineated corridor does not adequately include all the zone of influence as the landscape seen by the hiker includes the trail's "view shed."

CHAPTER 2

PLANNING A TRAIL PROJECT

AT-A-GLANCE

Interacting with landowners is an important step in the trail-building process.

- ➔ **Research landowners:** Consult local records and speak with residents and government officials to learn who owns the land on a potential trail site.
- ➔ **Communication:** Communicate with landowners to determine their concerns.
- ➔ **Permission and protection:** Make legal arrangements with landowners to establish a trail right of way and other use agreements.

Planning a new trail construction or rehabilitation project can be one of the most rewarding and challenging experiences that one may undertake. There are many reasons to build a trail, including the promotion of mental and physical wellness, enjoyment of nature, access to natural features or cultural landmarks, regional economic development, or the creation of a tool for future conservation efforts.

When approaching a potential new trail project, it is important to ask: "Is this trail needed, and will the effort put into the development and construction be worthwhile?" Hiking and other forms of outdoor recreation have become increasingly popular, but use is not uniform across all trail systems. In certain areas, trails may be overdeveloped to counter high demand, while in other areas there may be little demand for trails. Regardless of the scale of the project, AMC recommends working with a skilled and experienced professional to ensure that the effort results in an enjoyable and sustainable trail.

When considering the construction of a new trail, it may be necessary to involve many stakeholders. Proposed routes that cross public lands require an approval process that incorporates thorough environmental analysis. A wide range of specialists and agencies may be needed to ensure the routes will not adversely affect natural, historical, and economic interests. Agency personnel may also prepare an information packet for all those who are interested or involved with the planning process.

Trails proposed across private lands may also face a high level of public involvement and environmental assessment, depending on the scope of impact. Planning boards, conservation commissions, land regulatory commissions, and wetland bureaus may help determine the suitability as well as the positive and negative effects of a proposed trail over the short and long terms. It may be advantageous to speak with local officials to be certain that a trail concept is allowable.

Often, a trail designer/advocate may predetermine which groups will use the proposed trail. It may not be wise to limit intended users until others have commented on the proposal. However, establishing generalizations about a trail's purpose and deciding whether it will be nonmotorized, motorized, or multiuse can help clearly define the parameters of a given project. The trail's designer should know who will be using the trail, the estimated frequency of usage, safety considerations, and major obstacles or needs (such as bridges). The designer should also research landowner information and have preliminary discussions with any owners before submitting the proposal to the public. This is especially important when landowners' permission is necessary for the project to be successful.

➔ RESEARCHING THE ENVISIONED LOCATION

The envisioned location is usually one of two forms: (1) a route that is in close proximity to an established route or (2) a route that best serves the purpose of the scope of the project. Typically, a trail professional or someone with intimate knowledge of the surrounding land will have spent many days scouting around the woods, locating appealing features, or finding unique destinations.

One must find a site that will be both environmentally feasible and experientially pleasing. The planner/trail designer should know the general characteristics of the topography and terrain to get a comprehensive idea of the type and amount of work that will be involved to make the project a reality. Will the trail pass through wetlands? If so, for what distance? (Costs, wildlife disturbance, and environmental impacts will need to be considered.) Are there sensitive areas, such as deer wintering yards, that need to be avoided? Are there rare communities of plant or animal species? If so, where are they, and how will they be protected? What are the unique features that will make this an attractive project for others to support?

TOPOGRAPHY

During the planning phase, study topographic maps and other natural resource map layers for ideas about possible trail routes. Many Geographical Information System (GIS) map layers are free, usually provided by natural resource agencies and public education institutions. Check these maps to determine the lay of the land and to decide the best location for a route.

Aerial photographs can reveal features such as ledges, wetlands, watercourses, forest cover, and sometimes old roads that could be potentially usable for a trail.

Aerial photos are available from the USDA Natural Resource Conservation Service or, in the case of state or federal land, from a managing agency.

An hour in a plane or helicopter can often give a much better sense of the landscape than hours of studying maps or days walking the area. Fly over a proposed trail location several times at different elevations and from multiple directions. It is best to charter an aircraft or to find a pilot willing to volunteer to scout. Bring a topographic map, take photographs, and keep your eyes glued to what is on the ground. Of course, this option is very costly unless the pilot is sympathetic to the project and is willing to donate time and fuel. Recent advances in technology and imagery make drones an effective tool as well, but be sure to secure any applicable permits and landowner permissions. Online GIS data and satellite imagery have become increasingly helpful.

Studying an area's soil characteristics can help determine whether constructing a new trail system is feasible and if it will be sustainable. Certain soil types hold up well for constructing a natural tread trail, but others are poor choices. (See Chapter 4, page 38, for detailed information on soils.) Consider topography as well: flat terrain or steep slopes may prove to be equally challenging in regard to sustainability and will factor into the project's costs. Flat surfaces can be susceptible to water pooling, and steep grades can lead to rapid soil erosion. Streams and other watercourses also deserve special attention during the planning stage; identify suitable bridge or ford areas early so that the final trail route doesn't greatly deviate from the original concept.

During the planning stage, bring a camera to document the special features throughout the property. Special features can be any points of significance that are desirable for the trail to lead to or pass through, such as watercourses, views, and unique natural areas. Also bring (and know how to use) a topographic map, and consider using a global positioning system (GPS) unit to pinpoint features and to reference photos on a map location. The photos and points on a map will be beneficial when presenting the conceptual plan to those unfamiliar with the land. Before heading out onto the property, obtain landowner permission where necessary.

Anyone can scratch out a trail route on a map, but a well-developed plan is necessary to ensure a successful trail that people can use and enjoy. This is where layout and construction become part science and part art. Essentially, the trail planner is threading a simple path across the landscape, minimizing impact and ensuring durability while subtly influencing the hiker to use this predetermined route. The purposes of the planning phase are to develop a trail that will be interesting and satisfying and to anticipate and solve possible problems. Potential problems may be topographic features, such as steep slopes, ledges, or water crossings, or land ownership conflicts. Solutions may need to incorporate intensive trail engineering, permissions for water crossings, or negotiating land ownership agreements.

ORGANIZING TRAIL DATA

Use U.S. Geological Survey (USGS) topographic maps or GIS map data sets to record information gathered for the route. If a project is particularly complex, create a GIS layer and data files that can be referred to on a map. In these files, record all pertinent features for eventual use in the final on-the-ground layout. Describe the nature of each feature and whether it will improve or hinder the trail. Include other pertinent information, such as boundary lines and addresses of landowners or managing agencies.

As this information file develops, each feature will become a control point that will be avoided if it is a hindrance (for example, a bog or a steep slope) or be included if it is beneficial, such as areas of dry, well-drained soils. The final selection of the route will then involve connecting attractive features and circumnavigating negative ones.

TRAILHEAD AND PARKING FACILITIES

The proposed site of a trailhead needs careful study during the planning phase, as it will affect the usage and maintenance needs of the trail. The location and size of trailhead parking can, to some degree, limit the number of users. If the designer wants a small number of visitors, parking should be limited. If parking is plentiful and accessible, or if the trailhead is near a major recreational area, visitor use may become high and therefore increase trail maintenance needs. However, some trails become popular even where parking is limited, so careful analysis of the area's recreation needs and the expected number of users is critical.

Parking facilities provide a first impression and can be the most problematic part of planning a trail. Be certain to involve owners of abutting lands, local businesses, and the appropriate governmental agencies in the planning process. For safety, the location of parking facilities on highways must be carefully planned and must be coordinated with the state's highway department or local municipality to ensure clear sight lines. Highway department specifications for a parking facility will likely determine the location of the trailhead.

Try to coordinate parking facilities with other recreational uses. Use an existing picnic area or pull-off for the trailhead to eliminate the need for a new parking lot. A snowmobile trail parking area could be used for a summer hiking trail in the same vicinity. However, weigh your options carefully because some choices may invite unwanted conflicts, such as the overlap of foot travel and mechanized use on your trail.

Place a signboard or kiosk at the trailhead to post rules and regulations, allowed trail uses, map(s), management and emergency material, and other pertinent information (see Chapter 11, page 210). Reduce the possibility of vandalism by putting the signboard out of sight of the road, or 50 feet in from the start of the trail.

2

Proactive trailhead management can prevent problems associated with litter and human waste; remember that some preventive educational efforts (for example, Leave No Trace Ethics) are considerably less expensive than building new facilities to combat these issues. If you do need a more developed trailhead that could include toilet facilities and fee boxes, plan your facilities carefully to avoid problems after installation.

Buffer the trail as much as possible from the sights and sounds of unnatural features, such as roads, railroad tracks, industrial facilities, logging operations, and residential developments. In cases where the trail must cross a road or industrialized area, plan the route to reduce exposure as much as possible, crossing these areas in the shortest practical manner, preferably at right angles. Right angles are also safer for road and railroad crossings (see figure 2.1). Coordination with local and state highway departments is recommended to provide safe pedestrian crossing.

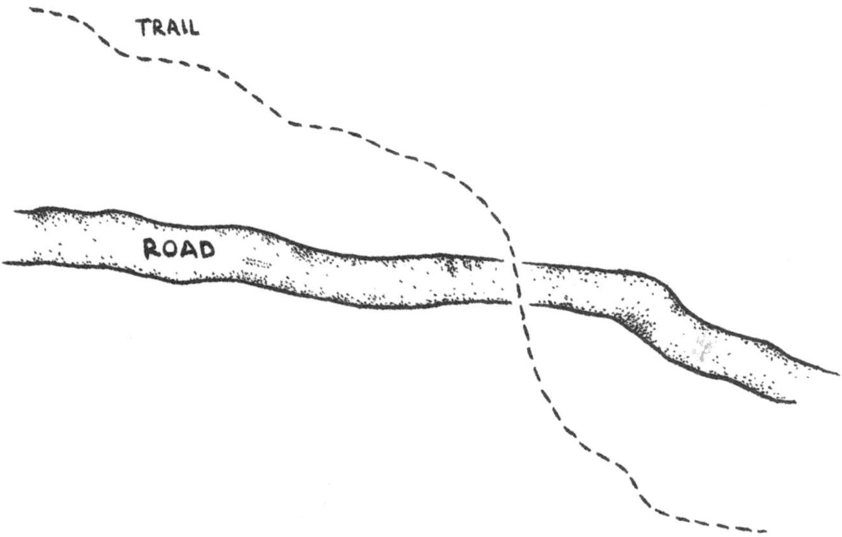

Figure 2.1. Cross at right angles to increase road-crossing safety.

➔ TRAILS ON PRIVATE LANDS

Trail building in the East, where much of the land is privately owned, often involves constructing a trail partially or completely on private property. In addition to the standard challenge of considering soils, topography, and vegetation, this introduces the complexity of multiple landowners who have requirements and conditions for use of their properties.

There can be distinct benefits to creating trails that incorporate private land. Greenways, suburban hiking, and multiuse paths, which increasingly cross private land, provide recreational opportunities close to population centers. These trails can enhance access to town, municipal, and state parks, offering activities that may be more commonly found outside of urban/suburban communities. Local trails may also promote environmental education, with some school curricula using trail maintenance and development as part of a broader nature study. Finally, local trails can provide a way to imbue the public with conservation values and ethics.

Despite these benefits, landowners have legitimate concerns about allowing trails to be built on their property. Although many landowners are primarily concerned about liability and future use, trail builders and maintainers may encounter a wide range of concerns. Use the information in this section to assist in securing permission and future protection for a trail proposal.

DETERMINING OWNERSHIP

Once the trail proposal is drafted, identify land ownership along the trail corridor. To maintain flexibility for negotiations with owners, initial planning stages should include a broad corridor, offering alternate locations. Inflexible proposals that rely on one key parcel of privately held land can be thwarted if that owner refuses to cooperate.

Review town tax maps. Tax maps are usually kept at the assessor's office, through the town clerk, and are increasingly available online. Tax maps are public information and are available for anyone to examine. Many municipalities now have digitized tax maps that can be reviewed and analyzed using GIS software. The information on the maps may vary from town to town. The most critical details are landowner addresses, acreage, deed and survey references (if on file), and rights of way that may exist. However, view the boundary lines presented on a tax map as guidelines only. For accurate boundary information, it is imperative to refer to a registered survey or deed.

Research deeds and surveys. With the landowners on record obtained from the municipal office, recorded deeds and surveys can be cross-referenced. In some areas of the country, registered deeds and surveys are at county offices, and in others these documents reside at municipal offices. If the town has incomplete tax map information, the process is far more complex—a bit like solving a jigsaw puzzle.

To solve this puzzle, start by piecing together deeds and surveys and cross-referencing them to ensure they agree regarding the boundaries of each property. From these, put together a conglomerate of properties that encompass the trail project area, including adjacent properties that may be useful for access. Depending on the date and thoroughness of the deed and survey, this work may require a professional surveyor or forester to help in determining land ownership and project bounds.

LANDOWNER/COMMUNITY RELATIONS

Regardless of the plans and proposals drafted, most often it is the relationships and communication with landowners, municipalities, and other vested interests that determines the success of a trail project. Here are some suggestions:

- Get to know the locals. Area residents may be useful sources of information because they are familiar with the use of land over time, attitudes toward development and conservation, financial status of individual owners, and future plans for the region. Ask local residents who are sympathetic to the trail project about general landownership, specific owners (if known), and ideas on who might be most favorably inclined toward the idea of a trail and land preservation.
- Talk to members of the select board, city council, or local equivalent. If they support a proposed trail, they can be a good source of information. The municipal office can give an idea of how much land is being sold in the town, what the various land uses are, and any known future plans that might affect the trail. Maintain a good working relationship with the governance members because they may be useful when you talk to landowners, and their opinions and counsel can be quite influential. The chairpersons of town conservation commissions are extremely helpful in most cases, especially since they are aware of the prevalent local conservation attitudes.
- Talk with consulting foresters and surveyors who work in the area. Often these individuals have been working in a region for a number of years and know the land and landowners well, particularly the larger holdings. They are a reliable source of information about existing woods roads, current land use, and outstanding natural features. Use foresters and surveyors who are in favor of a trail and have good relations with landowners and the town as references when you contact landowners. It is recommended that the trail designer communicate with these professionals, as the substance of their inquiries, concerns, and comments will likely be specific in nature.
- Contact conservation officers of state fish and game departments, county foresters, and consultants from the USDA Natural Resource Conservation Service. They often know a particular area well and can identify landowners who would be more favorably inclined to the project than others. Their greatest contribution, however, is their knowledge of the land and its features.

➔ TYPES OF OWNERSHIP

CORPORATE OWNERS: FOREST INDUSTRY AND AGRICULTURAL OWNERSHIPS

Land owned by corporations for timber harvesting and agriculture can be ideal for trail use. Well-planned trails can be easily adapted to the land management objectives of these owners and provide an opportunity for them to communicate their management values to the public. Additionally, negotiations with one corporate owner often can yield access to larger tracts of land.

However, corporate owners tend to have very specific concerns. Before approaching them with a proposal, develop the project vision in a manner that acknowledges their concerns, which generally are related to ways the trail will affect future use of the land. Allowing a public trail is often beneficial for corporate public relations, but corporate decisions tend to be based on financial issues and not hiker satisfaction. Accidents could pose an unacceptable liability burden to the corporate owner. Genuine concerns about fire hazards, parking congestion, vandalism, and sanitation problems can also make obtaining endorsement of trail proposals by these owners difficult.

Corporate Owners: Developers and Real Estate Investors

Owners whose purpose is to develop land holdings sometimes have unfavorable attitudes about proposals for trail use. From their perspective, trails may limit future development options. However, an increasing number of developers see recreational trails as a potential selling point for residential and economic development. Additionally, a local land use board may require dedicated "green space" as a condition for a major subdivision.

Designating land for development virtually precludes the possibility of high-quality trail design because such land tends to be subdivided into smaller units. Even existing trails sometimes must be closed because development has cut off access. Many informal, unmaintained paths in and around cities and towns have been effectively closed by development. Land held for development may present only limited trail options and narrow the possibility of successful public trail use.

However, if town land use boards and developers recognize the value and desirability of recreational trails as integral to a vibrant community and an asset to potential buyers, trail systems or connections can be designed as part of a subdivision plan. For this approach to be successful, it is important to have town planning boards and open space committees support the overall trail vision.

Residential Owners

In urban and suburban centers, most ownerships are residential, with owners living on their property. These owners require clear and thorough communication. Their attitudes are varied, and to satisfy different perspectives, trail design and planning becomes more complex.

Conservation-minded owners may not need much convincing of the social and environmental goals of the proposed trail. Document owner attitudes during initial research, and note which owners are most sympathetic. Approaching these landowners first will facilitate further negotiations. Endorsements from these owners may encourage their less sympathetic neighbors to accept the idea of public trail use. Protection of trails on residential land can be complex and may be unrealistic for some projects.

2

→ COMMUNICATION WITH LANDOWNERS AND STAKEHOLDERS

The use of land-protection mechanisms for trail corridors is an extensive process that at a certain stage usually requires legal counsel, considerable financial investment, and time-consuming negotiations. This section offers a cursory review of some of the available mechanisms and their benefits and drawbacks.

Direct and clear communication is essential. All parties involved must completely understand the goals of the trail project, how goals will be accomplished, the role each party will play, and how the project will affect each party. If policies and modes of implementation are not fully understood and collectively acknowledged, negotiations for agreements will likely be unsuccessful.

Tact and enthusiasm are critical for negotiating with landowners, and a good public relations profile in the proposed region is a great asset. To establish strong and positive public relations, make sure the goals of the project can be clearly understood, because conflicting information may spawn distrust and reticence. Develop a solid vision with flexible options before communicating with landowners. They may feel defensive about their private property rights, so use a low-key, restrained approach to reduce the likelihood that they will feel threatened. This is especially important as the demands on private land are growing. For example, private land holdings are increasingly being targeted to accomplish initiatives for water quality, regional conservation, and recreation.

Despite the need for a relaxed approach, be firm and clear about the proposal. Agreements that are not binding may help get a trail constructed, but they won't assure the long-term protection that the project will ultimately require. Only a legal agreement can guarantee that the trail or trail corridor will be protected for the long term and through potential landownership changes.

To facilitate all this, the project negotiator must be thoroughly familiar with the attributes of the land, land ownership, and legal status on which the trail is proposed. Before approaching an owner, the negotiator should have a general knowledge about the owner's perspectives on and concerns about the trail project. This will aid in the development of a successful proposal that best suits the landowner's needs and addresses concerns. Although arrangements can be adapted for each owner, all landowners should receive equal treatment. Mistrust can develop if special accommodations are made for one particular owner, especially regarding financial compensation.

→ LEGAL FORMS OF TRAIL PROTECTION

Five arrangements can establish a trail right of way or corridor: oral agreement, license, lease, easement, and land ownership known as fee simple. Between the two extremes of oral agreement and fee simple, there are three limited legal interests that can be placed on trail corridor land. These nonpossessory interests offer much flexibility and are excellent techniques for accommodating landowner wishes with respect to the land. To protect a trail and its corridor, the goal is to use the most binding arrangement that the landowner finds agreeable while providing the longest and most stringent protection to the trail. Any legal arrangement requires careful consideration of its respective characteristics.

ORAL AGREEMENT

A contract involving the exchange of real estate is not binding unless it is in writing. An *oral agreement*—sometimes referred to as a hand-shake agreement—is not legally binding. Enforcing an oral agreement is difficult because the parties may disagree over the original terms. An oral agreement is, therefore, inappropriate for a trail project except during the earliest preliminary planning stages. It may be appropriate to use an oral agreement to begin dialogue with a landowner and slowly develop trust to work toward a more binding written agreement.

LICENSE

The most limited nonpossessory interest in land is the *license*, which is revocable at the will of either party to the agreement. Unlike an easement, a license does not continue with the land; the death of the licensor generally will terminate the license, and the licensor often retains the right to terminate the license at any time and for any reason. A license simply permits the licensed party to enter the land of the licensor and to maintain a trail or other activities without being deemed a trespasser. The license is the simplest legal device and the least formidable to owners, who will be assured that there will be no threat of litigation should they decide that the arrangement is no longer in their best interest. The nonbinding nature of the license makes it fairly easy to consummate with owners; however, it has obvious limitations as a device to secure land for trails.

When negotiating a right of way for a trail, it is important to include an agreement regarding the landowner's use of the right of way, including potential obstacles and encroachments to the trail. It is recommended to establish a minimum distance around the trail or trail corridor that will be free of incompatible developments and aesthetic concerns, such as highways, structures, and off-highway vehicle use.

LEASE

A *lease* involves the granting of an interest in land upon the payment of an agreed-on fee. The fee does not have to be monetary, but to assure that the lease will be legally binding some consideration must be given for the right to use the land. For example, a nonmonetary lease might offer the percentage of an extracted forest product, such as firewood or maple syrup, in exchange for the use of the land. The benefit of a lease agreement to the landowner is that it can be terminated after a certain period of time. Remember, though, that the power of termination is limited to the terms of the written arrangement.

EASEMENT

The *easement* is the strongest of the nonpossessory interests in land. An easement grants a nonowner the right to use a specific portion of the land for a specific purpose. The extent of the interest conveyed needs to be explicitly outlined in the deed of conveyance, which is recorded in public records of title. An easement may be limited to a specific period of time or may be granted in perpetuity. Its termination may also be predicated upon the occurrence of a specific event (for example, the easement could include the following language: "so long as the bridge is maintained" or "unless and until the property is zoned for commercial development"). A trail corridor easement can range from 8 feet to a quarter of a mile wide, depending on the owner, the financial resources of the trail sponsor, and the vision for the proposed trail. An easement agreement usually "runs with the land," meaning it survives transfer of land ownership and is generally binding upon future owners until it expires on its own terms.

FEE SIMPLE

Fee simple is the highest possible ownership that can be held in real property. It is absolute title to a property with no limitations regarding the future inheritors. A fee simple acquisition would be a complete transfer of ownership from the landowner to the organization that will hold the trail ownership. Outright ownership may not be financially feasible or necessary, except perhaps where permanent facilities such as parking lots and campsites will be provided. However, a landowner may find the donation of land to a nonprofit landowner appealing because of tax or estate planning benefits. If comfortable with this topic, the project negotiator may want to explore it with the landowner.

➔ CONCERNS OF PRIVATE LANDOWNERS

A legally binding agreement may require a commitment too great for an owner to accept. Private property ownership is a highly valued constitutional right, and any restrictions should be considered with care and respect.

Owner concerns regarding public trail development and any accompanying proposed, legally binding arrangement are entirely legitimate. To see a trail proposal from the owner's perspective, consider the following points.

FUTURE USE OF THE PROPOSED TRAIL PROPERTY

The major concern for protecting trail rights of way or easements is the landowner's future right to use property proposed for the trail. Trails need not be protected with highly restrictive agreements, but without some protection a trail's future cannot be securely guaranteed.

Try to anticipate the owner's concerns so that the proposal does not sound unreasonable. The trail sponsor must enter negotiations with a firm sense of the owner's attitude. In initial transactions, it may be best simply to secure a written pledge from the owner to continue to work with the trail sponsor toward construction and eventual protection.

Trails can easily bisect property into compartments, which can seriously constrain the property's future use. The trail agreement should permit motorized crossing of the corridor and possibly allow limited use of vehicles along the trail treadway. For working forest land, this concession and the latitude to harvest timber according to prescription will protect the trail while giving the owner essential freedom to manage the land.

In some cases, the best course of action may be to begin by getting verbal or basic written permission from the owner to build the trail. This approach may work well with reticent owners. If construction of the trail proceeds with minimal trouble, maintenance work is top-notch, and the use of the land is not restricted, the landowner may be willing to consider a stronger agreement. Unfortunately, obtaining simple verbal or written permission for trail use is unlikely to protect the trail well into the future because of its very limited nature. The tenuous status of most trails on private land must eventually be fortified with viable agreements to protect and perpetuate these hiking opportunities.

LIABILITY FOR HIKER INJURY AND COSTS OF LEGAL SELF-DEFENSE

Landowners are frequently concerned that by approving a proposed trail, they are tacitly accepting liability for accidents that hikers may have on their property. They fear that failure to warn hikers about dangerous conditions on the land or failure to inspect trails regularly and draw attention to possible hazards will cause an injured hiker to sue them. This can indeed occur, and these lawsuits are usually based on an argument that the landowner was legally negligent by failing to protect the hiker from hazards even though the landowner knew that the hiker was going to use his or her land. To establish that a landowner has been legally negligent, the plaintiff must prove four elements, explained as follows.

Duty

The plaintiff must prove that the landowner had some obligation or duty recognized by law to protect the plaintiff from unreasonable risk. In law, the actions of the landowner are judged by a standard of conduct. For example, if landowners generally prune dead branches off trees that overhang a public walkway to make the walkway safe, a landowner who does not do so would not have lived up to the legal standard of conduct for landowners. In this case, the landowner might be liable for the injuries of a hiker who gets hit by a dead branch while using the walkway.

Breach

The failure on an owner's part to conform to the standard of conduct that the law requires is considered a breach. In the previous scenario, the landowner has not pruned the branches on the tree and therefore is in breach of the duty to do so.

Proximate Cause

The plaintiff must also establish a reasonably close causal connection between the conduct and the injury. Using the example above, the landowner's neglect was the actual reason the dead branch remained on the tree until it fell and hit the hiker. There is a direct relationship between the landowner's actions (or inactions) and the harm to the hiker.

Damage

The action or inaction of the negligent party must result in actual quantifiable loss or damage to the injured party. In the example, the hiker only has a cause of action if injured by the falling tree limb. If the hiker sustains a head wound and must be rushed to the hospital, that would be considered damage. If the branch simply startles or annoys the hiker when it falls, no actual injury has occurred and the plaintiff cannot recover for the landowner's actions.

Burden of Proof

In a lawsuit for negligence, the burden of proof is on the injured party. This means that the plaintiff must prove each element of the case by a preponderance of the evidence. The defendant, however, must still pay for a legal defense. Even though landowner liability is often limited by state recreational-use statutes, these statutes do not eliminate the right to sue, and defending against even a frivolous lawsuit can be expensive. Landowners are legitimately concerned about legal costs, even though few cases, if any, are likely to cause serious financial peril.

Extent of Duty

Identifying the extent of the duty that the landowner has to the hiker is important because, as indicated in the outline of requirements for negligence, landowner liability is predicated upon the breach of the duty owed to another person. The extent of the duty owed by a landowner to users of the owner's land depends on the legal status of the person using the land, as outlined below.

Statutory Law

Many states have recreational-use statutes that limit the liability of owners who allow the public to use their lands for recreational purposes, such as hiking, skiing, or mountain biking. Generally, these laws protect only landowners who permit use of their lands without charge. The statutes may also set a specific level of care below which the landowner is liable. To encourage landowners to allow the recreational use of their property, these laws help to minimize their duty toward recreational land users. The statutes also serve to keep the cost of liability insurance premiums fairly low, which makes it feasible for landowners to purchase insurance to protect themselves when they open their lands to recreational use.

Case Law

In some states, the law provides for categories of persons entitled to use land and establishes a hierarchy of land users (most generally called trespassers), licensees, and invitees. However, most states have abolished this hierarchy. Instead, the law considers whether the landowner's conduct toward a person on the land is reasonable. Some discussion of the different categories is useful to demonstrate "reasonable" treatment by the landlord.

A trespasser is a person who enters the landowner's property intentionally and without privilege or consent of the landowner. The landowner owes no duty to trespassers to use reasonable care to keep private lands safe for them; however, the landowner may not set traps for trespassers. If the landowner knows of a trespasser's existence, the landowner has a duty to warn the trespasser of serious or life-threatening conditions.

A landowner may have an additional duty to protect trespassing children because they cannot judge the degree of risk the way adults can. This is particularly true when the landowner knows that children are trespassing; in this situation, the responsibility to protect them from dangers on the land is high. For example, the law finds it unreasonable for a landowner to leave unsecured dangerous equipment where children might play. It would also be illegal, for instance, to fail to warn of thin ice on a pond if the landowner knows children often skate on the pond and knows that the ice is thin.

The landowner owes a greater duty to licensees—people who have been given permission to use land but who do so for their own reasons without benefit to the landowner. The landowner owes the greatest amount of duty to invitees, people the owner invites to enter the property at some benefit to the owner—social, financial, or otherwise. The landowner must protect invitees from known hazards but also has an affirmative duty to protect invitees against hazards that they might, with reasonable care, discover when exploring the land.

The reasonableness test does not make a clear distinction between the licensee and the invitee but instead examines the landowner's conduct. The court looks at what a particular person was doing on the land and what that person could reasonably have expected from the landowner. For example, if the landowner lets people fish in a pond, the owner may only have a duty to warn people of known dangers, such as underwater structures that could damage watercraft. However, if the landowner suspected that the bank of the pond was eroding and unsafe, the court may determine that the owner had a duty to check the bank of the pond and ensure that the anglers were safe.

Opening land to the public implies that it has been prepared for their reception. While there may seem to be some inherent risks involved with hiking, the legal duty owed to hikers by landowners has not been established clearly, and no determination would cover every circumstance. It seems likely that the courts will enforce greater responsibility on owners in the future because of a generally increasing concern for users' safety.

Indemnifications

Indemnification of landowners by the responsible trail club is one way to alleviate the very real concern about liability. Indemnification should be done only on a case-by-case basis and only after the trail club has obtained a qualified legal opinion. Insurance is available to private landowners concerned with the liability they may incur by opening land to hiking, and most landowners have homeowner's insurance policies that adequately cover their risks. However, if the landowner lacks insurance or if additional coverage is deemed necessary, the trail sponsor could purchase it with the landowner as the beneficiary.

A local insurance agent usually knows a landowner's needs. It is important for the agent to understand the nature of the recreational program as well as the volume of recreational use and potential hazards. The agent should also know the state laws limiting landowner liability.

Sponsors

Two types of liability insurance policies are available to managers (sponsors) of recreation facilities on private land: the Owner, Landlord, and Tenant policy (OL&T) and the Comprehensive General Liability policy. If possible, someone familiar with insurance terms and definitions should review policies to determine the extent of the coverage.

The OL&T policy is the basic method for covering legal liability to the public. Campgrounds and parking areas may be covered by this type of policy. The Comprehensive General Liability policy offers extensive coverage unless specific risks are excluded. Its major advantage is coverage of almost all trail hazards.

OVERUSE, VANDALISM, PARKING, AND OTHER MANAGEMENT PROBLEMS

If the landowner's reservations regarding future use and liability are quelled, concerns about the actual management of the proposed trail may become the greatest cause for reticence to support it. All the problems that can develop on public-land trails can develop on trails on private land as well. They range from environmental concerns, such as soil erosion, to social concerns, such as overcrowding, vandalism, parking congestion, and littering. These trail management problems and their solutions are described in Chapter 8 (page 159). A responsible trail organization will convince owners that problems have solutions and can be controlled by effective management and that the organization has the knowledge to effectively manage the trail.

The basic point, then, is to inspire trust in the maintenance organization that will be responsible for the trail. (It is presumed that the sponsoring organization has the capability to meet this responsibility.) This is essential before winning landowner support; however, if management tasks exceed capabilities when problems develop, the owner's trust in the organization will be diminished, and it will not bode well for future negotiations with other landowners.

A prudent procedure for new trails is to slowly release information on the trail's availability and to clearly explain the landowner's property rights in trail information that is posted and disseminated. Management problems are almost directly proportional to the level of trail use and perceived hiker and landowner rights. A maintaining organization will obviously not be as heavily burdened on a trail with low or moderate public use. Gradually increasing the dissemination of information about a trail serves to gradually increase the number of hikers on the trail. This may be difficult with the variety and proliferation of online trail applications. Therefore, prudence and an eye to future issues and conflict are imperative. The gradual start will help the trail manager develop and adapt a management style to support the higher profile that comes with more use. This way, problems can be solved before they become full-blown irritants to the landowner.

Once the trail is constructed and in use, the trail-managing organization should remain in regular contact with landowners to ensure continued support. This includes tracking changes in ownership and establishing communication with new landowners, ensuring landowners know whom to contact with management issues or questions, and sharing general updates about the trail.

CHAPTER 3

DEVELOPING AND USING TRAIL MAINTENANCE INVENTORIES

AT-A-GLANCE

Before performing maintenance or relocating a trail, fieldwork is necessary to assess problem areas and to determine work priorities.

➔ **Objectivity vs. subjectivity:** Consider the experience of the assessor and the style of reporting used to determine whether information gathered is objective or subjective.

➔ **Trail condition reports and logs:** Write down or make an audio recording of work to be done on the trail.

Before beginning work on a trail project, it is helpful to create inventories and assessments of trail conditions and maintenance needs. Inventories are useful in a variety of ways to trail maintainers, land managers, and others for project planning, scheduling maintenance, budget preparation, specific project guidance, and many other aspects of trail management. Their uses can range from the prioritizing of small, specific project areas to the creation of baseline data for trail conditions in a land management area.

➔ OBJECTIVE AND SUBJECTIVE ASSESSMENTS

Most trail condition assessments tend to be completed by trail organization staff or volunteers who hike and take notes on general conditions. In the case of a trail log (discussed in detail later in this chapter), a measuring and recording device is used to note problem areas on the trail. These assessments are subjective because most of the information gathered is not quantifiable. For example, assessments often include a rating system; the assessor decides whether a section of trail is "good" or "bad," which can be difficult to quantify since a rating of "good" or "bad" will vary depending on overall conditions and user/land manager experience and expectations of the area.

It's important to note that assessors possess different levels of trail management experience, which can lead to inconsistent data. Experience in the region and with a certain character of trail can also vary. Despite these limitations, subjective trail condition assessments are still beneficial. They can be done quickly and by a variety of people who do not need any special training aside from general trail maintenance experience.

There are ways to make trail condition assessments more accurate and consistent. One way is to create clear standards and to communicate them to all assessors. This can include written descriptions of what constitutes "bad" or photographic examples of "bad" versus "moderate." Another way to maintain consistency is to be sure that all assessors have a specified amount of training and experience and are familiar with local trail standards. In addition, have a qualified person make a field assessment if the quality of the initial assessment is in question.

Other types of trail condition assessments are considered more objective; for example, measuring and calculating the amount of soil that is displaced on eroded sections of trail. Objective assessments provide valuable and accurate information on trail conditions, but because a high level of training and a significant time commitment are necessary to collect the data properly, they are not very practical for most trail managers. However, for those who have the time and resources, objective assessments can provide accurate, quantifiable information for many levels of trails management. A training program called UTAP (Universal Trail Assessment Process) is taught through Beneficial Designs. This program includes in-depth assessment and the measuring and recording of features along a certain segment of trail. Parts of the process involve multiple people and can be quite labor-intensive, measuring the grade of each section and evaluating all features and trail improvement needs. UTAP training is offered at different locations around the United States.

➔ TRAIL CONDITION REPORTS

Most maintainers use reports completed by assessors in spring to prepare for the summer maintenance effort. Like other organizations and trail system maintainers, AMC has crews that hike all AMC trails in the White Mountains in spring to remove winter blowdowns and to identify problems; crew leaders then fill out a Trail Condition Report for each trail. Volunteer trail adopters also file reports on minor and major maintenance needs.

It is important to note that trail conditions vary from season to season and are affected by recent weather. Regional and local experience is invaluable when assessing trail conditions and recommending maintenance. For example, a certain degree of poor trail conditions may occur seasonally or intermittently, but drier conditions will naturally rectify the problem.

Most trail groups and land managers have their own assessment forms to collect information on specific problems (for example, a missing sign) or general maintenance needs (for example, a boggy or eroded section of trail). Specific problems may require a follow-up field check to thoroughly assess the situation and to prepare for eventual correction. Some forms provide spaces for comments about guidebook descriptions, facilities along the trail, parking accommodations, off-trail or bootleg camping, and other trail-related matters. Some also double as work reports.

Bear in mind that the degree of detail provided will vary depending on the questions asked and the trail maintenance experience of the person recording the inventory. The assessors' experience and knowledge of standards count, but assessors are not likely to provide more information than asked for on the form. Therefore, in addition to making sure assessors are qualified, be sure that the form specifically requests all the information needed. Finally, acquire input from both maintainers and land managers to compensate for biases if only one or two evaluations are considered.

Those not trained in trail problems and their solutions can find help in this book and the *Appalachian Trail Fieldbook: A Self-Help Guide for Trail Maintainers* (developed by the Appalachian Trail Conservancy) or the Student Conservation Association's *Lightly on the Land: The SCA Trail Building and Maintenance Manual*. However, none of these substitute for the firsthand experience of building and maintaining trails.

➔ TRAIL LOGS

One method of collecting very specific, detailed information on a particular section of trail is by creating a trail log, also called a work log. A trail log consists of an inventory of each problem or deficiency on a trail, with possible solutions for each specific site. Logs can be created using GPS applications or a measuring wheel, which measures distance as it is rolled across the ground. Both tools help establish distance reference points along the trail, making the log as specific and detailed as possible. Work logs are especially useful for prioritizing and scheduling projects, as well as for estimating time and expenses. Logs provide a way for project managers/planners to learn about potential projects, which helps them create detailed project plans for field crews. Because logs also serve as a way to quantify the amount of work to be done, they can be used to calculate the amount of time the crew and project managers need and the expenses for which they must budget.

Work logs should be prepared by experienced trail personnel. Two people are ideal because expertise and knowledge can be combined to evaluate and develop a prescription for difficult situations. Generate work logs while traveling uphill; the view of the treadway is better, which allows for more thorough assessments. Also, travel tends to be slower going uphill, allowing more time to consider issues thoroughly. Spring is often the best time to complete work logs because water-related problems might not be evident in summer or fall. This timing coordinates well with preseason project planning. However, always note the weather while creating the log, because recent precipitation can make trail conditions appear worse than they actually are. Although many drainage problems may exist in drier weather, they might not be as dramatic without a serious water event.

DIGITAL/GPS WORK LOGS

Digital work logs can be useful in many different trail management applications. Although most trail crews very rarely bring GPS devices into the field due to the nature of the work, tools carried, and crew culture, this equipment would make it possible to find very specific work sites and location of materials according to GPS coordinates. GPS cataloging work does have its limitations when notating extensive structures and work needed in a concentrated space. In these cases, the GPS can be used for the general area with additional notes about the specifics.

Thorough, useful work logs require time and detail. On a trail needing extensive work, it may take an experienced person a full day to log 3 or 4 miles.

CREATING A TRAIL LOG

Before beginning work, the following tools will be needed:

1. GPS device or its equivalent application
2. Data logger or digital voice recorder
3. Fully charged spare batteries
4. Paper and pen (backup for digital devices)
5. Map
6. Gear for the day

Begin by recording the name of the trail, the date, and the names of those generating the log. Note weather conditions and trail conditions (for example, wet, snowy patches and so on) and the wheel conversion rate (if any). Describe the exact location where the log begins.

Head up the trail. Look for notable features, such as a sharp turn in the trail or a viewpoint, that can serve as geographic reference points to existing structures and problem areas.

Upon reaching a feature or proposed work site, note and record the location; if using a wheel, record the number on the ticker. Briefly describe the feature or problem, and suggest a solution in a clear, concise, quantifiable way. For example: The problem is that the trail is eroded and gullying. The solution is to install four to five rock stairs.

Continue noting features and trail problems and suggesting solutions for the entire section of trail. List all trail junctions, streams, and outlooks. It may be helpful to record notes about priority of work, possible camp options, or water sources.

Transcribe or download the work log directly onto a computer. Doing this immediately after completing the log makes it more likely that you will remember additional details.

Don't forget that someone else is most likely going to use this log in the field, so make it as detailed, concise, and comprehensible as possible, with adequate reference points.

USING A WORK LOG IN THE FIELD

Because a work log is literally a list of work needed on a trail, it serves as a guide for projects along a specific section of trail. A log should be detailed enough that, with a little discussion on prioritizing, an experienced crew leader can take it into the field. Using the detailed reference points, the crew leader should be able to identify all the trail problems and deficiencies and the proposed solutions.

As mentioned earlier, work logs provide a relatively thorough inventory of the needs of a specific section of trail. However, no work log can ever be considered completely accurate or contain the best solution for every trail problem—two logs done by the same person for the same trail at different times will vary. Plan flexible procedures to accommodate variations from the work log.

To save time for the work crew and to support the log descriptions, flag the work on the trail shortly before the project begins. Use flagging tape to mark each work site, and use a permanent marking pen to write on each piece of tape either the instruction (for example, three rock steps) or a reference point from the log. Remove all flagging when the work is completed. The crew leader can also use the log to note which projects are completed each week to supplement weekly work reports.

→ TRAIL PROJECT PLANNING AND PRIORITIZING

Detailed work logs are invaluable when prioritizing projects. Setting priorities requires not only using the information on the trail log but also taking into account many other factors, such as users, amount of use, general trail conditions, and potential instabilities. For example, one might decide that a poorly laid-out, severely eroded trail (whether popular or not) in need of major reconstruction is a lower priority than a trail in adequate shape that has no drainage. Because installing drainage is faster and cheaper than major reconstruction and will potentially stabilize an entire section of trail, it may be of greater benefit. However, a case could be made for prioritizing the severely eroded trail if it goes to a very popular local destination. Decisions such as this are made based on management style, management plans, and funding availability.

CREATING TIME AND COST ESTIMATES

Logs are also helpful when estimating time and money required for a project. However, this requires knowledge and an educated estimate of the productivity of the crew assigned. Factors such as availability of material, commute time to the project site, and difficulty of the project need to be integrated. Often, volunteer crews take more time to complete a project than professional crews, but a larger volunteer crew size may be able to compensate for that. So, keeping a general record of work reports and being familiar with crew output can be useful to get an idea of the average productivity, which can then be applied to make an estimate for project planning, which will be discussed in Chapter 5 (page 43).

WORK LOGS FOR THE FUTURE

Because trails are dynamic and prone to change, detailed work logs might become outdated quickly. AMC crews have found little difference in overall tread quality on most trails over a few years, but conditions tend to deteriorate rather than improve. Trail conditions can change abruptly if use levels change dramatically or a natural catastrophe occurs (for example, a landslide or a stream jumping its course and flooding the trail). For planning purposes, refer to the most recent accurate work logs, which should be good for up to four years.

CHAPTER 4

TRAIL LAYOUT AND DESIGN

AT-A-GLANCE

Careful attention must be given to layout and design for a trail to be durable and sustainable.

➔ **Layout:** Familiarize yourself with the project area, organize and document data on a map, and place flagging tape to mark the route the trail will take.

➔ **Design:** As the trail is laid out, incorporate design features that anticipate potential problem areas and allow for sustainable building.

Creating a trail typically has four major phases: visioning, planning, layout, and construction. Visioning, which was discussed in Chapter 2 (page 9), starts with the broad view and often includes various ideas for possible trail locations. Planning, also discussed in Chapter 2 (page 8), is a conceptual stage where various factors are analyzed and carefully considered. Planners form ideas about how the proposed trail area should be developed by integrating the intended purpose with the landscape and natural resources.

During layout, trail builders go into the field and apply preliminary results from the planning stage to the proposed area. Once information is gathered during the field survey, conceptual plans are revisited and altered to reflect the reality on the ground. Layout prepares the area for trail construction and is the final step before breaking ground. For new trails, planning and layout phases blend together with field scouting and feasibility studies.

This chapter covers topics relevant to layout and design so that you can anticipate and become familiar with the wide range of issues that may arise.

➔ TRAIL LAYOUT

This is the stage of venturing into the woods and beginning the initial task of trail building. Designers navigate, hang flagging, and apply aesthetic virtues for a proposed route. During the layout process, keep in mind grade reversals and other drainage considerations, best practices for stream crossings, and effective ways of turning the trail. Patience and experience are needed to keep the primary objective in focus: to provide recreation interest with the least amount of impact on the land. Good layout can and should satisfy this objective.

DEFINING THE LINE

Check the proposed route. Then check it again. And again. Scout around to find the best trail surface and appropriate grades. The more time designers spend in the field during the layout phase, the better the trail location will be. Remember, an hour of time spent scouting can save weeks of a trail crew's time and can save years of maintenance troubles. Part of the proposed route simply may not work, or a solution to an unresolved problem may seem elusive. A designer may get lost or confused and, after hours or days of working the proposed line, could meet a dead end. All of this is par for the course and will help the designer understand the immediate environment. Designers must be willing to abandon what is not working.

Working knowledge of map and compass skills is a prerequisite. Laying out a trail demands following the best line, which often will not be a simple compass-bearing trajectory. Designers need to know where they are even if they drift into multiple dead ends. A partner is highly valuable in this effort. Trail layout is safer and faster and often provides better results when people work in pairs. One person can scout ahead while the second person hangs the flag line, or two people can scout in different directions when unforeseen obstacles impede practical advancement.

A GPS receiver can be helpful but can also be fickle when adjusting the proposed line. GPS units allow features to be mapped quickly, plus they store data, track movements, and can be used to pinpoint locations. Nonetheless, GPS units rely on clear signals from satellites. Various factors, including deep valleys or a dense canopy, can limit a GPS unit from calculating reasonable triangulations, producing no data or, worse, undependable data. Therefore, GPS accuracy may not be very useful at microscale during layout. Bring a GPS unit as a supporting tool and use it if it is receiving a strong signal, but rely primarily on maps, sketches, and good sense.

Fall is the best time of the year to lay out trails in the Northeast because leaves are off the trees and sight lines are excellent. Once the ground is covered with ice and snow, it is unrealistic to continue with anything other than scouting to establish points of interest, mark difficult terrain, or check grades. Try to view the route at different times of the year: in spring for indications of drainage; in summer to confirm that scenic objectives are visible; and in winter if the trail is intended for ski touring.

The layout process is one of trial and error. Continually backtracking and reflagging the route is common until a final location is confirmed.

FLAGGING THE ROUTE

Different colors of flagging may be helpful. Choose one color for initial "try lines." Flag control points (scenic features, boundary corners, unsightly areas, and difficult ground) in a separate color. Pick a bright color of reasonably permanent tape to define drift lines (a generalized route that could support a trail). Use another color of heavy-duty tape to mark the center line of the final trail route. Be sure to share all the details of your color scheme and the methodology of the flagging system with the workers who will be building the trail. Make relevant notes directly on the flagging tape with permanent marker, such as "Install drainage here." Use consistent abbreviations for regularly referenced information.

Place flags no more than 50 feet apart on the final line or close enough that trail builders can see more than one flag at any one point. In very dense growth, this might be only a foot or two apart. Tie flagging securely on living trees and branches. Choose tree trunks whenever possible; flagging on branches breaks in the cold, blows away, or is yanked off more often. Avoid leaving long tails on your flags—they shred and become litter. Biodegradable tape, although reasonable for initial try lines, breaks down too quickly to use for layout.

Flagging tape gives a general idea of the trail's location, but pin flagging (wire flags placed in the ground) or wooden stakes define where the tread should be. Some designers stake or flag the hinge, center line, or downhill edge of the trail. Be sure that the designer and builder have the same understanding of the trail's layout.

While flagging the line in the field, keep these ideas in mind:

- During layout, pay careful attention to the environmental concepts covered in this chapter.
- Where possible, always use a sidehill trail location, and check soil characteristics at regular intervals. Ideally, keep the trail gradient below 10 percent or, if not possible, below 20 percent with a plan to harden the steeper grades with erosion-control structures during construction.
- Incorporate frequent grade reversals to move water off the trail.
- Blend the trail into the natural surroundings. Be sensitive to various ecological communities, bypassing rare plants and fragile areas. Avoid too much meandering or sudden changes in direction.
- Record all important information for later discussion.
- Remind trail builders to remove all flagging tape when the project is complete.

When flagging the route, first determine the "control points" that the trail is certain to travel to, such as viewpoints, passes, and other notable features (see figure 4.1). Then identify the "pinch points" that limit the trail's passage connecting these points, such as wetlands, steep terrain, and ledges. Avoid crossings, but if that isn't possible, mitigate the trail's impact on the wetland and/or riparian environment by using narrowing crossings at a right angle to the stream or other watercourse with existing durable embankments that are stable and are not vulnerable to severe erosion. Take advantage of south-facing slopes because they tend to exhibit better drainage.

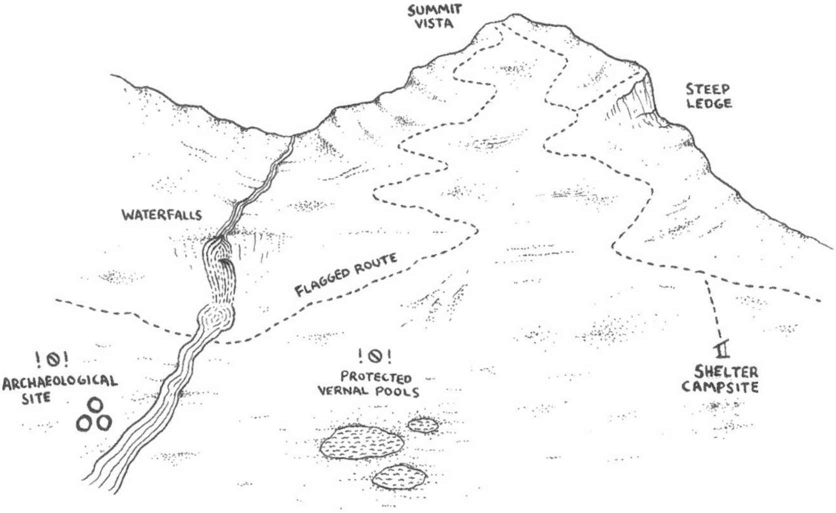

Figure 4.1. Flagging helps with trail vision as you work through terrain and determine control points. Take time and allow for line adjustments during this process.

Topographic features, such as ledges, knolls, and views, make trails interesting. Let the route drift across the land; this may limit difficult construction and later allows hikers a greater sense of anticipation when traveling. To provide visitors with an interesting and satisfying experience, include subtle turns and undulations in grade steepness, dramatic climbs to unobstructed views, or the sudden appearance of a waterfall.

Rocks, cliffs, ledges, caves, and other potentially dangerous areas offer points of interest along a trail. Do not avoid these rigors of the landscape when designing the route, but use caution when placing trails over shale slides, talus slopes, or cliff edges. Scarred trees and talus with recently fractured surfaces indicate falling rocks. It is unreasonably dangerous to locate trails under unstable ledges and cliffs. Clearly define trails skirting the tops of cliffs.

Wet, mossy areas that form ice in spring and fall are as dangerous as any cliffs and generally must be avoided. However, if these limiting conditions are not serious, take every advantage of dramatic topography.

Prudent topographic layout is essential to minimizing potential environmental impacts. Significant erosion could develop on trails that ascend long, steep gradients. Find a balance between the need for the trail to gain elevation and the tendency of foot traffic and water to erode trails. Rolling contour trails built at appropriate grades with regular grade reversals allow for natural drainage. Outsloped sidehill trails let flowing water cross over rather than running down, therefore reducing water volumes that aggravate erosion.

SIGNIFICANT ELEVATION GAIN

To climb a long, steep grade on a mountain, a sidehill trail alone cannot provide the needed rise in elevation. Often the lateral area available for a trail is limited, so the trail must turn and start a lateral motion in the opposite direction. This turn, aptly named a *switchback*, has been used for centuries in road and trail design. When setting a series of switchbacks, seek enough space to maneuver around unforeseen problems, such as a spring or ledge bands. Ideally, the available area for a route is wide and allows room for switchbacks, climbing turns, and contouring trail sections. Plan long stretches between switchbacks and minimize the number of turns to avoid monotonous repetition.

Draining water from the trail can be difficult around switchback turns and usually involves shedding water from the same source several times or reversing the outslope of the trail briefly to shed water at the corner.

On a well-designed trail, one switchback leg should not be visible from another. Switchbacks often fail when their upper and lower portions are built within sight of each other. Descending hikers who can clearly see the turn ahead will drop off the trail before the turn and take a shortcut. Water will drain using these shortcuts once they are developed enough, causing erosion and forcing maintainers to manage multiple steep trail sections.

Control shortcutting on switchbacks by using a wide turn (see figure 4.2). Run a short section of the turn straight up the fall line. Where the likelihood of shortcutting is greatest, such as in open hardwoods or above treeline where hikers can see for long distances, this tactic can be the best design choice. Harden the steepest part of the turn with steps to keep it stable and durable (see figure 4.3). Another tactic is to set the outer edge of a turn near a good view to attract hikers' attention to the corner and away from shortcuts. Placing large rocks, logs, and brush on the inside of a switchback often reduces shortcutting near the turn. Clearly mark switchbacks and any abrupt change in a route's direction to prevent hikers from walking off the trail at a turn or its corresponding drainage. When possible, use natural features, such as rock outcroppings, boulders, and dense stands of vegetation, to form barriers against shortcuts. Retaining walls can also help support the tread and prevent shortcutting at switchbacks.

Avoid areas with landslides and rockslides; if the trail will be used in winter, bypass areas with evidence of avalanches. All such areas may be prone to severe soil and vegetation movement that can be hazardous to hikers.

Do not build switchbacks on short, frequently used trails, such as those between a water supply and a campsite or between a parking lot and a view. Switchbacks require a large area with adequate vegetative screening between legs. Short trails do not offer enough space for proper switchback design.

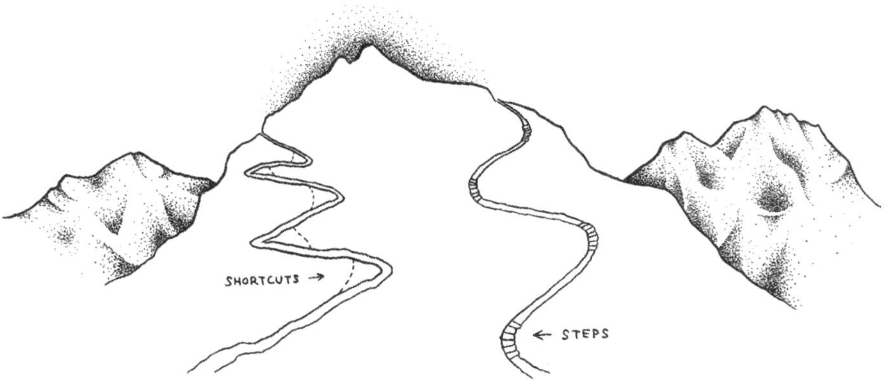

Figure 4.2. Switchbacks can be cut off by users. Good design and foresight are paramount.

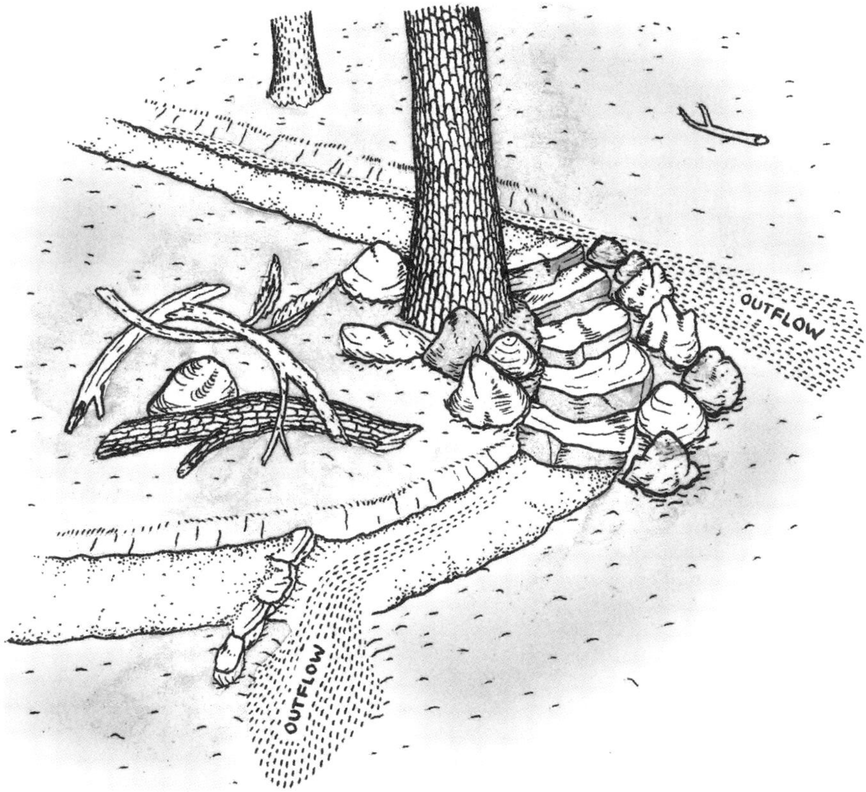

Figure 4.3. Steps at turns limit shortcutting and increase trail durability.

SOIL COMPACTION

Traffic on a trail causes compaction of the surface soil, which reduces its permeability and increases surface water runoff. Compacted surfaces lose their porosity and ability to absorb water. If water is not absorbed, it will either pool on the trail or flow over land and cause surface erosion. These tendencies make draining water off the trail critical for soil retention, even on flat trails.

SURFACE EROSION

Trail layout, existing soils, and type and frequency of use are the most important factors when considering the erosion potential of a trail. Erosion is a natural process in which soils are worn away by wind, water, and other mechanisms. On trails, this process is aggravated by soil compaction and the churning agitation of foot traffic. Water flowing over the compacted soil surface detaches smaller, lighter particles and carries them downhill (see figure 4.4). The greater the velocity of flowing water, the greater the mass of soil carried.

Trail gradient, water flow, and elevation increase surface erosion, especially when combined. Water velocity increases with slope steepness. As a result, increased water volume amplifies the force acting on the soil. Higher elevations pose additional

Figure 4.4. Water trapped in the treadway can lead to significant soil erosion and difficult maintenance solutions.

challenges because they generally receive more precipitation and have thinner soils. These factors, exacerbated by steep slopes and foot traffic, create significant erosion hazards that can quickly destroy a trail treadway.

Erosion is easy to spot on a trail. After the smaller stabilizing sand and silt particles have washed away, loose stones and gravel remain (see figure 4.5). The material offers poor footing, and hikers often walk the uneroded edge of the trail to avoid the difficult surface. This starts the vicious cycle of trampling more vegetation, compacting soil, and initiating more erosion that can change a trail into a wide, boulder-strewn gully.

Erosion can cause resource damage beyond the trail as well. After sediment-loaded water settles on the forest floor, it can disrupt neighboring plant communities. If sediment finds its way into streams and ponds, it can decimate aquatic organisms, degrade water quality, and load additional nutrients that may cause eutrophication, which decreases the dissolved oxygen available. In addition, soil loss around the base of a tree can expose roots, causing greater likelihood of disease and possibly weakening their anchoring function, allowing the tree to become more susceptible to wind throw.

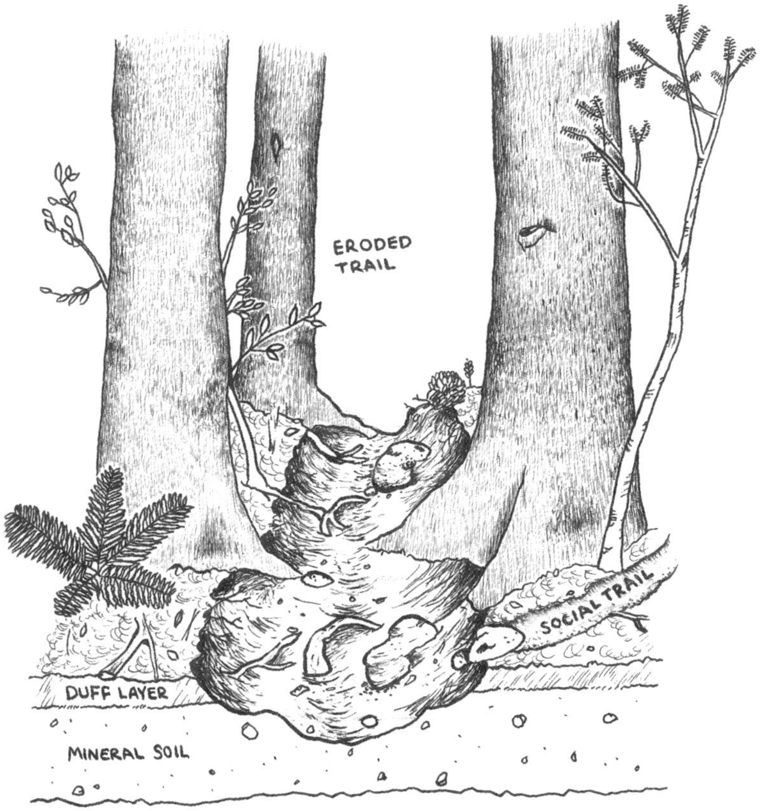

Figure 4.5. Water, compaction, and grade all factor in trail erosion. Over time, burdensome issues will arise, making maintenance more challenging.

Due to the threat of resource degradation, trail layout must carefully evaluate soil characteristics. Where possible, locate trails on soils that are capable of withstanding the anticipated use without eroding or becoming unstable.

SOIL

Trail planners must consider soil characteristics and should know how different soil types respond to compaction and alteration. If the plan calls for a trail to reach the top of a high mountain, trail designers will likely have to deal with a delicate alpine environment. Or, if the trail is designed so hikers can experience a bog, designers will need to work with devolved mull soils that contain a high level of organic matter. For a trail on a seashore, expect unstable sand. Soil is also an important, yet subtle, part of the outdoor experience—just as critical as the flora or vistas.

Vegetation and ecological communities can indicate broad soil characteristics. Tree size, age, and quality indicate soil fertility: large, young trees indicate deep, well-drained soils, while small, stunted trees accompanied with wetland species indicate marginal soil conditions. The preponderance of a species can suggest soil composition, depth, and wetness. For example, pine and oak tend to grow in sandy, well-drained soils; balsam fir, spruce, and hemlock may signify more shallow soils. Red maple, cedar, and tamarack tend to grow in soils that are moist. However, designers must consider the broad landscape and not simply rely on these generalizations.

Soil is a complex mix of minerals, organic matter, organisms, pore space, and water. The soil in a given area from the ground to bedrock is called the soil profile (see figure 4.6). Each soil profile is composed of layers (sometimes very small or thin). The local USDA Natural Resource Conservation Service office or Agricultural Extension office have detailed soil maps that show prevalent profiles, including the approximate depth of each layer and best uses for it. These maps can be very helpful.

The ability of soil to withstand traffic depends on the combination of wetness, texture, and depth. Planners must consider these qualities when determining the best location for a trail.

Soil Wetness

Groundwater moves through the landscape and saturates the surface of soils, especially during periods of heavy rainfall and the spring thaw. Groundwater fluctuates with the seasons. Seasonally high groundwater in shallow or poorly drained soils will create problems on a compacted treadway. In very poorly drained soils, such as in bogs or depressions near lakes and streams, water moves extremely slowly, such that the soil surface may be wet for much of the year. Avoid building trails in these areas, or use bog bridges from the outset to protect trailside vegetation and soils (see Chapter 8, page 151).

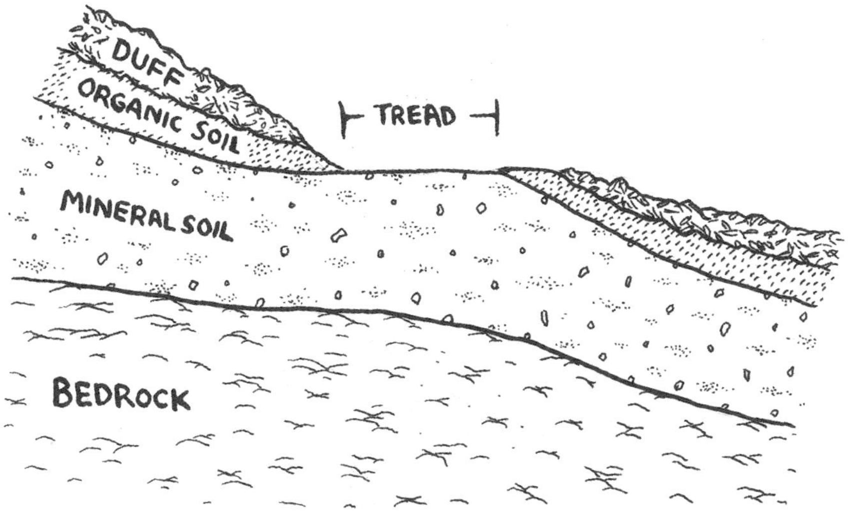

Figure 4.6. In general, good-quality and sustainable tread uses the mineral soil layer as the main contact surface.

Evaluate soil wetness after long periods of rainfall or during the spring snowmelt. Check that minimal surface water is present. If water is flowing across the ground in many rivulets, the site may not be appropriate for a trail. One option is to dig a shallow hole where the proposed trail would be; if it fills with water or if water placed in it does not percolate out, then the water table is high or the soil inhibits adequate drainage. Trails across soils like this will degrade quickly or demand significant amounts of work to stabilize. Often it is better to locate the trail elsewhere.

Soil Texture

Soil texture refers to the relative proportions of various-sized groups of grains in soil. Texture is an important factor in how well soil can sustain compaction. In general, loamy soils with a mixture of sand, clay, and silt will resist compaction and erosion most successfully. The smaller sizes of silt and clay particles add cohesion; sand and gravel lend porosity and water absorption. Coarse fragments in the treadway increase the durability of the soil. Gravel-sized fragments embedded in the soil matrix help to hold the more easily eroded sand and silt in place. Rocks, stones, and loose gravel on the surface act as natural erosion retardants.

Moderately sandy soils will resist compaction and will absorb a large amount of water, making them good for trail use. However, use caution when building trails across pure sand because it tends to support natural communities of little diversity and therefore fewer plants for soil retention. Avoid building trails on soils composed mostly of silt and clay. They become muddy when saturated, cracked and dusty when dry, and erode easily.

Also avoid soils with high organic matter and minimal mineral material. Organic soils are five times lighter than the more common mineral soils. They compact quickly, erode easily, and become very mucky. Organic soil can hold two to twenty times its dry weight in moisture, but a mineral soil will hold only about a fifth of its weight in water.

Soil Depth

Soil depth is the distance from surface level to bedrock. Avoid shallow soils when possible, especially on steeper terrain. Shallow soil over bedrock or hardpan (an impervious layer of subsoil) can lead to problems. Water cannot drain through the substrate and will saturate the soil above. The saturated soil sloughs easily when compacted and erodes quickly.

The limitations of soil depth are especially critical in alpine environments, where soil is only a few inches thick at most and should be carefully preserved. Vegetation is small, often shallow rooted, and easily damaged by foot traffic. Trail builders must take special care to delineate the trail, contain foot traffic on durable surfaces, avoid abrupt turns that could lead to shortcutting, and bypass areas with sensitive vegetation.

In summary, erosion from a simple footpath can add an immense amount of soil to watersheds. Soil depth, soil texture, and trail gradient are the most important factors in determining appropriate trail locations and can be easily measured in the field with a soil auger and a clinometer. Evaluate these characteristics during the initial phases of a proposed trail and strive to locate the trail on the most suitable soils.

SUMMARY OF SOIL INDICATORS FOR EVALUATION OF A PROPOSED TRAIL INSTALLATION

Conditions	Conditions Posing Slight Limitations for Trail Installations	Conditions Posing Moderate Limitations for Trail Installations	Conditions Posing Severe Limitations for Trail Installations
Soil Wetness	Depth to seasonal high water table 4 feet or more; well drained to moderately well drained	Depth to seasonal high water table 1 to 4 feet; excessively drained	Depth to seasonal high water table less than 1 foot; poorly drained
Soil Texture	Particle mixture of sand, clay, silt; 20–50 percent of content gravel	High sand content; less than 50 but greater than 20 percent of content gravel	High clay content; no gravel
Soil Structure			Hardpans less than one foot from soil surface; peaty, mucky soils
Soil Depth to Bedrock	Greater than 3 feet	1½–3 feet	Less than 1½ feet
Slope*	0–5 percent	5–20 percent	Greater than 20 percent

*Slope is the number of feet of vertical rise per 100 feet of horizontal distance, expressed as a percentage—that is, a 10 percent slope rises 10 feet vertically for every 100 feet traversed horizontally.

CHAPTER 5

DETERMINING THE COSTS OF TRAIL PROJECTS

AT-A-GLANCE

Before beginning a new trail project, you will need to estimate how much it will cost.

- ➔ **Break down costs:** Use the cost of each structure, the number of weeks of labor, and the cost of a trail per foot or per mile to estimate a total expenditure.
- ➔ **Labor costs:** Consider the experience level of the trail builders when determining the duration of a work project and the inherent labor costs.
- ➔ **Funding resources:** Seek funding from the government or private donors.

Calculating the cost to construct or perform maintenance on a trail is an important part of the planning and implementation process, and it requires a thorough understanding of many components and variables. Factors include site conditions; use of professional trail crews, volunteer labor, and/or contracted services; terrain; use of native or non-native materials; engineering standards; and choice and use of equipment. It is also prudent to consider land acquisition, permits, project management, and associated administration expenses. The plan should include a budget that identifies each item or major task. On larger, complex projects, estimates may need to be broken out into phases over a period of years due to availability of funding and the construction timeline. A successful endeavor requires that expenditures be carefully thought out ahead of time to ensure that funds will be available to complete the project. Having an accurate budget is essential. Employ people with a solid background in trail construction to estimate all costs before breaking ground on a new trail. Funding organizations will likely need to know projected material and labor expenses before offering financial support.

➔ HOW TO ESTIMATE COSTS

Trail managers and designers often use one or more of the following methods to estimate trail project expenses: unit costs, crew weeks of labor, and per-foot or per-mile costs.

Unit costs are predetermined for each structure to be built along the trail. For example, it might be estimated that installing a native rock water bar would cost $50 (considering materials, equipment, and labor). Sidehill construction might cost an average of $10 per linear foot. A tally of structures multiplied by their costs equals a total project expenditure. It is important when using the unit cost method to have a completed trail log (see Chapter 3, page 26) from which to work. This method of estimation should be employed only when there is significant organizational experience with construction and labor requirements. It can pose serious risks of underestimation due to unforeseen circumstances.

When estimating by using crew weeks of labor, determine the amount of time it will take to complete a project and then add this to material costs. For example, a professional trail crew of four people might contribute 160 hours per week of labor to a project, so each "crew week" will consist of 160 hours. Experienced crew leaders can estimate how much work a crew is capable of completing in a week and divide the project into the number of crew weeks. Project material costs would be estimated separately and added to labor costs to provide an overall expenditure. This method of determining trail project costs is widely used for both volunteer and professional trail crew labor. The person doing the estimating should have experience in trail work and firsthand knowledge of the labor a crew can perform in a given time period.

The per-foot or per-mile method is used when an accurate figure is available from previous experience. For example, a per-foot cost may have been determined in the past for a 5-foot-wide wooden boardwalk of similar design or an 8-foot-wide Americans with Disabilities Act (ADA) trail that uses bituminous asphalt as surfacing. This method isn't recommended when the trail has a range of variables, such as a variety of involved structures, but it can be helpful when applied to discrete parts of the route.

Trail designers and managers often use a combination of the methods discussed above and factor in other considerations, such as:

1. The commute to the project site. How long will it take for the crew to drive to the trailhead and then pack-in to the project site? Will the crew be staying on-site?
2. Availability of native/project materials. For example, is rock for a retaining wall nearby and available, or will it need to be transported a long distance?

3. Safety concerns. Is the project in an area that could be dangerous to the crew members and/or the public during construction? Will the site be open to the public? The need for additional materials or precautionary measures to make the area safely passable may drive up costs.
4. Available tools and equipment. Are any tools or equipment prohibited from being used on the site? Can motorized equipment be used, or is the project limited to hand tools only? Will it be necessary to purchase or rent additional tools and/or equipment?
5. Possible weather extremes. Is the project in an alpine region or an area that receives large amounts of precipitation? Extreme weather conditions can slow production or cause the crew to cease work for periods of time.

These are general guidelines to use when considering variables that may play a large role in reaching an accurate construction or maintenance cost figure. For more specific information, consult professionals who are familiar with local conditions. Take care not to underestimate or overlook costs for trail design, layout, and project management. Be sure to include drafting proposals, stakeholder meetings, mapping, procuring cost estimates, and any other time or materials costs that contribute to the administration of the project. These can be significant expenditures but are often omitted in a trail project budget. Design and management expenses can account for 20 percent of total costs, although that figure can vary widely from project to project.

➔ SOURCES OF LABOR

When preparing cost estimates, decide who will build or maintain the trail. Trails get built and maintained in a variety of ways. Nonprofit trail clubs who have professional and volunteer trail workers, such as AMC, construct trails throughout the Northeast. Other trails are built by trail contractors, landscape companies, or construction firms. Youth conservation corps (YCC) often build trails on both public and private lands. On state and federal lands, construction may be done by a combination of agency staff, trail contractors, and volunteers.

AMC is a member of the 21st Century Conservation Corps and is a partner of the Corps Network (the National Association of Service and Conservation Corps). AMC is one of the 130 Corps across the country that provides young adults and veterans the opportunity to serve our country through projects on public lands and in rural and urban communities. See corpsnetwork.org for more information.

For some projects—and almost all established historical trails in the Northeast—volunteers are solely responsible. Before finalizing the project budget, obtain estimates that reflect the specific type of labor being used to complete the work. Costs will vary widely depending on the source (contractors, YCC, nonprofit trail clubs, and so on). Even if you are using only volunteers, be aware of hidden labor costs such as food, safety equipment, and travel expenses that are often overlooked.

➔ RESOURCES FOR FUNDING

After a cost estimate for the trail project has been established, the question becomes: "Where will the money come from?" Funds from federal, state, and local governments and private sources are often combined to pay for project costs. Sometimes user fees, taxes, or bonds are also available. Funds may come from donations from area businesses, individual sponsors, foundation support, or creative methods such as "buy a mile" programs or fundraising events.

One grant source that is available annually is the Recreational Trails Program (RTP), which is a program of the Federal Highway Administration. The RTP is funded and administered through individual states for the purpose of developing and maintaining both nonmotorized and motorized trails. Each state administers and awards this grant money yearly.

Seek funding sources and apply for grant opportunities. When considering federal or state grants, do research well ahead of time. Speak with past recipients and discuss your project with the granting organization to be certain the project and application meet the requirements. Grants are often very competitive, so set aside a sufficient amount of time to prepare an excellent application. Be aware of application deadlines, award dates, and the reporting process to avoid surprises. Also, develop contingencies for moving forward if a grant is not awarded. It is always important to have a backup plan.

Raising funds for new trail projects is often easier than raising funds for trail maintenance projects. Be sure to include a maintenance plan for the near future when applying for grants because it indicates to the grantor that the intention of the project is looking to the long term. It is also easier to raise funds if strong partnerships with other organizations, businesses, and agencies are developed. Don't overlook the importance of having strong community support in place before seeking funding. Consider breaking your project into components so that you can tailor your funding requests through a number of different sources. Follow up with donors by submitting progress reports and writing thank-you notes when appropriate.

CHAPTER 6

SAFETY, PREPARATION, AND TOOLS

AT-A-GLANCE

Protect yourself while working by taking precautions and using care with tools.

- ➔ **Personal protective equipment:** Prevent injury by wearing appropriate attire.
- ➔ **Food, water, and first aid:** Eat and drink to prevent exhaustion and dehydration, and be prepared to administer first aid when necessary.
- ➔ **Tools:** Use the correct tools properly and ensure they are maintained well.

Trail work is satisfying, challenging, exhausting, frustrating, and fun, but the element of danger is always present. Cutting wood, digging ditches, and moving stones—the basics of trail work—are fraught with perils and inconveniences, ranging from cuts, scrapes, and bruises to blisters, achy muscles, and dehydration. Any of these can temporarily affect your enjoyment of trail work, reduce your effectiveness, and hinder the extent to which you can contribute to the project. If you ignore these problems for too long, they can keep you from performing your work.

Hypothermia; heatstroke; injuries from tools, rocks, or falling trees; and similar serious conditions are usually caused by minor mistakes or blunders that culminate in a major mishap. These hazards and injuries require immediate attention. In the long term, people who dedicate considerable time to trail work can develop chronic health conditions such as carpal tunnel syndrome and knee and back issues. What follows are the fundamentals of preparation that are essential for protecting yourself and other workers on the trail.

➔ PERSONAL PROTECTIVE EQUIPMENT (PPE)

Use of personal protective equipment while performing trail work can make the difference between a successful, injury-free day and one that is plagued with problems. Having the right PPE for an activity and being sure it is functioning properly should be at the forefront of any trail maintainer's mind. For most organizations, employers, and/or sponsors, using the appropriate PPE is not optional but mandatory and, for the safety of the individual and crew, should always be considered as such.

BOOTS AND SOCKS

Sturdy leather boots are one of the most important pieces of gear a trail worker can have. A well-made pair of boots with lugged soles will keep you comfortable and protect your feet while you work. Lightweight cloth boots provide inadequate protection for common trail-building activities, such as moving large rocks or logs. Steel-toed boots offer an extra level of protection but can be very uncomfortable on long hikes.

Help protect your feet from blistering by wearing the right socks. Use heavy-weight wool or wool blends; cotton socks will absorb moisture and increase the chances of blistering. As soon as you feel the onset of a blister or a hot spot, pause in your work. Remove your boots, let your feet dry thoroughly, and apply moleskin, Molefoam, or duct tape to prevent further injury. You may want to wear a light inner polypropylene liner under your socks to wick moisture away from your feet and to reduce friction.

GLOVES

Gloves should be worn for most trail work, although certain tasks require finger mobility and additional dexterity that gloves limit. Some work, such as operating a chain saw, a Griphoist, or similar equipment, requires operators to wear gloves to protect their hands from possible serious injury. Trail workers often choose leather gloves because they offer more protection than cotton gloves and generally hold up better with heavy use. In wet climates or periods of wet weather, woven nylon/polyester gloves with rubber grips provide good traction and dry quickly.

EYE PROTECTION

Safety glasses and safety goggles are inexpensive and lightweight. Use the impact-resistant option that offers additional protection on the sides. Safety glasses can be clear or tinted and are designed to be shatterproof. There are even mesh glasses that won't fog up. Some safety goggles are designed to fit over prescription eyeglasses. Eye protection is suggested for all trail work, but be absolutely certain to wear safety glasses or goggles when using axes, hammers, or chain saws or when splitting or drilling rocks. Use safety glasses or goggles that meet American National Standards Institute (ANSI) Z87.1-2010 standards or higher. Mesh face shields mounted on hard hats can also serve as eye protection while operating a chain saw or brush cutter. However, it is recommended that the chain saw operator wear safety glasses in addition to the mesh face shield.

EAR PROTECTION

Some trail maintenance activities, such as using chain saws, rock drills, and other forms of gas-powered equipment, require users to wear ear protection to prevent hearing loss. Two types of ear protection are generally available: plastic ear muffs, worn on the outside of the ear, and foam plugs, which are worn in the ear canal. Both are designed to reduce external noise to a level that prevents or limits hearing loss. It is important to know the decibel level of the equipment being used so you can choose the appropriate ear protection. Hearing protection should have a noise reduction rating (NRR) that specifies the number of decibels (dB) reduced when worn correctly. Use hearing protection that meets ANSI/ASA S12.6-2016 standards or higher. (Visit ansi.org for more information.)

HARD HATS

Hard hats should be worn when doing any trail work activities and are required in all situations in which falling or flying objects could present a danger. Always wear a hard hat when working in an area with unstable rocks overhead, when felling trees, and when working around standing trees with dead limbs. Hard hats should meet all ANSI/ISEA Z89.1-2014 safety standards in their design for the intended activity. Color, although seemingly insignificant, can make a difference—lighter colored hard hats are much cooler on hot, sunny summer days. Hard hats that are not designed or approved for trail work or construction activities might not provide adequate protection. Replace hard hats if they have been damaged or if they have reached their expiration date (usually about three years after the manufacture date stamped on the inside of the brim). UV exposure, sweat, and repeated use contribute to the breakdown of materials. Periodically test hard hats by squeezing the brims; replace them if there are any cracks or brittleness.

LONG PANTS

Long pants should be worn for most trail work activities to protect the user from cuts, scrapes, and bruises. It is not practical to do trail work in shorts. If hot weather makes wearing long pants uncomfortable for hiking, consider walking to the work site in shorts and changing into long pants there.

SHIRT

Long-sleeved shirts are recommended, but at the very least, a trail worker should wear a T-shirt. Even though it may be tempting to wear less in hot weather, it is impractical and unsafe to go without the minimal layer of protection of a long-sleeved shirt or T-shirt.

CHAIN SAW CHAPS

Chain saw chaps are worn over pants and cover a person's legs and lower torso to provide resistance to cuts and to prevent serious injuries. When punctured by a running chain, the fibers in the chaps catch and clog the drive sprocket, stopping chain rotation quickly—ideally before serious personal injury occurs. Chaps should be approved by Underwriters Laboratories (UL) and must fit the operator correctly to provide maximum protection. Chaps that wrap around and behind the ankles are best because they are more comprehensive in their coverage.

DUST MASKS AND RESPIRATORS

Dust masks and respirators filter out undesirable contaminants from the air. It is important for trail workers to be trained in hazardous material identification and safety practices so that they can choose the proper mask or respirator. Dust/particle masks are intended to filter airborne particulates created when performing activities such as drilling and splitting rock, crushing stone, or sanding wood. Be sure to check the directions and instructions for proper application and wear.

Respirators have a filtration component that filters out substances such as hazardous fumes from stains, paints, epoxies, chemicals, or gaseous materials that a trail worker might be exposed to. Respirators and dust masks vary in quality and application. Do some research to be sure you purchase the correct model. Read the directions carefully.

RAIN GEAR AND INSULATION

Wearing and carrying high-quality outerwear that will protect you from the elements is important. Pack rain gear and insulating layers appropriate for your location and activity. For example, a rain jacket and light sweater might be sufficient in protected or low-lying areas in summer, but when working in alpine areas or above treeline, pack rainwear, a wind suit, and insulating layers appropriate for a worst-case weather scenario. This might require several layers of clothing, including a warm hat and gloves, even in summer. Be sure to choose wool or synthetic blends that are designed to keep a body warm even when wet.

MAINTENANCE, INSPECTION, AND RETIREMENT OF PERSONAL PROTECTIVE EQUIPMENT

All PPE should be stored appropriately and inspected on a scheduled basis at least annually and more often with frequent use. Certain projects may require PPE inspection daily due to the hazards and risk involved. Clean all PPE and check it for damage before putting it in storage when the season ends. (Damage is easier to detect after cleaning.) Look for hairline cracks in helmets, cracked safety glasses, tears in gloves, and any other signs of damage. Store hard hats, safety glasses, ear protection, and similar plastic items out of direct sunlight to prevent prolonged exposure to UV rays, which prematurely break down some plastics. Label and date all PPE at time of purchase unless it is already marked. Keep up-to-date records of the number of times each piece of equipment has been used and of the stress placed on each piece.

Replace PPE when an item has reached its expiration date or sooner, depending on use and wear. Certain events, such as a severe impact to a hard hat or cutting into chain saw chaps, exposing the protective layers, could force the retirement of a piece of PPE much earlier than anticipated. PPE is far too important to be negligent in its care and use.

FIRST-AID KIT AND OTHER CONSIDERATIONS

Every trail crew unit or solo worker should have a first-aid kit at all times. The contents should be based on the number of people in the crew, hazards posed by the work, and the remoteness of the work location. Inventory first-aid kits regularly and replenish any used, damaged, or expired supplies. See page 51 for suggested first-aid kit contents for a one-person crew and an eight-person crew. Trail workers should, at the very least, receive training in wilderness first aid and CPR to be prepared for emergencies. It is recommended that trail crew leaders obtain more advanced training in first aid, such as Wilderness First Responder certification.

Know how to identify and protect yourself from the local harmful plants and insects. Warn others if they will be working in an area infested with poison ivy, poison oak, or other poisonous plants. Bring Tecnu skin cleanser or Fels-Naptha soap so workers can wash off the irritating oil if they are exposed. Similar advice applies to venomous snakes: identify the species to avoid, warn the crew, and have a first-aid and evacuation plan should someone get bitten and become ill.

Insects can test a trail worker's patience, and in extreme cases their bites may produce an allergic reaction. Carry plenty of bug repellent that has been proven to be effective. Individuals allergic to bees or other stinging insects should have their own EpiPen or anaphylaxis kit. It is imperative that the crew leader or person responsible for medical emergencies knows who on the crew is allergic and who carries this medication. The crew leader or responsible person should also be trained in administering an EpiPen (epinephrine) if applicable, considering state and local EMS protocol. (*Note*: EpiPens and anaphylaxis kits can be obtained only with a prescription.)

PERSONAL FIRST-AID KIT FOR ONE TRAIL WORKER

- 1 package of moleskin or Molefoam
- aspirin or ibuprofen
- 1 triangular bandage and safety pins
- an assortment of Band-Aids
- 1 Ace bandage
- 3 4 × 4 in. gauze dressings
- 1 roll of tape or Kling bandage
- gloves
- pocket mask
- antihistamine capsules
- iodine antiseptic or iodine antiseptic wipes
- shears or scissors

FIRST-AID KIT FOR A TRAIL CREW OF UP TO EIGHT PEOPLE

ABSORBING

- 4 triangular bandages
- 3 rolls of 2 in. × 4½ yd. cling gauze
- 6 4 × 4 in. gauze pads
- 6 2 × 2 in. gauze pads
- 2 Ace bandages
- 2 maxi pads
- 2 5 x 9 in. combine gauze
- 6 safety pins
- 8 tampons

STICKY

- 1 roll duct tape
- 1 roll ½ in. medical tape
- 1 roll 1 in. medical tape
- 1 roll 2 in. medical tape
- 1 tube Neosporin
- 20 assorted Band-Aids
- 5 large Band-Aids
- 8 butterfly bandages
- 2 pkgs moleskin
- 1 pkg SecondSkin bandages

CLEANSING

- 6 alcohol pads
- 6 iodine pads
- 1 baby toothbrush or iodine scrub brush

DRINKING

- 1 bottle Potable Aqua
- 1 pack Aquamira

RELIEF

- 6 Pepto-Bismol tabs
- 8 Benadryl caps
- 10 ibuprofen (Advil)
- 10 acetaminophen (Tylenol)
- 1 tube Insta-Glucose

WASTE

- 2 1 gallon Ziploc bags
- 4 1 quart Ziploc bags
- biohazard bags

IN THE OUTSIDE POCKET

- 8 pairs of medical gloves
- 1 SAM Splint
- tweezers
- trauma shears
- pocket mask
- lighter

RECORDS

- incident reports
- workers' comp form
- patient care form
- first-aid handbook
- notepad
- pen, pencil, permanent marker

➔ TICKS AND DISEASE PREVENTION

Ticks are and have been an increasing concern for all outdoor activities as tick populations expand and the season becomes prolonged. Ticks can carry various infectious diseases, the most notable and infamous of which is Lyme disease. Be vigilant in monitoring for ticks on your body. Here are a few tips regarding ticks and disease prevention:

1. Wear long pants tucked into your socks when traveling through long grass or scrubby areas that are more likely to harbor high tick populations.
2. Every 12 hours do a full-body tick check. Ticks are often found in moist, dark places, so carefully inspect your hairline, armpits, waist, groin, behind the knees, and similar areas.
3. Wear light-colored clothing to be able to spot ticks better.
4. Check your gear and other materials that travel with you and remove any ticks you find.
5. Know protocol for removing a tick if engorged. Know the symptoms of Lyme disease and get medical treatment if necessary.
6. Check cdc.gov/ticks for more information on ticks, bite prevention, Lyme disease, and more.

➔ FOOD AND WATER

Stay properly hydrated—be a safer, happier, and more efficient trail worker. Proper hydration helps prevent hypothermia, heat exhaustion, and heatstroke. A dehydrated person is often sluggish, is susceptible to injuries, and can have impaired judgment. Headaches are often an indicator of dehydration. Another indicator is the color and amount of urine. A properly hydrated person will have clear and copious urine.

Bring at least 2 quarts of water into the field (more if the weather is hot and humid). Drink small amounts often rather than a quart in one sitting. Follow the guideline that if you are thirsty, you are already dehydrated.

Never drink water directly from untreated water sources, such as ponds, streams, and rivers, as there is a risk of becoming ill. If obtaining water from these sources, several methods for purification are recommended. Boil the water for five minutes, use a commercial water purifier, or treat with iodine or a chlorine-based treatment. For the trail maintainer working for a day, iodine tablets or a lightweight commercial water purifier might be best.

Bring plenty of food and eat it. Hard work requires a lot of calories. Choose food you know is healthy and will provide energy. Food and diet is a very individual practice. Therefore employ a diet rich in calories that can sustain your energy for the entire day. Frequent snacks can bridge between meals to ensure sustained energy.

➔ SAFETY

Before setting out on the trail, get in the right mindset. Safety for you and the others in the work party is the first priority. When making decisions, always err on the side of safety. Remember that if you or another member of your party gets hurt out in the woods, you cannot expect an immediate response from emergency workers. While the crew leader is usually responsible for ensuring that safe work habits and techniques are used, ultimately all individuals are responsible for their own safety.

Crew leaders should hold a safety meeting each morning to review the day's work and to discuss safety considerations, including an evacuation plan. Make certain that everyone has adequate layers, appropriate PPE, and enough food and water for the day. Go over the goals for the day and tools needed. Do not assign people to work for which they have not been trained. Crew leaders should monitor crew safety levels continually and communicate with the crew if changes are needed. Leaders should especially be aware of their own behaviors and practices, since their actions will set the tone.

SAFE WORKING TECHNIQUES

Before going into the woods on their first trip, trail workers must know, at a minimum, how to safely lift heavy items, carry tools, and identify safe proximities relative to other coworkers and the work environment. These topics can be covered in a safety talk at the trailhead, on the project site, or before beginning a new task.

Lifting

Many trail workers develop back problems because they fail to heed this simple advice: Lift with your knees, not with your back! Improper lifting may lead to an injured back or a more serious chronic condition.

Trail work can require lifting a variety of objects, such as branches, logs, rocks, and tools (see figure 6.1). Many strenuous trail work activities can cause a sore back, but lifting improperly can lead to worse problems. Always consider how you can limit the stress on your back. When lifting, start with your knees bent, back straight, and feet shoulder-width apart. Keep your shoulders and neck straight. Lift the object gradually rather than jerking it up. If you are pushing a heavy ob-

Figure 6.1. Lift with your legs to minimize risk of injury to your back.

ject along the ground, keep your back straight and parallel with the direction you are pushing. Exert force on the object with your knees.

Carrying Tools

There is a right way and a wrong way to carry tools. When carrying a tool with a blade, a point, sharp teeth, or a sharpened surface, hold the tool at your side with the sharp or pointed end facing away from you (see figure 6.2). Should you trip, stumble, or fall, this makes it easier to toss the tool to the side to avoid injuring yourself or the person in front of or behind you. Distance yourself from the person in front of you, especially when carrying difficult-to-hold tools. Use blade guards and sheaths on sharp edges when you are hiking to or from a work site. Switch hands often to avoid fatigue, and if you can do it comfortably, strap your tools onto your pack to leave your hands free. Don't carry tools on your shoulder, as this increases the likelihood of injury if you fall.

6

Figure 6.2. Carry tools at your side with the more dangerous ends pointing down.

Circle of Danger

The *circle of danger* is the area that surrounds a worker who is using or carrying a tool (see figure 6.3). The primary, or inner, circle of danger extends as far as the tool can reach while the worker is using it. The secondary, or outer, circle of danger is the distance the tool could travel if the worker were to let go of it. Be especially aware of the outer circle when tools such as axes and swizzle sticks are in use; the quick swinging motion of those tools is more dangerous when combined with a broken handle or a lost grip. Workers should never enter someone's inner circle of danger while that person is working and should never enter the outer circle in the direct path of a swing (see figure 6.4). The person using the tool must always be aware of people in the immediate area and ask others to move away if they are too close.

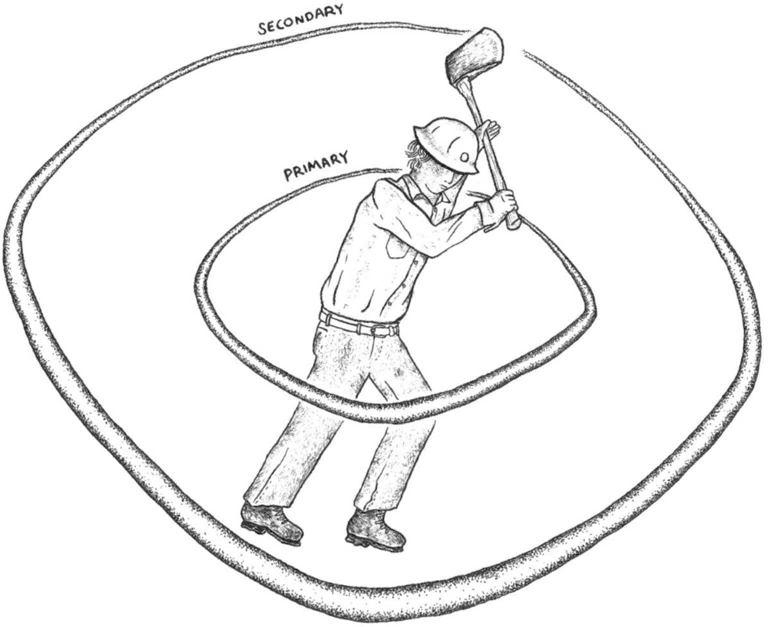

Figure 6.3. Your circle of danger emcompasses arm length plus tool length.

ACQUIRE THE SKILLS

Get training for trail work from a local trail club, land management agency, or contractor. Training with other trail workers is fun, increases ability and skills, and provides an opportunity to ask questions about trail work. Many trail clubs require training for people who want to maintain a section of trail on their own.

Leading crews is challenging and requires skills beyond basic trail work. At a minimum, acquire first-aid certification and leadership training. First-aid training will provide an extra measure of risk management and is required by most organizations to lead groups of individuals. Leadership training helps with the finer points of group management and is available through many trail-maintaining organizations.

In short, use common sense and go through the fundamentals of preparation before heading out. Work safe and work smart.

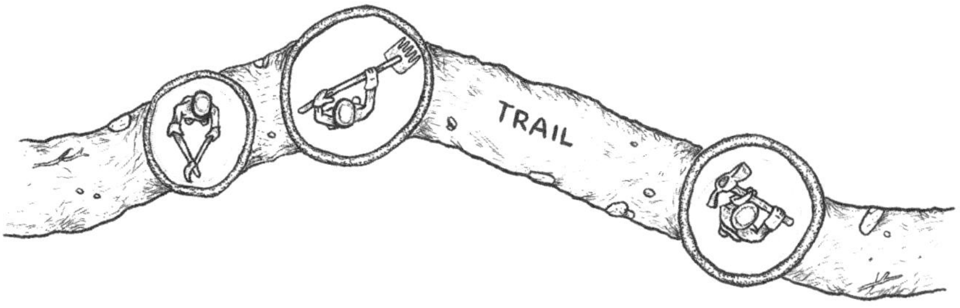

Figure 6.4. Be mindful of others' circles of danger as well as your own.

→ MANAGING YOUR CREW

Set an attainable goal each day—one that is ambitious but not out of reach. Examples of good goals would be to clean all the drainages on a section of trail, brush one mile of a trail, or install six rock steps. Goals will keep the crew focused and provide a sense of accomplishment at the end of the day.

Be sure to check in regularly with the crew. Trail work can be more exhausting than some people anticipate. Offer regular rests for water, snacks, and foot care, and to simply take a break. Finding appropriate tasks for all crew members can be challenging due to varied skills, experience levels, and interpersonal dynamics. Plan a variety of tasks that offer something for everyone. Above all, be sure the crew is safe, busy, and having fun.

→ THE RIGHT WORK PLAN AND TOOLS

Plan and prepare trail projects ahead of time and determine the types of tools and the number of personnel needed. Know exactly the work to be done and the location of the site. If necessary, have the work site marked in advance. With a volunteer crew, planning and preparation is especially important. It minimizes the amount of time the leader needs to get oriented to the work; during this time volunteers are likely to just stand around, waiting for instructions.

It is critical to bring the proper tools, and in the correct number, so that the crew can work effectively. There is no formula for this—use experience and judgment. Obviously, don't bring unneeded or excessive numbers of tools that will load up workers' packs or make the crew doubt the project leadership. The more information known about the work ahead of time, the more precisely tools and tool quantities can be selected. Avoid scheduling extra work that requires additional tools. Focus on one task, such as cleaning drainage, and bring only the tools needed for that job.

For more information on leading a crew, see Chapter 13 (page 222).

TOOLS: USE AND CARE

The types of tools used in trail maintenance and construction will vary depending on the type of work and, in some cases, regional and cultural preferences. One should always have the proper tools for the job. The purpose of this section is to discuss various types of tools and equipment and to outline proper use, care, and applicable safety procedures.

Although this section covers some basic power tools, the information provided is limited. Professional users and manufacturers can supply many more details about selecting and safely operating power equipment. Remember, proper training is extremely important for safe and efficient use of all power tools.

Strive to purchase top-quality tools. Bargain tools will usually cause headaches for trail workers and could possibly compromise their safety and efficiency, especially in a backcountry setting.

➔ MEASURING AND MAPPING TOOLS

GPS

There are many GPS units and applications on the market, ranging from amateur to professional grade. Most applications are widely available on portable devices and have varying capabilities of storing specific data. Because technology is constantly changing and new features are always being added, do some research before investing in a GPS unit, a GIS program, and any other software needed for collecting, organizing, and managing data. There are many options for mapping software, from expensive GIS programs with annual subscriptions to free applications for download.

CLINOMETERS

A clinometer is a simple, useful tool for determining grade of the existing terrain or desired line of the trail. Most optical analog clinometers show grade in percent (%) and degrees (°). It is standard to discuss grade as a percentage. Measurements through the device are usually read with the right eye while the left eye sights the target object simultaneously. Due to personal sight differences reading with the left eye may be easier. It is important that both eyes are kept open when reading the scale through the device. In the case of reading grade for trail layout or construction, aim at an object that is the exact height of your eye. This is easiest to do with a partner; as the partner walks in the direction of the desired trail, aim at the point on the partner that aligns with your eye height. The partner flags locations at desired grades as you both move along. If you must take readings alone, tie flagging to a tree at eye height, walk ahead to a tree along the desired path, and "backsight" the tied flagging. This gives you the grade along that sight line.

STRING LINES

String lines can be used as a guide with a tape measure and line level to lay out stairs and to determine their desired rise and run (see Chapter 8, page 136). String lines can also be used in the general trail construction process or in applications with bridge construction to guide the outside edge of the structure as it's built.

FLAGGING

Flagging or marker flags can be used to mark out new trail, possible campsites, potential projects, and other important locations. Pieces tied to trees can be written on in permanent marker with shorthand instructions. However, be sure to remove flagging when it is no longer needed so as not to leave litter in the woods. Pin flagging is best in treeless areas or for projects that require more engineering precision. Biodegradable flagging tape can be good for trail work, depending on the climate and length of time it needs to be used.

➔ GENERAL PURPOSE TOOLS

SHOVEL

The commonly used spade shovel comes with either a long handle (see figure 6.5) or D-handle (see figure 6.6). The shorter D-handle shovel is more appropriate in congested situations. Some also find lifting with this type of shovel to be easier, since the load is closer to the body. Others favor the long-handle shovel because it offers a longer reach and usually requires less bend. Do not pry too aggressively with either kind of shovel or the handle will break. Use a mattock or rock bar if large rocks impede digging. Some maintainers sharpen the shovel's edge slightly to facilitate cutting roots.

Fire shovels are often well sharpened and are used to scrape away the duff (organic matter) in the building of a fire line. A well-sharpened shovel should be marked or labeled and kept separate from the other shovels to maintain its edges.

6

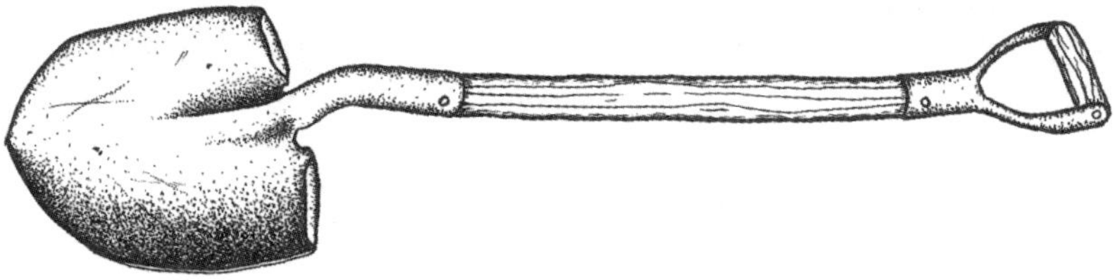

Figure 6.5, top. Long-handle shovels have wood or fiberglass handles.
Figure 6.6, bottom. A D-handle shovel adds hand control and comfort.

ROCK BAR

The rock bar (see figure 6.7) is an essential tool for moving large and small rocks. Hardened-steel rock bars that are 16 to 18 pounds and about 4½ feet long with a beveled tip are best. Lighter ones tend to bend; shorter ones provide less leverage. The bar's length allows for various ways to level and push rocks, and its chisel-shaped tip provides additional mechanical advantage for moving extremely heavy objects. Lifting strength is dramatically increased when a rock bar is used in conjunction with a small rock or log as a fulcrum. Techniques for using this tool will be further discussed in Chapter 7 (page 93).

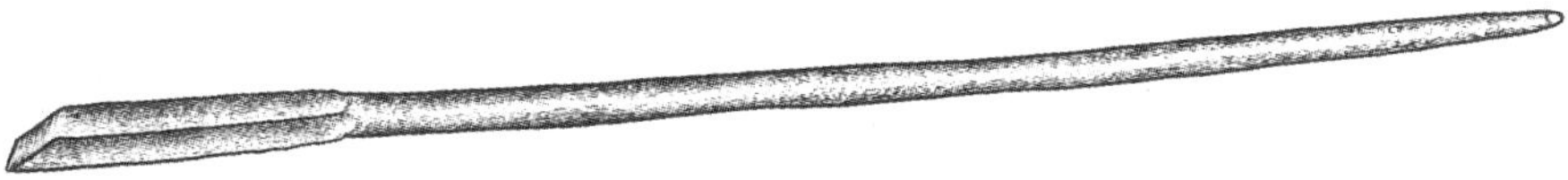

Figure 6.7. The 18-pound single-bevel steel rock bar is a popular choice for trail builders.

➔ **Safety Tips:** Never have fingers and tools on the rock at the same time; the possibility of crushing a finger with a tool or shifting rock is too great. Communicate clearly if working with anyone, and make a plan ahead of time. Always lift with your legs, keeping your back straight. Be aware of other hazards that might be encountered while rolling a rock. Never place yourself downslope from a rock while moving it.

PICK AND CUTTER MATTOCKS

Mattocks are heavy, rugged tools that do not break easily. They can be used to chop through roots, loosen compacted soils, and pry rocks. Two types of mattocks are available, both of which have an adze set at a right angle to the handle for grubbing out roots, stumps, rocks, and debris. They differ by having either a pick or a cutter blade at the other end (see figure 6.8). The cutter mattock may be more effective in areas with deeper soils that contain more roots than rocks.

The pick mattock (see figure 6.9) is one of the most useful and versatile trail hand tools. In addition to its effectiveness when digging, it can also be used in some situations to facilitate rock moving. When the pick is placed against the rock, the mattock acts as a fulcrum for both lifting and pulling the rock. Take care when using this technique. Be sure to use a pick mattock designed for trail work, made of strong metal and with a strong handle in good condition. A rock that is too heavy could break the handle or bend the tool head. It's easy to lose your grip and fall while using a pick mattock to fulcrum, so take time to determine if a rock bar might be a more effective and safer tool for the job.

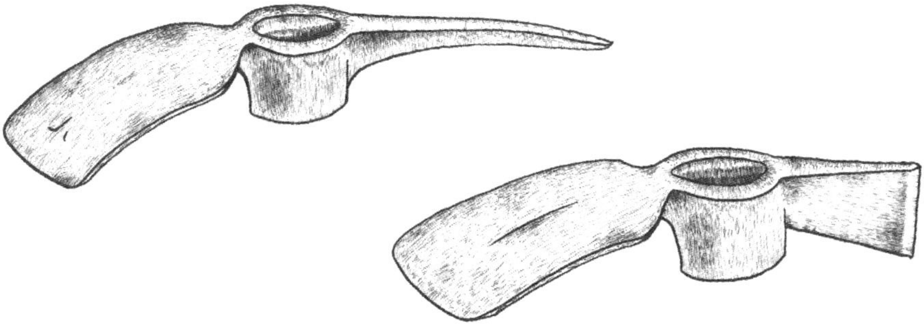

Figure 6.8. Pick and cutter mattock heads.

6

To care for a mattock, slightly sharpen it periodically to maintain a rudimentary edge capable of effective digging and root cutting. An electric grinding wheel, carefully used to avoid overheating the edge, reduces labor time when sharpening. Give handles an occasional coating of boiled linseed oil; replace any damaged handles.

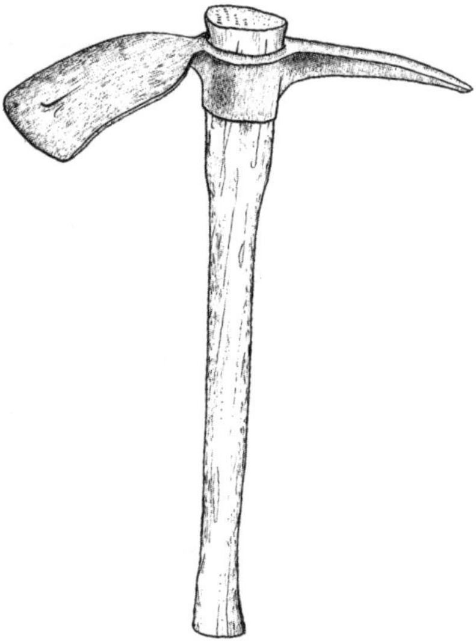

Figure 6.9. The pick mattock is a popular hand tool for trail builders as it can be used for many tasks.

To keep handles from loosening, drill a pilot hole and then screw a 3⁄16-inch-by-1-inch lag bolt into the handle up against the mattock head. Do not place it in the side of the handle, because this may cause it to split. (This should be done to grub and adze hoes also.) However, some workers like having the option to remove the mattock head from the handle for easier transport. To do so, tap the end of the handle on a rock or other hard surface, carefully watching as the head becomes loose and drops down the length of the handle to the ground. To reattach the head, hold the handle upside down and drop the head (also upside down) onto the handle. Tamp the entire tool (still upside down) on a rock to secure.

➔ **Safety Tips:** Maintain a well-controlled swing and stay aware of people around you. Pay attention to your lower back when using the mattock to fulcrum. Also, be ready if the pick slips on the rock . . . it's very easy to end up on the ground.

FIRE RAKE

Fire rakes (see figure 6.10) are very useful for duffing (removing the organic layer of the soil) new trail and are also good for cleaning drainages that are primarily clogged with leaves and loose soil. If drainages are maintained annually, this can be the ideal tool for cleaning them.

➔ **Safety Tip:** Be sure to set fire rakes in a safe place, teeth down, when not in use.

Figure 6.10. Fire rakes are typically used for duffing or for clearing wide drainages.

MCLEOD

The McLeod (see figure 6.11) is a tool named after Malcolm McLeod, a U.S. Forest Service Ranger at the Sierra National Forest in the early twentieth century. A flat metal head with rake tines on one side and a straight beveled edge on the other is attached to a long handle. The McLeod originated in the West and was initially designed for work on the fire line, but it can also be used to tamp. It is very useful when breaking new trail (especially on trails with a lot of duff), when finishing natural surface trail tread, and when maintaining drainage structures.

Figure 6.11. McLeods are great for new trail construction, shaping, and tamping.

HOES: GRUB HOE AND ADZE HOE

Hoes of various styles are used in trail construction and maintenance. They are particularly useful for duffing new trail, sidehill grubbing, and building and cleaning drainages.

Adze hoes are essentially mattocks without cutter blades or picks. These hoes have a blade 3 to 4 inches wide and have a handle like a mattock. Adze hoes are heavy but are preferable where soils are rocky.

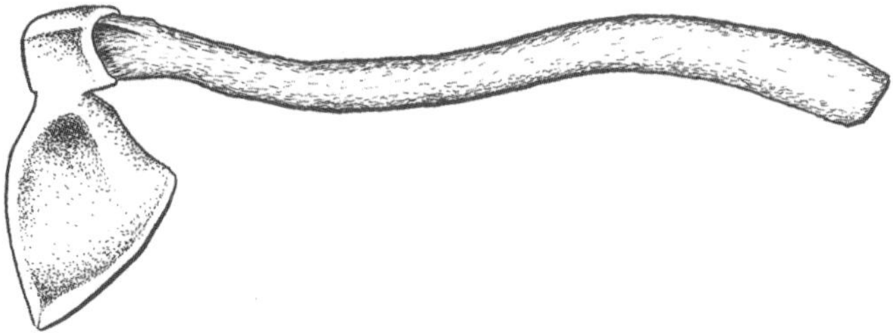

Figure 6.12. A grub hoe, hazel hoe, or Rogue hoe is a good tool for trail construction and cleaning drainages.

A grub hoe (see figure 6.12), or hazel hoe, is lighter than an adze hoe and has a wider blade (6 to 8 inches), sharper edge, and curved handle. This tool is most useful where a significant amount of sidehill grubbing has to be done—except where soils are very rocky. The wider blade moves more soil, the sharper edge cuts roots well, and the curved handle facilitates use.

Recent entries into the hoe marketplace, such as Rogue Hoe, offer products that have very sharp blades and longer handles and combine hoes with rakes and other features.

➔ **Safety Tip:** Be aware of shins while swinging.

SLEDGEHAMMER (DOUBLE-JACK)

Sledgehammers, sometimes referred to as double-jacks, are used to hit rock directly and to hit other hammers or chisels. They are also necessary when pounding spikes during wood construction projects. Their heads generally weigh 6 to 12 pounds. As with all softer metal hammers, the head may mushroom with extended use. File off metal spurs and mushrooming when necessary. To shape rock, use a hammer set. They are produced with metal that is meant to be struck by another hammer.

SINGLE-JACK HAMMER

This lightweight hammer (3 to 4 pounds) with a short handle can be used for single-person rock work and placing spikes.

PICK

A pick is rarely necessary in trail work, since its function is adequately served by the pick mattock. However, picks may be more appropriate than mattocks for loosening compacted earth or for chipping rocks. They are particularly helpful for aerating compacted soils when closing and revegetating trails.

➔ **Safety Tip:** Be sure to maintain a controlled swing.

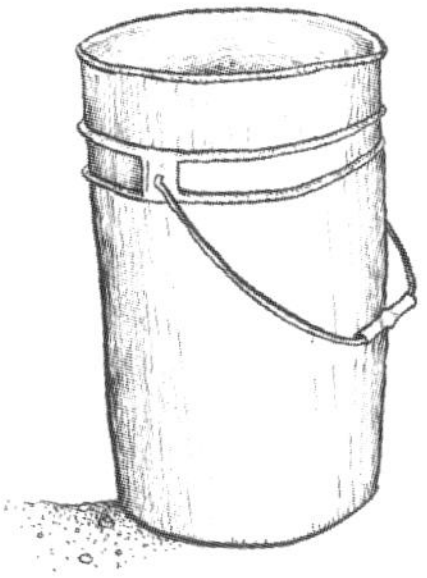

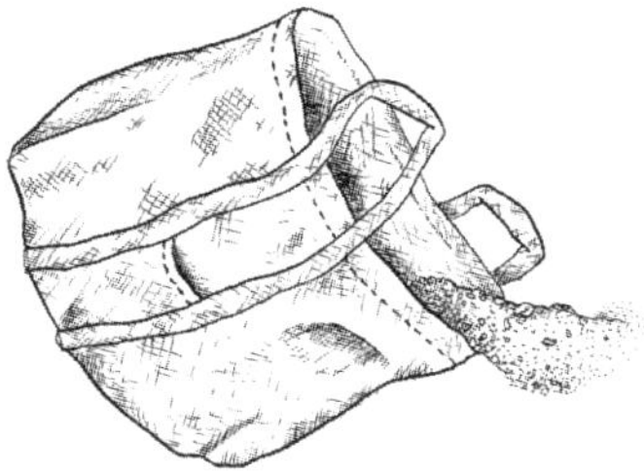

Figure 6.13, above left. A wheelbarrow with one or two wheels can help move mineral soil or rock fill easier.
Figure 6.14, above center. Five-gallon buckets are indispensable on any trail project.
Figure 6.15, above right. Canvas bags are similar to five-gallon buckets but harder to find. They are collapsible and packable.

OTHER TOOLS

Wheelbarrows (see figure 6.13) can be used for moving rock or soil along a moderate trail. (*Note*: Wheelbarrows are not permitted in Wilderness areas.)

Five-gallon buckets (see figure 6.14) are great for carrying soil or stone for projects such as cribbing, scree walls, or turnpiking. They are also useful to carry leaves for finishing brush-in of project sites.

Canvas bags or coal bags (see figure 6.15) can be handy for moving smaller, lighter amounts of material.

Garden rakes are good for spreading material but must have strong metal tines.

➔ CUTTING TOOLS

Cutting tools are some of the most important tools for trail work. They are used to clear trees and brush from trails during their initial development and annually thereafter. In addition, cutting tools are used to build various wooden trail structures.

Cutting tools require more care and maintenance than other tools; in addition, high-quality products may be harder to find. Many stores carry axes, saws, and pruners; however, most of these "off-the-shelf" tools tend not to stand up to the rigors of heavy use. Purchase well-made tools that are designed to withstand the demands of trail work.

In addition to their usefulness, cutting tools can be some of the most dangerous tools to work with, so be especially careful when using them and always wear PPE.

AX

The ax is one of the world's oldest tools. It has played a tremendously important role throughout history. In America, the ax reached its highest form; nowhere else in the world has it been used so much, undergone so many changes, and seen so many adaptations to different uses. Unfortunately, the ax is losing its importance and popularity due to several factors: abundance of alternatives (for example, chain saw, pruning saws), lack of market demand from the forest industry, and required skill needed. This makes it very difficult to find a good ax made of high-quality steel.

Although fewer people use the ax today, it continues to be important in trail work. For example, it is the AMC trail crews' primary tool for cutting logs for trail reconstruction and removing winter blowdowns. If used correctly and maintained properly, the ax can be a very effective, efficient, and safe tool for trail jobs. However, without proper training in its use and with poor maintenance, an ax can be very dangerous. Trail organizations and land managers have developed ax training programs for staff and trail adopters. Training is highly recommended and sometimes required before performing any trail work with these groups.

An ax is lighter than a chain saw and does not require as many accessories. In addition to being a very practical tool for trail work, the ax is also aesthetically pleasing because of its ancient roots and has great appeal for many trail workers.

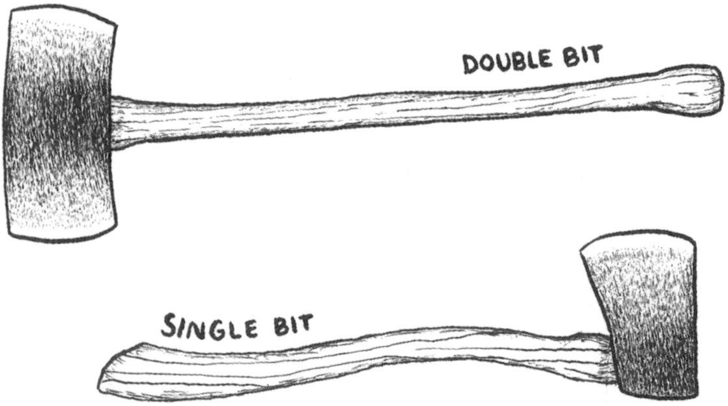

Figure 6.16. Single-bit and double-bit axes.

Aside from replacing the handle when necessary, maintaining an ax is a relatively expense-free proposition, unlike the continued cost of operating a chain saw.

The two basic kinds of axes are the single bit and the double bit (see figure 6.16). Both can be used for removing blowdowns, felling trees, limbing (removing limbs from fallen trees), cutting notches and water bars, and squaring off bridges. The double-bit ax was more popular in the past, but the single-bit ax is the most popular today. Although the flat head of the single-bit ax can also be used for pounding stakes or driving wedges in a pinch, it is best to use a sledgehammer for heavy pounding or when driving spikes or other metal. Both types of ax heads can have different shapes (see figure 6.17).

The size of the ax is a personal preference. Chopping work is often done with a 3- to 3½-pound ax head, although some prefer a heavier head. The correct handle length is determined by the user's height, body type, and personal preference. Unfamiliarity with an ax and lack of maintenance are the most common causes of injury.

A high-quality ax is often made of two different kinds of steel. Mild steel, which is softer and more resistant to impact, composes the body of the ax, or the eye. The edge of the ax is made of harder carbon steel that is forged to the body; it will take and hold a sharp edge. Most axes today are drop-forged and made of soft steel, which generally doesn't hold a sharp edge for very long. When shopping for an ax, look for a seam and hammer marks between the eye and the edge of the ax; this indicates that it is made of two different kinds of steel. An ax head that is painted or otherwise obscured, especially in the vicinity of the edge, is probably drop-forged. A good place to look for a high-quality two-piece ax is an antique store. The older axes found in such places are often handmade and of generally higher quality than those purchased new.

In addition to axes for cutting clean timber, most crews also have a root ax, usually a lower-quality single bit. Root axes are used when cutting in or close to the ground, where the edge of a good ax could be damaged.

6

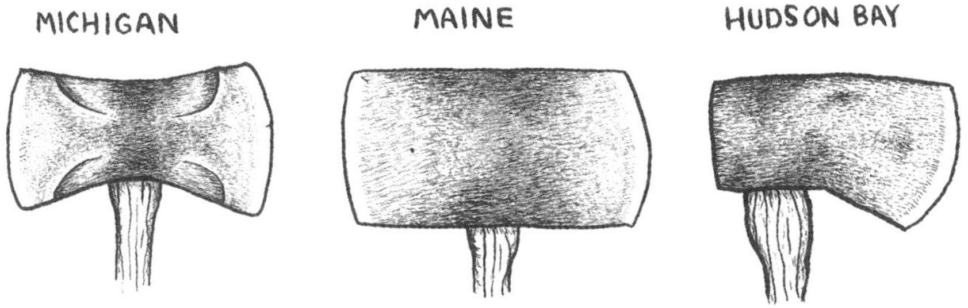

Figure 6.17. Older ax heads can be found with a variety of shapes and styles, many based on specific regions.

Ax Sharpening and Maintenance

Sharpening

All cutting tools, including axes, are safest when kept sharp. A sharp edge easily penetrates wood, reducing fatigue and hazardous glancing blows.

Sharpening an ax can be tedious, but it is a fairly straightforward process, requiring only time, practice, and a few simple implements. The most critical aspect of the ax edge is the *bevel*, which is the shape of the edge itself.

Look at figure 6.18. Bevel A usually develops in an older ax that has been improperly maintained. Sharpening has obviously been concentrated on the edge, which has rounded out the steel into a fairly blunt profile. Bevel B is the proper bevel. The ax is thin enough to penetrate deeply into wood but not too thin, as in bevel C. A thin bevel is apt to stick in wood without knocking the chips loose, which makes the edge fragile and prone to breaking. To work a bevel down and get it into shape, as in bevel B, use a good manual stone wheel or a mill bastard file (see figure 6.19). The mill bastard file gets its name from its traditional use sharpening saws in sawmills. This type of file comes in many configurations for various tools that have a cutting edge.

6

When using a manual stone wheel (see figure 6.20), always keep its surface wet to carry away any grit that could clog the sharpening surface and to prevent unnecessary friction and overheating of the ax head. Never sharpen an ax with an electric grinding wheel. This can lead to overheating the metal, which will destroy the temper of the steel.

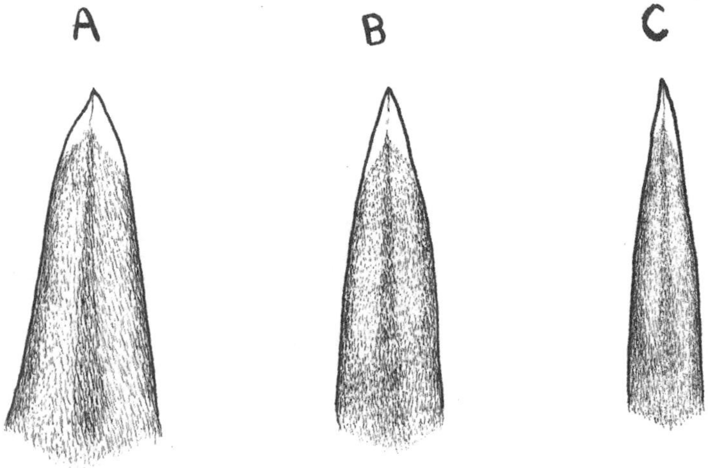

Figure 6.18. When sharpening axes, aim for "B."

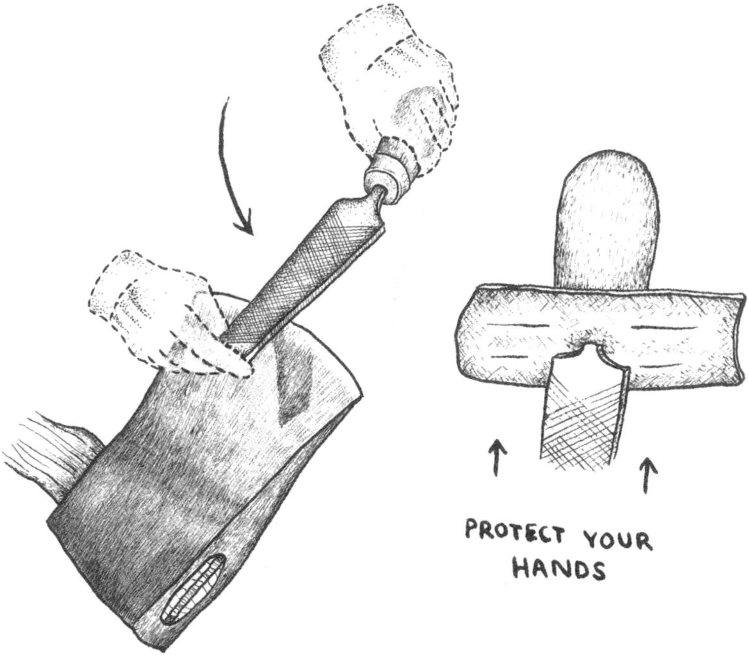

Figure 6.19. Hand-filing allows for a slow and methodical process. Use a mill bastard to take off large amounts of material and a second cut file for more fine-tuning.

6

A mill bastard file works well for sharpening axes and other hand tools; it is also inexpensive and can be brought to the work site. Always sharpen into the blade; otherwise, the edge will develop a small piece of wirelike metal that will break off with use. By sharpening into the blade, little or no burr will form. Use extreme care when sharpening with a file, because your hand will be pushing toward the blade. For extra protection, a file can be fitted with a handle and hand guard. Cut a 4-inch square of leather or old fire hose, cut a hole through the center, slip it over the tang of the file, and put the handle on. Wear leather gloves to prevent cuts when sharpening an ax.

Work the bevel down until it looks thin enough to cut properly (bevel B) and has

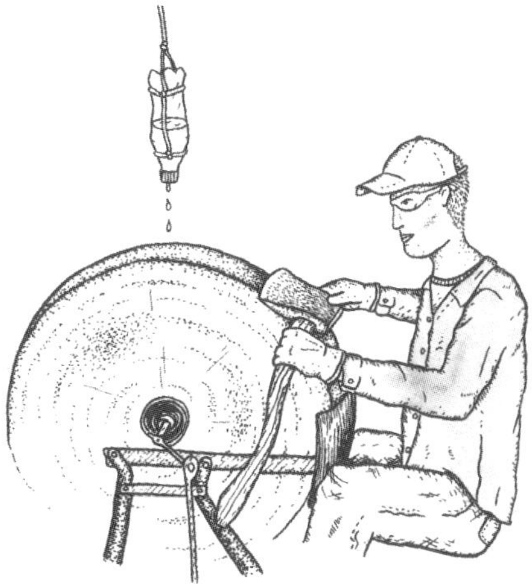

Figure 6.20. Large stone wheels may be hard to come by. Electric slow revolution stone wheels can be found more easily and achieve the same results.

a consistently even and slightly curved shape. Once the proper bevel is attained, use a round handstone to hone the edge smooth. Put water or a light honing or mineral oil on the handstone. If a very keen edge is desired, use a finer grit stone. This final part of the process can produce an edge fine enough to shave a hair, although many people achieve an excellent edge using only a file. A sharpening stone may be preferable for maintaining a good edge, since frequent filing rapidly wears down the blade.

Again, an ax should be kept as sharp as possible at all times. Maintaining a keen edge is well worth the effort because it will greatly increase ease of use, efficiency, and safety.

Rehandling

Handles eventually must be replaced because over time they will warp, crack, break, or shrink. A loose ax head can also make handle replacement necessary. The first step is removal of the old handle. An easy way to do this is by sawing the handle off close to the ax head. Then place the head in a vise or on wooden blocks and drill out as much wood as you can from the eye of the ax with an electric or hand-operated drill. Boring out these holes relieves the pressure of the wood within the ax head so that the wood can be pounded out with a hammer and a blunt metal object.

Choose a new handle with a length suitable for the user. Keep in mind the importance of choosing the correct length for safety reasons and efficiency. When purchasing a new handle, closely observe the grain of the wood. The grain of the wood should be fairly straight, close together, and parallel with the axis of the handle and the ax head (see figure 6.21). Look carefully for knots and other defects. Hickory is often considered the best choice for handles because of its overall strength and elastic qualities. Avoid purchasing handles that are painted, since painting often conceals faults in the wood, and the paint can contribute to blisters forming on hands.

The next step is fitting the handle into the eye. Shape the handle to closely match the eye of the ax to ensure a tight fit. Use a draw knife, wood rasp, or spoke shave to whittle the top of the handle down to the size of the eye. Remove wood cautiously, a little at a time, so that you do not make the handle too thin. Once you can get the handle to slide into the top third of the eye, test the fit by pounding the handle into the head. Hold the handle, ax head down, and drive the handle down into the eye by pounding the base of the handle with a wooden or leather mallet or old mattock handle. You can also drive the ax head down onto the handle by setting the head on the handle and pounding the base of the handle straight down onto a block of wood on the floor or a stump. Be careful to prevent the head from springing off the handle. Check the fit and see if you need to take off more wood. If you do, knock the head off the handle with a block of wood or mattock handle, and shave off more wood where needed. Try the fit

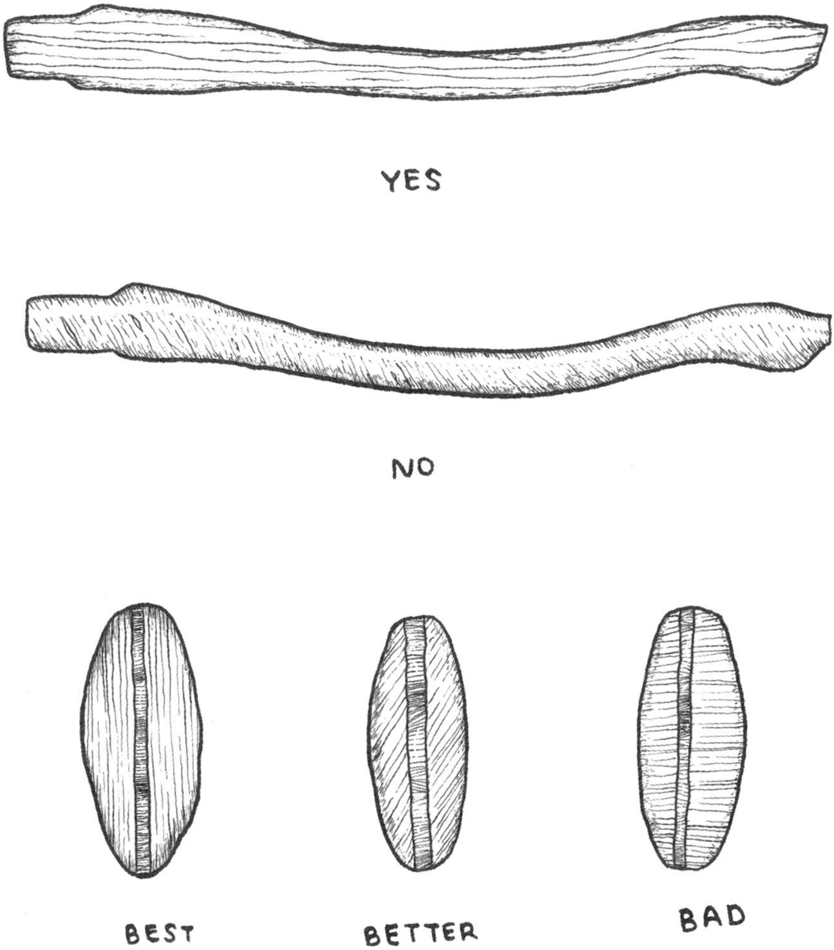

Figure 6.21. Wood grain running parallel to the wedge slot will make the strongest handle.

again. You'll probably need to test and fine-tune the handle a few times until you achieve the desired fit.

Once you get a snug fit, pound the handle all the way in so that the ax head wedges tightly on the handle at its proper place (see figure 6.22). An inch or so of the top of the handle should be sticking out past the top of the ax head; saw off this excess wood, leaving a quarter to half an inch protracting above the eye; when this wood swells with moisture it tightens the handle's fit. Next, drive a hardwood wedge into the cut handle slot, now inside the eye of the ax head. Cut off any excess wedge when it will not go deeper. Wooden wedges, usually supplied with a new handle, compress as they are driven in and then expand inside the head, securing it tightly. The wedge may split as you drive it in; that's fine because some pieces will go deeper and fill wider gaps. Avoid small steel wedges, but if you have some, you may want to save them for emergency use if the ax head becomes loose while you're in the field. Once steel wedges are driven into the ax, the grain of the handle becomes cracked and weakened. Thus, it is hard to use the same handle to rehang your ax.

Caring for the handle

When purchased, new handles are often either painted or have a hard varnish finish that can lead to blisters on hands and cause the handle to dry out and crack. Sand off the paint or varnish and rub in a coat of boiled linseed oil with a rag; this keeps the handle flexible and protects it from rot and drying, which can lead to cracking and shrinking. A periodic coat of boiled linseed oil will prevent these problems and give the handle a smooth finish.

To help extend the life of a handle, periodically pour boiled linseed oil in one or two holes drilled into the end of the handle (see figure 6.23). The holes should be about ¼ inch in diameter and ½ inch deep. At the end of each work trip, carefully pour several drops of linseed oil into the holes and set the ax handle upright (ax head down) to soak overnight. The natural capillary action of the wood will draw the oil into the grain.

If a handle shrinks and loosens within the ax head, soak the ax head in a bucket of water overnight. Soaking in water causes the wood to swell and tighten within the head. However, this is only a temporary solution. Replacing or adding a wedge may help, but the handle probably needs to be replaced.

Do not store an ax for a long period of time by leaning it in a corner, because the handle could develop a bend. Hang it up instead.

Sheaths

Axes should be sheathed when transported or stored to protect both the edge of the ax and people. Many kinds of sheaths can be purchased (see figure 6.24) or made. The most common ones are leather sheaths with snaps or straps.

Sheaths can be made using rubber from an old garden hose or fire hose. Cut the hose the width of the blade and

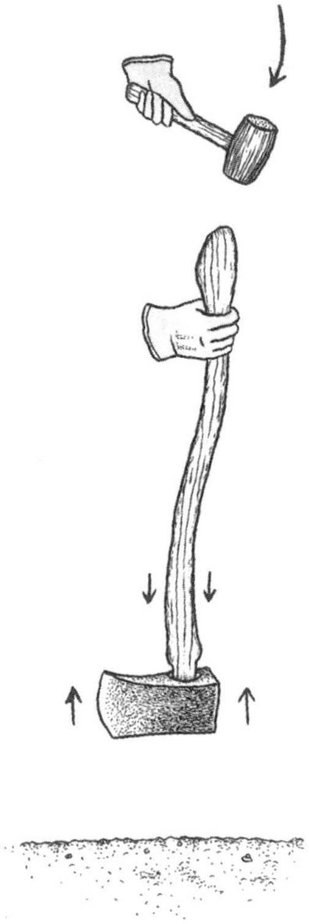

Figure 6.22, above. Use a wood or rubber mallet to strike the bottom of the ax handle. This is a slow, back-and-forth process.
Figure 6.23, below. Adding linseed oil will help with handle preservation. Once the ax is hung, soaking the head in linseed overnight is another good option.

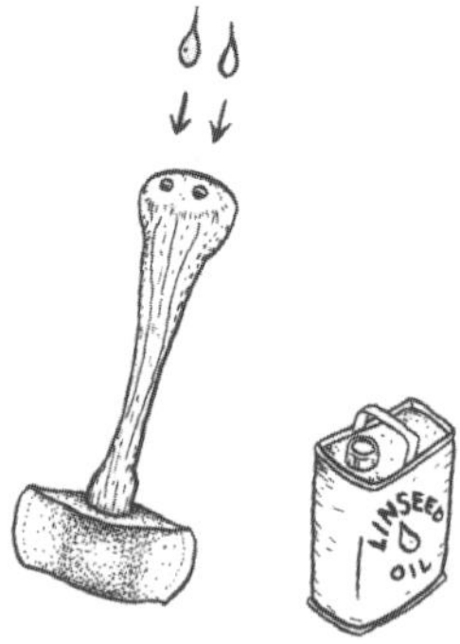

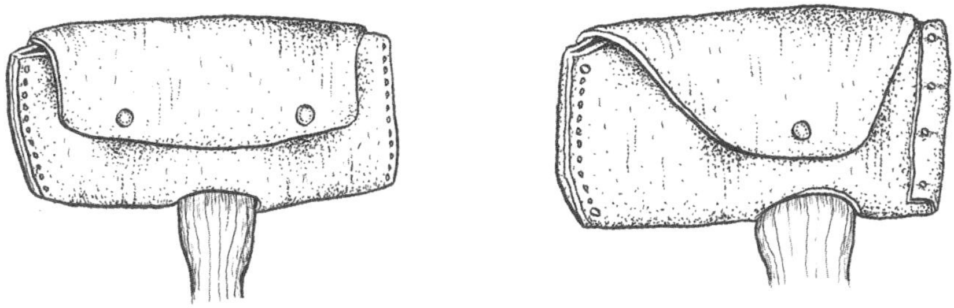

Figure 6.24. Store-bought ax sheaths tend to fit only factory-made axes.

slit it lengthwise. Insert the edge of the ax in the hose and secure it by wrapping a piece of rubber inner tube around the hose and the poll or butt of the ax head. Another type of sheath can be made by hollowing a block of wood to fit over the edge of the ax (see figure 6.25). Wood is less prone to slip off the blade and is stronger than rubber hose. Staple or screw the inner tube to the wood sheath. The sheath is then held in place by the tension between the wood block and the inner tube wrapped around the butt of the ax.

CROSSCUT SAWS

There are two main types of crosscut saws: the one-person crosscut, generally 3 to 4½ feet in length, and the two-person crosscut, usually 5 to 8 feet in length (see figure 6.26). The basic two-person saw is further split into two different patterns: The felling saw, for cutting down trees, has a concave back and is relatively light-

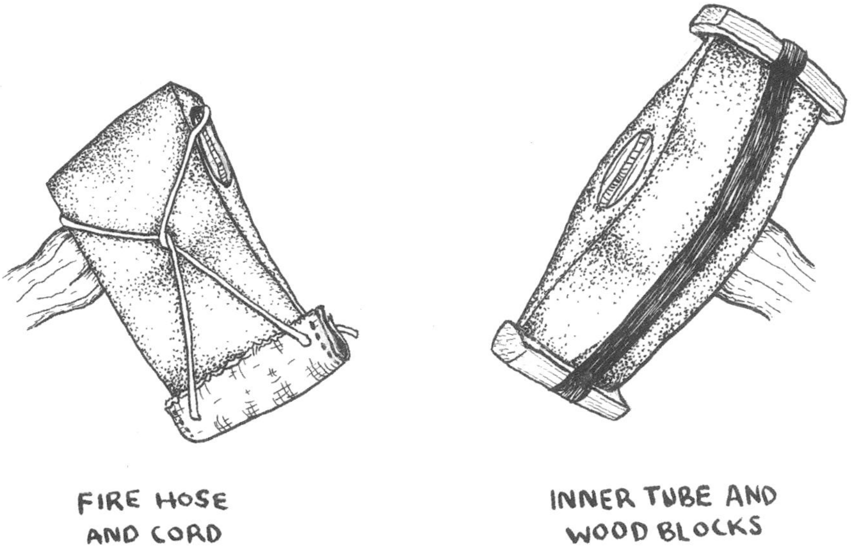

Figure 6.25. Handmade ax sheaths add character and allow flexibility to fit the unique shape of the ax head.

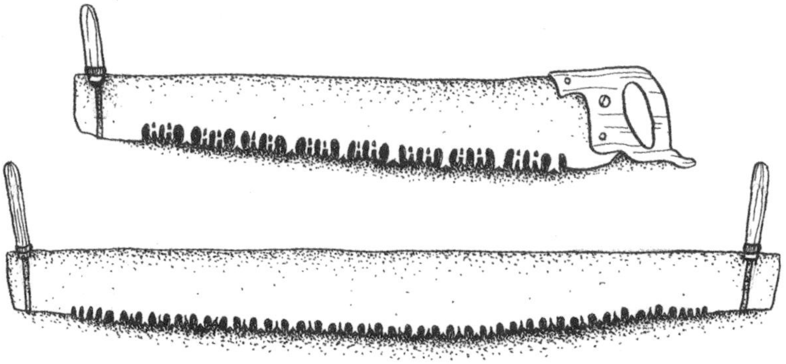

Figure 6.26. Crosscut saws for one for two people. One-person saws can generally be adapted for use as a two-person saw.

weight and flexible. The bucking saw, for cutting up felled trees, has a flat back and is heavier and stiffer.

Crosscut saws have three common tooth patterns, each designed for a specific type of wood. The perforated-lance tooth is best for cutting softwoods (see figure 6.27). The champion tooth (see figure 6.28) is ideal for cutting hardwoods or frozen timber and is most often used with one-person saws. The plain tooth (see figure 6.29) is designed for cutting dead, dry wood.

A plain-tooth saw both cuts the wood and removes the shavings. Perforated-lance saws and champion-tooth saws sever the wood fibers on each side of the cut. The raker teeth on these two saws, cutting like a plane bit, peel the cut fibers, collect them in the gullets between the cutting teeth and raker teeth, and carry them out of the cut (see figure 6.30). A properly sharpened crosscut saw cuts deep and produces thick shavings.

Most important, when using a crosscut saw, make sure these different teeth are at the appropriate levels. The raker teeth need to be a bit lower than the cutting teeth so that they are not the first to cut into the wood. The U.S. Forest Service publishes a manual about using and caring for crosscut saws, which can be accessed online at www.fs.fed.us/eng/pubs/pdfpubs/pdf77712508/pdf77712508dpi72.pdf.

Few people today know how to properly maintain and use a crosscut saw. The ax, chain saw, and bow saw are more commonly used. With the introduction of the chain saw, the crosscut saw—like the ax—has fallen out of favor.

Crosscut saws do have some advantages over axes and chain saws, which makes them a good choice for certain projects and applications. They are inexpensive, lightweight, and nonpolluting; they are generally safer than axes and relatively easy to operate. They are often used for trail work in Wilderness areas where motorized equipment is not allowed. They can be just as effective as chain saws, especially when tools must be carried long distances. Finding someone to properly sharpen a crosscut saw can be difficult sometimes, but you can purchase small, relatively

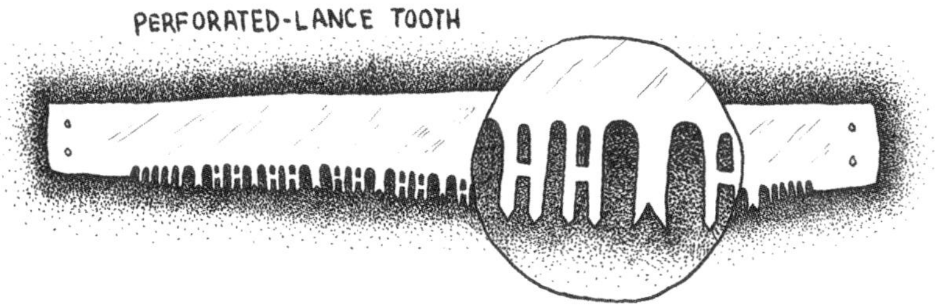

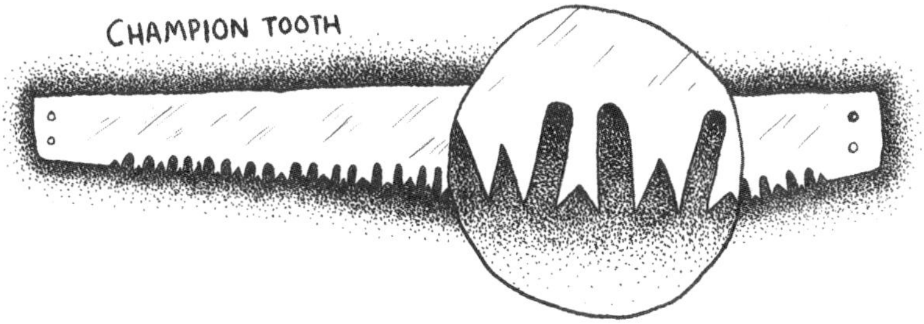

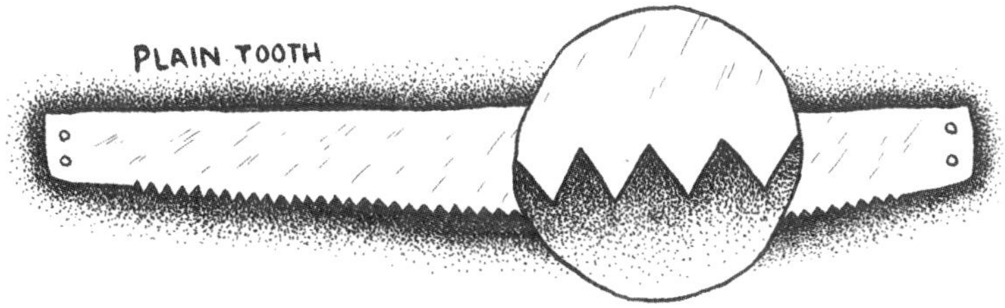

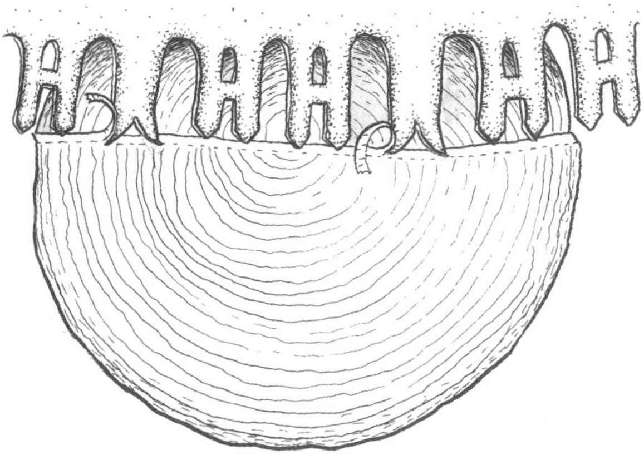

Figure 6.27, top. Perforated-lance tooth profile. Good for cutting softwood.
Figure 6.28, middle above. Champion tooth profile. Good for cutting hardwood.
Figure 6.29, middle below. Plain tooth profile. Good for cutting dead, dry wood.
Figure 6.30, bottom. Perforated teeth both cut and remove wood shavings.

inexpensive sharpening kits, and it is fairly easy to find excellent instructions online and elsewhere for performing your own maintenance.

Keep a few use and safety factors in mind. When felling timber, use the same basic technique as outlined for felling with a chain saw or an ax (see Chapter 7, page 99). When transporting a crosscut saw, make a sheath from a section of old fire hose by slitting it along its length and tying or strapping it over the teeth. You can also use three or four bolts to fasten two strips of plywood together over the blade.

➔ **Safety Tip:** Be aware of where wood will roll or shift when it is cut in relation to your position and the threat of binding the saw.

BOW SAWS AND PRUNING SAWS

Bow saws (see figure 6.31) and smaller, curved-blade pruning saws come in a variety of sizes and shapes. Bow saws cut on both a pulling and pushing stroke; pruning saws generally, but not always, cut on a pull stroke only. The choice of saw depends on the size and amount of wood to be cut. Bow saw blades typically range in length from 16 to 36 inches; pruning saw blades range from 10 to 24 inches. Some bow saws and pruning saws conveniently fold up like a jackknife.

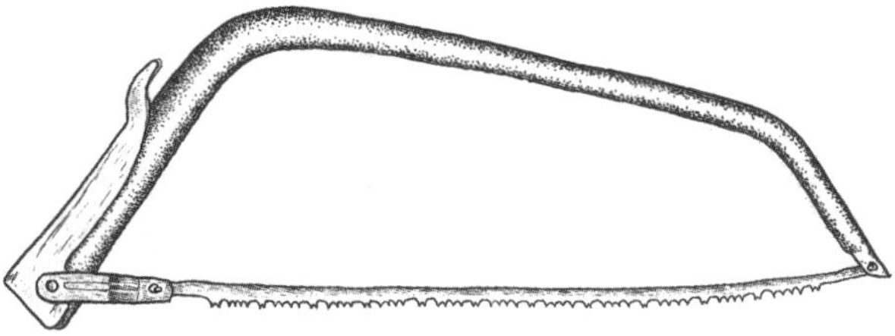

Figure 6.31. Bow saw with removable blade. The space between the blade and handle will limit the diameter of log that can be cut.

Larger bow saws can be used for cutting moderate-sized timber and for removing blowdowns. Smaller bow saws and pruning saws are good for small-diameter timber and for clearing trails where saplings or limbs are too large for clippers. They also won't leave undesirable pointed stumps, which sometimes happens when using an ax or brush hook. Some collapsible bow saws are handy for occasional use but are generally too lightweight for continuous heavy-duty use.

Various types of pruning saws with long handles (see figure 6.32) are useful for cutting high limbs when clearing ski touring trails. When using these saws, be sure that moving parts, such as nuts and bolts, are secure and that blades are set at the right tension. Blades that are too loose or too tight can break or get pinched in the wood. Experienced trail workers favor saws with the fewest number of movable parts (such as wing nuts), which may get lost.

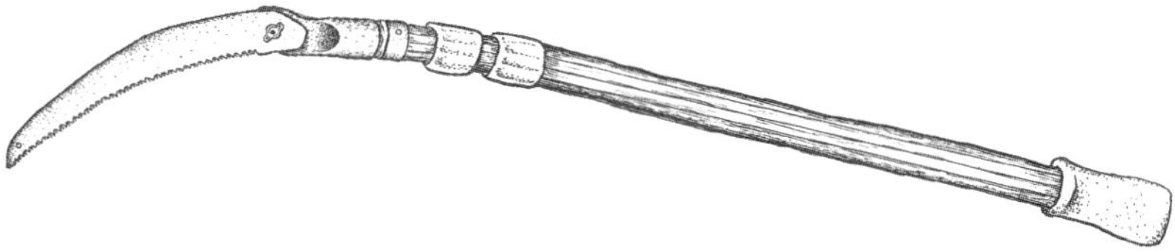

Figure 6.32. Pruning saws with long handles can reach very high limbs. They are often made with fiberglass and have telescoping handles.

Most bow saws and pruning saws have blades that are replaced rather than sharpened. Bring spare blades and parts when working in the field so that minor repairs can be made.

➔ **Safety Tips:** Be aware of what you're cutting and where your body is in relation to the blade. Always have a sheath nearby. Also, saws tend to "jump" when being used, especially before they get a good purchase on the wood. Use caution, as this has led to many a hand injury. Never stand directly below the branch being cut.

➔ **Safety Tip:** When transporting or storing a saw, cover it with a sheath to protect the worker and the blade. Wood, leather, or pieces of garden hose make good sheaths. Many bow saws come with hard plastic sheaths. All unpainted metal parts of a saw should be kept lightly oiled to prevent rust.

PULASKI

This tool is a single-bit ax with a small adze/hoe blade (see figure 6.33). The Pulaski was originally created for digging fire lines in wildland firefighting because it combines two traditional tools for working with wood—the ax and the adze. However, a well-sharpened Pulaski will prove more versatile. Pulaskis are mostly used for sidehill grubbing, cutting roots, removing blowdowns, cleaning drainages, and other trail maintenance. A Pulaski sharpened to be a wood tool should be marked as such and never used in the dirt.

➔ **Safety Tips:** Beware of hitting your shins with an overswing. Be sure to swing in a controlled fashion—never over the shoulder. Also, beware of eye hazards and flying debris.

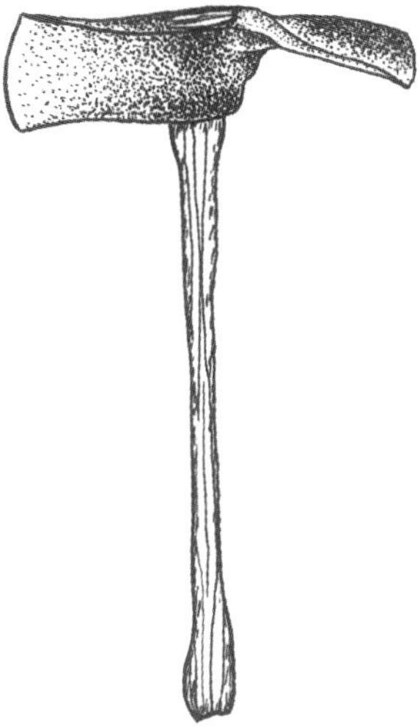

Figure 6.33. The Pulaski is a versatile tool that can be used for chopping small-diameter wood as well as for grubbing with the adze.

SWIZZLE STICK

The swizzle stick (see figure 6.34) is an important and versatile tool. Also known as a weed whip, it was developed for clearing brush and low growth along hiking trails. Some swizzle sticks have straight edges, and others have serrated blades.

A swizzle stick is used in a swinging motion, like a golf club. When equipped with a double-edged blade, it enables the worker to cut on the backswing as well. Sharpen a swizzle stick similar to the way an ax is sharpened, using a flat file and stone (see figure 6.35).

Use a blade sheath when carrying and storing the swizzle stick (see figure 6.36). Wrap a strip of heavy canvas or old fire hose around the blade and hold it in place with inner tube rubber shaped in a figure-eight. A sheath fashioned from wood or leather will also work. Adhesive tape can be used in a pinch.

➔ **Safety Tips:** Never swing above the waist. Be aware of those around you. Always swing the swizzle stick firmly, with both hands on the handle to fully control the swing. A rock or stump may deflect the tool unexpectedly; therefore, always wear heavy boots when using this tool.

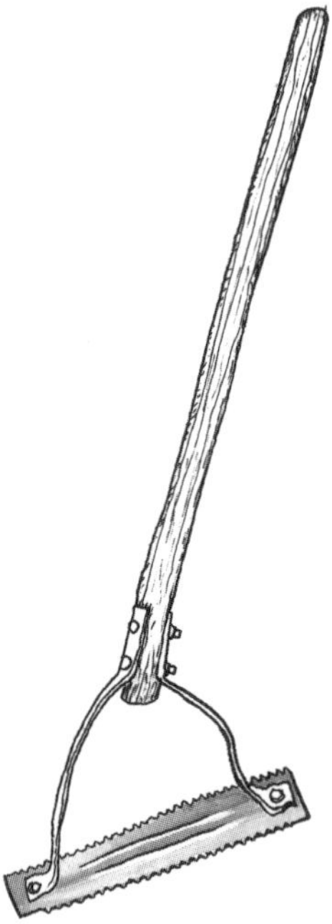

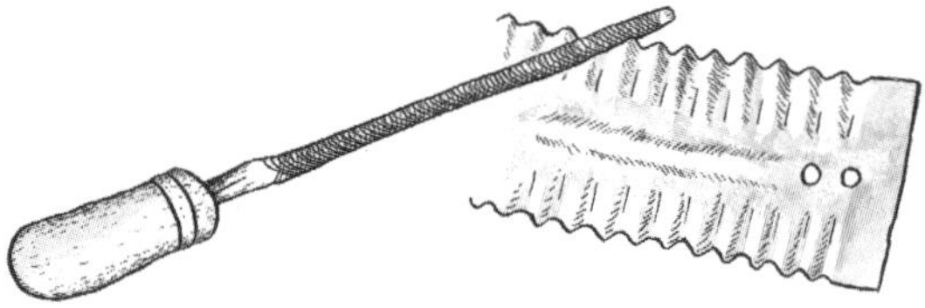

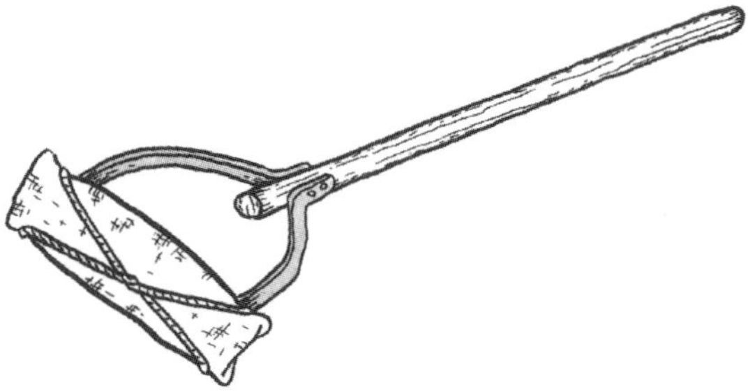

Figure 6.34, left. The swizzle stick is a lightweight option if brush maintenance is a longer distance hike in.
Figure 6.35, right, top. Use a small flat file to sharpen the swizzle cutting teeth.
Figure 6.36, right, bottom. Homemade sheath for a swizzle stick.

LOPPING SHEARS, POLE CLIPPERS, AND HAND PRUNERS

Long-handled (pole) clippers, hand pruners, and lopping shears (loppers) come in many styles. Handles are made of wood, steel, or aluminum. Cutting heads are either the sliding-blade-and-hook type or the anvil type. Some have simple pivot actions, and others have compound or gear-driven actions for increased cutting power. Most cut limbs between 1 and 1¾ inches. As a general rule don't cut anything wider than the diameter of the handle.

A variety of pole clippers (see figure 6.37) are manufactured for professional tree trimming and specialized work, such as clearing ski touring trails. These are suitable for clipping high limbs up to 1 or 1½ inches in diameter. Generally, a 6- to 8-foot handle is sufficient for ski touring trail work, although longer handles are available.

Small hand pruners (see figure 6.38), of the sort common in home gardening, can be quite useful for occasional light pruning. These also come in a variety of styles.

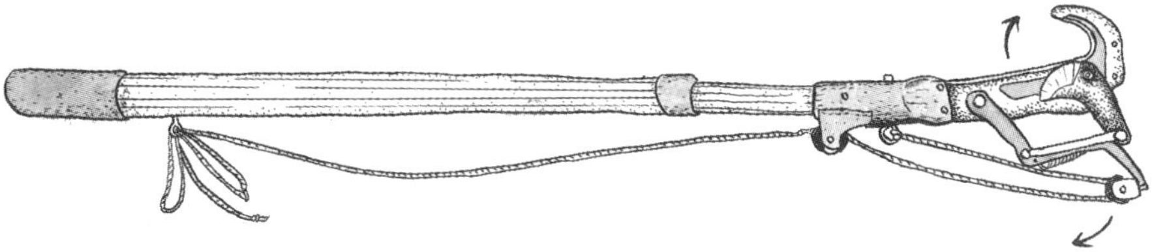

Figure 6.37, above. Pole clippers can reach upper limit, small-diameter limbs. The attached rope is used to create the action needed to make the cut.
Figure 6.38, below. Hand pruners are good for small and numerous branches and twigs.

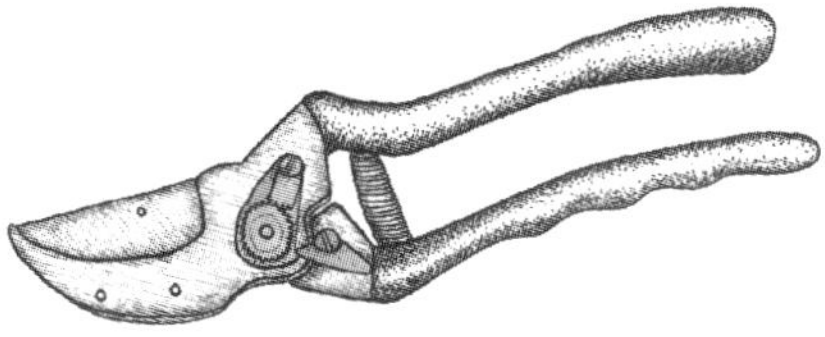

Since loppers are one of the primary tools of the trail maintainer, it is important to purchase high-quality ones (see figure 6.39). Look for well-made brand-name shears that are built for rugged, professional use and are simple to maintain and repair. Anvil-type loppers are sharpened on both sides of the cutting blade with a stone, like a pocketknife. Take care to sharpen these blades evenly along their length. The soft metal anvils should be adjusted to meet the cutting blade evenly when the lopper is closed.

Clippers should be kept sharp, with all metal parts lightly oiled. A flat file or handstone works well for sharpening the blade. For sliding-blade pruners, which work like scissors, sharpen only the outside, beveled edge of the cutting blade (see figure 6.40).

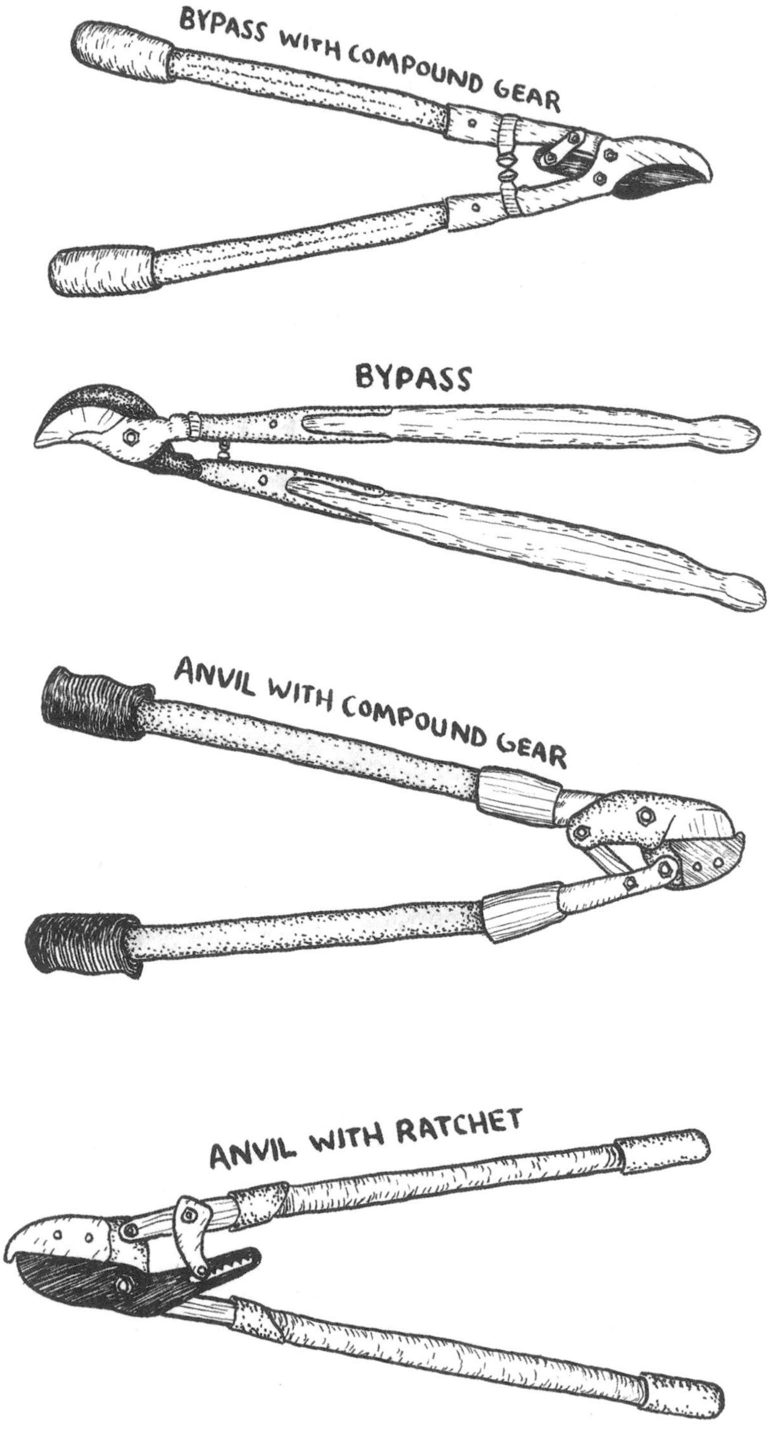

Figure 6.39. Loppers can be found in a variety of styles.

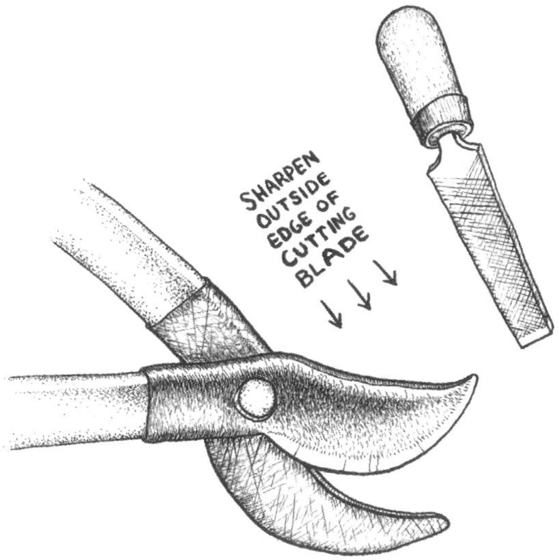

Figure 6.40. Sliding-blade pruners can be sharpened with a flat file.

➔ **Safety Tips:** Keep fingers out of hinges and from between blades by transporting with both handles secure. Also, be aware of your grip and where the branch will fall when cutting above the shoulders.

SAFETY AX AND MACHETE

Safety axes and machetes can be handy, although somewhat hazardous, supplements to the more classic tools used for trail clearing. They require care, sheathing, and sharpening similar to that described for the ax. AMC generally recommends against their use for trail work due to the likelihood of injury, but in some areas, they might be necessary.

The safety ax, as the name implies, is a good choice for most trail workers, because the blade is less exposed than that of a machete. If the blade is damaged, it can be replaced. Safety axes (also known as sandviks) are particularly effective on young, springy hardwood growth and for brushing in dense softwood.

The best machete for trail clearing is probably the Woodman's Pal. Some of its features, such as a cutting hook, are unavailable on conventional machetes. It is also not as long as the conventional ones, which allows a shorter, more controlled swing.

Because these tools can be hazardous and often leave a sharply pointed stub when limbing or brushing, most trail workers prefer handsaws or clippers for limbing and other brushing, which leave a cleaner, smoother cut and are much safer to use.

➔ **Safety Tips:** Use these tools with care. A good grip at all times, plenty of space between workers, and looking and concentrating before swinging will prevent accidents and damage to the tools.

➔ WOOD TOOLS

LOG CARRIER

A log carrier (see figure 6.41), or timber tong, consists of a pair of hooks that grip a log and are attached to a handle that extends on both sides (often with the ability to swivel). This allows two people to lift or drag a log without getting underneath it.

➔ **Safety Tips:** To make sure the tongs are equally well set, both workers should lift the log in unison. Be careful of your back while lifting. Communicate clearly with others working with you.

PEAVEY

A peavey (see figure 6.42) is a traditional wood tool used by loggers to roll and manage logs. It has a hook and point to help rotate logs. The hook bites into the wood, and the handle can then be pulled in the other direction to lever the log.

➔ **Safety Tip:** Always be careful when working with a pile of logs; assess what can move, where it will go, and who is in the immediate vicinity.

BARK SPUD AND DRAW KNIFE

In spring and early summer, when tree sap is plentiful, bark can be easily peeled away with a bark spud (see figure 6.43). Late in the season, when the bark is tight and dry and the wood does not peel easily, a draw knife (see figure 6.44) is the better option.

➔ **Safety Tips:** When working around felled trees and logs, be aware of where a log could shift and if anyone else is working on it. Also, wood tends to be very slippery when peeled, so be careful when transporting it. One way to do this is to brace the log between rocks or other pieces of wood.

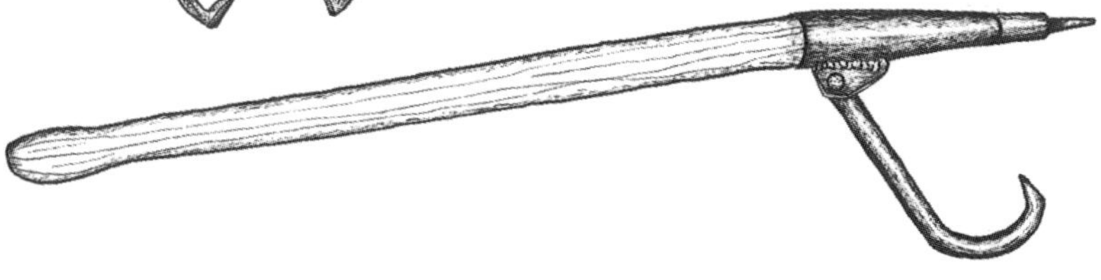

Figure 6.41, top. Log carriers are strong and sturdy, with steel prongs.
Figure 6.42, bottom. The peavey is a traditional wood-moving tool that helps roll and shift logs too heavy to move by hand.

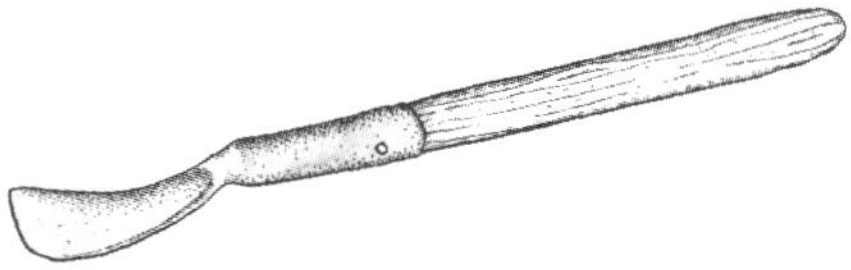

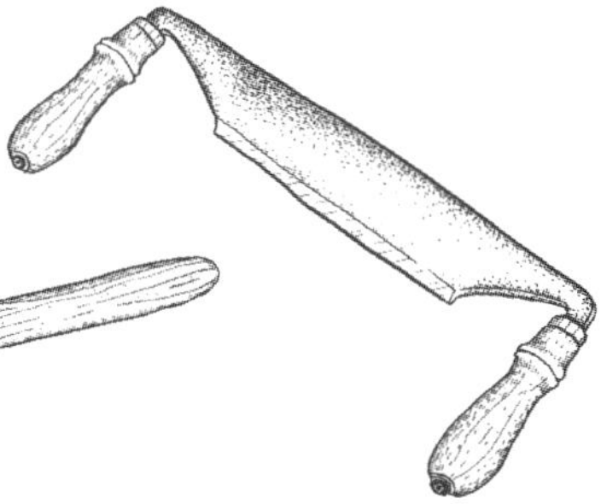

Figure 6.43, left. The bark spud is used to get under the bark layer of freshly cut trees in order to peel logs.
Figure 6.44, right. A draw knife is used to remove wood in small amounts.

➔ ROCK WORK TOOLS

ROCK HAMMERS

Many different kinds of rock hammers are available, but all of them are used to shape stone. Some strike stone directly, some are held against the stone and struck by another hammer, and some only strike other tools. Each type is tempered and hardened for its specific purpose. Using a hammer in a way it was not designed for can be very dangerous. Hard, brittle metal can chip and crack with incorrect use. Softer tempered metal, meanwhile, tends to mushroom with use. This is natural, so hammers must be monitored, and edges and blades must be ground down to remain safe. Hammer heads and handles should be checked for cracks or weaknesses before use.

Hand hammer

This hammer (see figure 6.45) is designed to strike other tools (thus it is also called a striking hammer). It is tempered to do so and will last a long time. It should never be used to strike rock directly.

Figure 6.45. A hand hammer is used to strike the top of another hammer or chisel. Not to be mistaken with a single jack or stone buster, which can be used to strike rock directly.

Mash hammer

A mash hammer, also called a mason's hammer, has both a blade and a flat, square face. The blade is used to break rock into smaller pieces, and the flat side is used to break edges off stone.

Spalling hammer

Spalling hammers have a blade on one side and a hammer on the other. Because the metal is soft, it tends to mushroom with use. This tool is very versatile and can be used for chipping, shaping, or scoring rock.

Rifting hammer

The rifting hammer is used to score rock along a rift line. It is designed to be held flat against a rock and struck with another hammer while tracing a line. Sometimes a rifting hammer alone can split rock, but other times it makes drilling more precise.

Bull set

The bull set (see figure 6.46) is also designed to be held against the stone and struck. It is used less for splitting stone and more for breaking flakes of stone along a parallel plane.

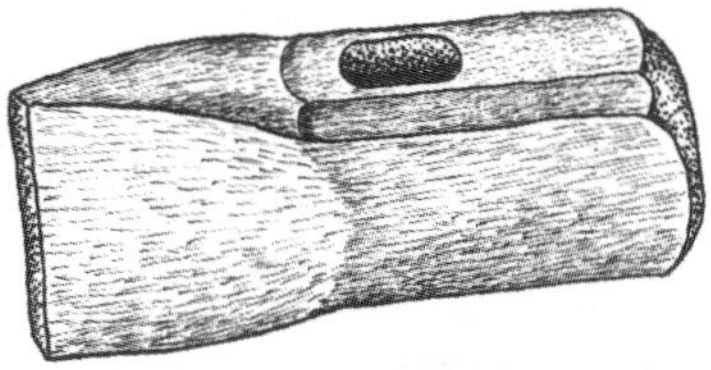

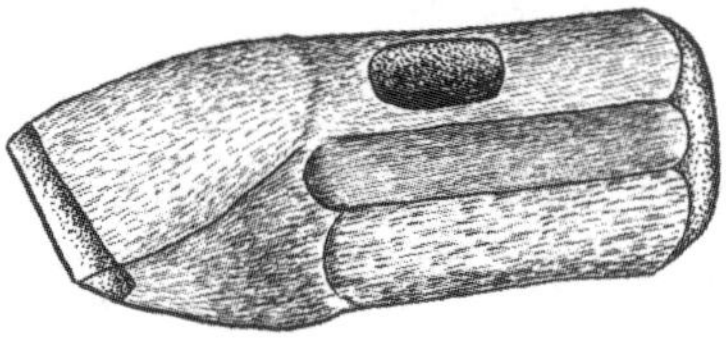

Figure 6.46, top. A bull set hammer is used in conjunction with a striking hammer. **Figure 6.47, bottom.** The stone buster is a versatile, lightweight hammer that can strike rock or other hand tools.

Stone buster

Stone busters (see figure 6.47) are versatile, effective tools. They can be used to strike other tools, can be struck with another tool, or can be swung alone to shape rock. The stone buster has a carbide blade on one side and a flat face on the other.

Hammer point

A hammer point is rounded on one side and pointed on the other. It is designed to strike a boulder directly or to be struck by another hammer to chip off small pieces of rock.

Bushing hammer

A bushing hammer is used for light shaping and texturing soft stone. It can also "naturalize" drill holes and cut edges.

Other hammers

There are a few other types of hammers used for shaping and breaking stone. The important thing to remember when using a hammer is what the metal is tempered to do. Never strike metal with a hammer that is not designed for it.

➔ **Safety Tips:** Be aware of those around you when swinging, especially when hazardous rock shards will fly. Always know the proper use of a hammer. Check handles and hammer heads for compromised integrity. Pay close attention to the target object and beware of injuring fingers.

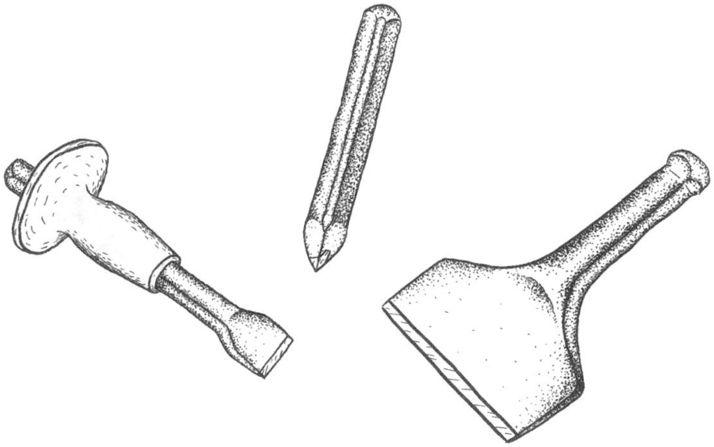

Figure 6.48. Hand chisels come in a variety of shapes and designs for a number of applications.

CHISELS

Many chisels (see figure 6.48) are used for similar purposes as their hammer counterparts listed above. However, they are all designed to be struck on the head. Swings should be relatively small and always controlled and sustainable. Some common chisels are the hand point, hand chisel, hand set, and hand tracer. The hand point is generally used to remove high spots or smaller features, the hand chisel to do general shaping, the hand set to remove overhangs or bulges when the surface is flat, and the hand tracer to trace a fracture line for splitting.

When striking a chisel, make the first hit relatively light to set the chisel into place. Also, when working with a chisel that has a blade, be sure that as much of the blade as possible is contacting the rock.

➔ **Safety Tips:** Be aware of the wear and tear on your striking hammer and the striking surface of the chisel. Be sure to grind down any mushrooming when it becomes apparent. Of course, be careful of your aim when swinging.

FEATHERS AND WEDGES

When splitting rock by drilling—either by hand or with a pneumatic gas or electric drill—use feathers and wedges (see figure 6.49) to actually break the rock. The process will be discussed in Chapter 7 (page 97). Two feathers and one wedge compose a set. Place the feathers into the drilled hole with the wedge in the middle. Pound the wedge down evenly, and it will push apart the rock due to the weakness caused by the drilled hole.

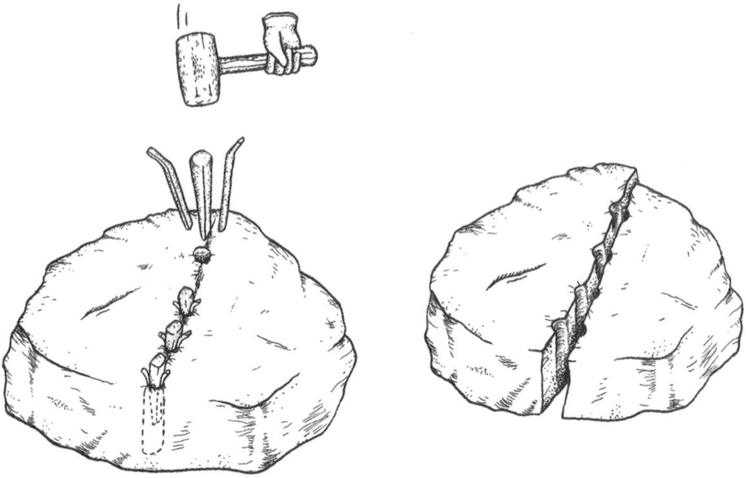

Figure 6.49. Feathers and wedges are used in combination to split larger stone into workable sizes.

6

- **Safety Tips:** There are plenty of safety concerns when drilling and splitting rock, which are discussed in Chapter 7 (page 91). Remember to use the proper hammer and to inspect the hammer and wedges for mushrooming and integrity of the metal before striking.

HOISTING TOOLS

GRIPHOIST

Griphoist (see figure 6.50) is the brand name for a winch-like tool that uses a wire rope available in varying lengths rather than a cable of fixed length, as with a ratchet winch. Griphoists are built with exceptional safety mechanisms and are powerful trail-working tools and systems. However, the rigging associated with the Griphoist requires prudence and attention to be safely employed. Although some basic techniques are discussed in Chapter 7 (page 105), it is vital to have adequate training before setting up and operating a Griphoist system. This training can be obtained through trail organizations, land managers, and trail contractors.

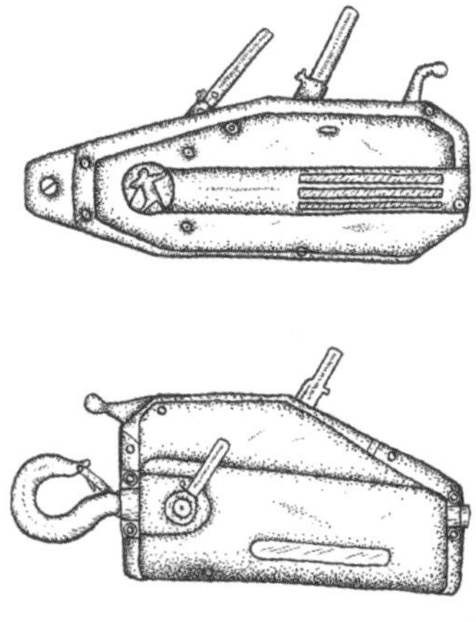

Figure 6.50. Griphoists can be found in working load limits of 1 ton, 2 ton, and 4 ton. Different models may have slight differences in operation and maintenance.

TRIPOD

When operating a Griphoist highline system in an area that lacks natural spars, use a metal tripod (see figure 6.51). Tripods are helpful, but the operator of the highline system must have adequate knowledge and training. Highline systems are very useful in areas such as alpine zones, where rock construction is usually necessary and the protection of vegetation and soil are imperative as materials are lifted and maneuvered aerially.

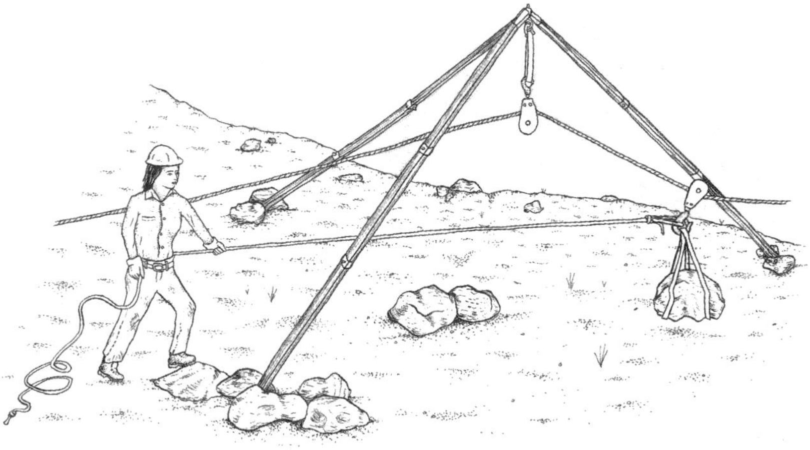

Figure 6.51. Tripods can be found in steel or aluminum models and provide another option to create lift in a rigging system.

6

➔ POWER TOOLS

Although the bulk of trail work is done with hand tools, some occasions call for power tools. This section gives information on the chain saw, motorized brush cutter, and rock drill. Only a broad description of each tool and its specifications is provided; obtain specific details from manufacturers on the use and care of these tools.

CHAIN SAW

When shopping for a chain saw (see figure 6.52), consider safety and the operator's guidelines (operator's manual) that manufacturers supply with the saw. The opinions of friends and fellow maintainers can also be helpful when comparing different saws. Chain saws are built by a variety of manufacturers and come in different sizes and types—each suited to a particular job. Major manufacturers carry a full line of equipment that ranges in size and power from small light-duty saws to large machines for the forest products industry.

Choosing a make and model is mainly a matter of personal preference. First determine the type of work in which the saw will generally be employed, and then find a local dealer who can help you purchase the appropriate model. Make sure

Figure 6.52. Chain saws come with different size powerheads, bars, and chains. Course participation and buying from certified retailers is strongly encouraged.

Figure 6.53. Sighting the fall line and using this stance are components of safe chain saw use and proper felling technique.

the saw has the best current safety features and is easy to operate and maintain in the field. A dealer who provides prompt and efficient service and thorough operating and safety instructions is equally important.

Smaller saws are the most popular choices for trail work because of their light weight. Larger, more powerful saws are best for heavy cutting, such as the clearing of a trail strewn with fallen trees following a major storm or during timber harvesting.

Safe chain saw operation

Constantly stress to workers the importance of safe chain saw–operating techniques (see figure 6.53). Chain saws operate at a fast cutting speed, and the slightest slip or miscalculation can cause serious injury or death.

It cannot be stressed enough to be properly trained in safe chain saw operation (see Chapter 7, page 99). Land managers, trail organizations, and contractors offer various professional use and safety programs. In addition, some land managers require certifications, so make sure you possess the necessary certifications for a project before you commence operation. When operating a chain saw, always wear eye and ear protection, a hard hat, and chain saw chaps.

SAFE AND EFFICIENT OPERATION OF YOUR CHAIN SAW

- Read your owner's manual and all supplements thoroughly before operating your saw. Use the personal protective equipment listed on pages 46–49.
- Don't use any other fuel than that recommended in your owner's manual.
- Refuel in a safe place. Be careful not to spill fuel, and do not start the saw where you fuel it.
- Never attempt to fuel a running or hot saw. If fuel spills on the unit, be certain the saw dries thoroughly before you start it.
- Don't smoke while fueling or operating the saw.
- Don't start a saw on your leg or knee. Do not drop-start.
- Never operate a chain saw when you are fatigued.
- Keep all parts of your body and clothing away from the saw chain when starting or running the engine. Before you start the engine, make sure the saw chain is not in contact with anything.
- Beware of kickback! Hold the saw firmly with both hands when the engine is running; use a firm grip, with thumbs and fingers encircling the chain saw handles, and watch carefully what you cut. Kickback (saw jumps or jerks up or backward) can be caused by the following actions:

- Striking limbs or other objects accidentally with the tip of the saw while the chain is moving
- Striking metal, cement, or other hard material near the wood or buried in the wood
- Running the engine slowly at the start of or during the cut
- Using a dull or loose chain

- Do not cut above shoulder height.
- Use the chain brake as often as possible, even when moving a couple of steps while the saw is still running.
- Do not operate the saw while in a tree, on a ladder, or on any other unstable surface.
- Be sure of your footing and preplan a safe exit from a falling tree or falling limbs.
- When cutting a limb that is under tension, beware of springback to avoid being struck when the tension is released.
- Use extreme caution when cutting small brush and saplings because slender material may catch in the saw chain and be whipped toward you or pull you off balance.
- Be aware of the effects of vibration. Avoid prolonged operation of your chain saw and rest periodically. Stop using the saw if your hand or arm starts to have a loss of feeling, swells, or becomes difficult to move.
- Avoid exhaust fumes. Do not operate your chain saw in confined or poorly ventilated areas.
- Observe all local fire prevention regulations. It is recommended that you keep a fire extinguisher and shovel close at hand when you cut in areas where dry grass, leaves, or other flammable materials are present.
- Turn off your saw when moving between cuts and before setting it down. Always carry the saw with the engine stopped, the guide bar and saw chain in the rear, and the muffler away from your body.
- Use wedges to help control felling and to prevent binding the bar and chain in the cut. Don't touch or try to stop a moving chain with your hand.
- Keep the chain sharp and snug on the guide bar.
- Don't allow dirt, fuel, or sawdust to build up on the engine or outside of the saw.
- Keep all screws and fasteners tight. Never operate a chain saw that is damaged, improperly adjusted, or not completely and securely assembled. Be sure that the saw chain stops moving when the throttle-control trigger is released.
- Keep the handles dry, clean, and free of oil or fuel mixture.

GAS-POWERED BRUSH SAW

Similar to heavy-duty weed trimmers with metal blades for cutting wood, gas-powered brush saws (see figure 6.54) are useful for extensive trail clearing through young, heavy growth. However, most clearing can be done by hand, and few maintainers find it necessary to invest in this specialized piece of equipment. If one is used, the operator should be trained and experienced and must maintain a safe working distance from others.

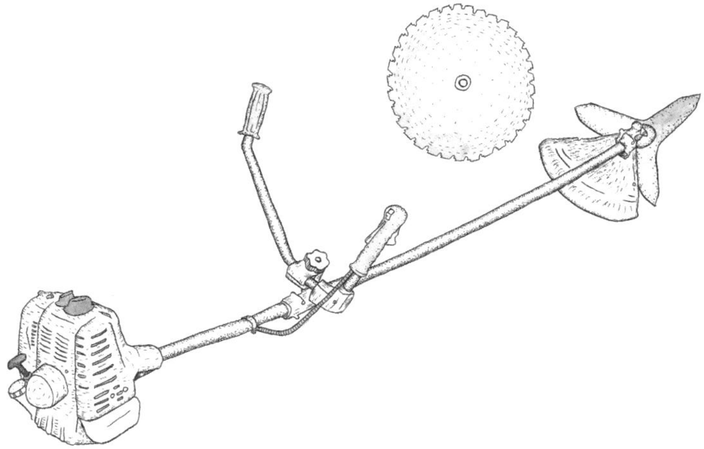

Figure 6.54. A brush saw with common cutter heads.

ROCK DRILLS (PNEUMATIC HAMMER DRILLS)

Often referred to as rock drills, pneumatic hammer drills are used in specific construction applications. They can drill holes to be used for pinning rocks, installing metal rungs or ladders, or splitting rocks with feathers and wedges; on a chisel setting, the drill's chisel bit can break rock. Holes drilled in rock can also be used for blasting or filled with an expanding compound. Gas-powered, electric, and battery-powered drills are available (see figures 6.55 and 6.56). Gas-powered rock drills are heavier, tend to break more often, and are difficult to find due to a decline in manufacturing caused by stricter emissions standards. Electric rock drills are lighter and must be powered by a generator. These are advantageous because the generator can be kept far from the work site, which decreases fatigue caused by noise and the operation of a heavy machine; also, the exhaust will not be in the vicinity of the operator. With the advent

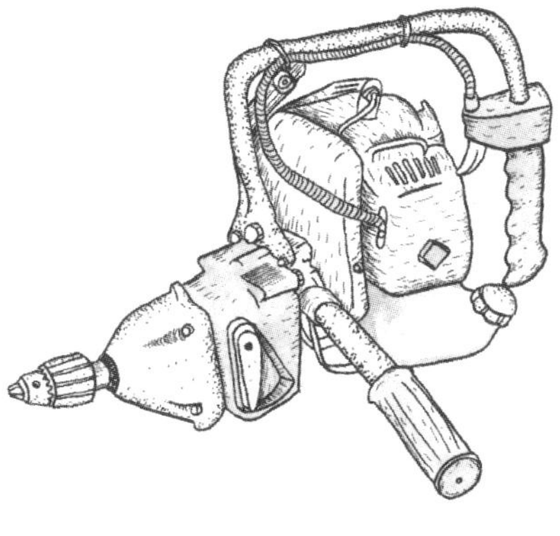

Figure 6.55. Gas-powered drills can still be found but are less common today.

of smaller, lighter generators, electric rock drills have become a more feasible option for backcountry applications.

Special safety concerns when using a rock drill include injury from repetitive impact, vibration, body positioning, and inhalation of particulates. Operators should take turns drilling so they do not become fatigued. In addition to ear and eye protection and a hard hat, be sure that everyone in the area is wearing OSHA-approved dust masks at all times.

Figure 6.56. A corded rock drill in combination with a properly sized generator is easy to use and has easy-to-find components.

➔ DON'T LOSE YOUR TOOLS

Wood and metal hand tools quickly become dirty and drab after use and therefore easily blend into trailside brush and woods. Remember where tools are set down and keep them close by or on the trail. At the end of the workday gather up all tools and make sure everything is accounted for. A list of tools can be useful, especially when managing large projects that require a lot of equipment and personnel. Store tools in one stash or cache at camp or near the work site, just out of sight of the trail. To keep tools visible in brush and woods, liberally paint a good portion of the heads and handles with a bright color, such as orange or red. (*Note*: Do not paint the cutting or digging edges of the heads or the gripping parts of the handles.) Use a drab-colored tarp to keep tools dry when left in the cache overnight or on days off. Be sure the sides are tucked in well so the tarp will shed water.

➔ TOOL SOURCES

Purchase tools at hardware stores and from catalogs and suppliers of forestry, farm, and construction equipment. Look for inexpensive but well-made used tools at garage sales, used-tool outlets, and antique shops. Often the best woodcutting hand tools, such as axes and crosscut saws, were made decades ago. See Appendix A on page 235 for suggestions on where to buy tools.

CHAPTER 7

BUILDING MATERIALS FOR TRAIL CONSTRUCTION

AT-A-GLANCE

After determining whether to use wood or rock for trail construction, employ different techniques to move, shape, and set materials at the project location.

➔ **Moving, shaping, and breaking rock:** Use correct tools and proper lifting procedures to move rocks. Break and shape rocks with hammers, chisels, drills, and wedges.

➔ **Felling trees:** Assess the utility of the tree to be used and the surroundings before felling with an ax, saw, or chain saw.

➔ **Hoisting materials:** Use a Griphoist to move rock and materials efficiently and in complex situations.

Having learned the requisite trail construction and reconstruction techniques, next comes field planning and choosing materials for construction.

In frontcountry trail operations, having materials delivered to a building site can be more efficient in both time and cost. However, this is impractical for most trail projects, which have a backcountry location and terrain. Instead, native materials must be found near the site and moved to the treadway. This laborious process should be undertaken carefully to ensure safety, minimize damage to the trail environment, and maximize the efficiency and quality of construction.

The materials—usually rock, wood, or soil—are either found on the surface or dug/cut from areas near the trail, preferably out of view, and with minimal effect on the surroundings. Construction material and its sources should blend into the local environment. Any spikes or other fasteners removed from old structures can be hiked out to prevent non-native materials from littering the woods. With diligence, trail crews can minimize their impact during the construction process, ensuring that their work causes as little harm to the ecosystem as possible while mitigating future impact on the environment.

➔ WOOD VS. ROCK

When constructing and reconstructing trails, choose natural materials to preserve the aesthetic quality and character of the landscape. These materials are usually native rock or wood. Metal is occasionally used for trail structures, but due to the non-native and permanent nature of this material, it should be used rarely, generally only for fasteners, pinning, or staples.

Because many structures can be built with rock or wood, a decision must be made as to which is most appropriate. There are advantages and disadvantages with either, and often the final decision is based on proximity, availability, and economics.

Before rock was used to build trail structures, wood was the dominant material. It is lighter and easier to transport, can be shaped, can be moved in larger pieces, and is abundant at most locations. Various species of trees can be used, and woodworking tools are relatively lightweight. However, wood has one major disadvantage: it rots. Regardless of how well built a structure is, wood (especially wood that is in contact with the ground) will always rot.

Rock is heavy and can be difficult to maneuver but is practically permanent. Rock setting and building take considerably more time to learn than working with wood. Rock can be shaped, but it is labor-intensive and sometimes inefficient. Finding good rocks can be challenging because they are often not readily available and must be extracted from the earth. However, well-placed rock on a well-planned trail structure has the potential to last until the next glaciation.

The problem of whether to choose wood or rock as a building material is not solved by simply considering longevity. The decision also depends on the situation. Many managers choose rock due to its durability and because it blends more easily with the character of the trail and landscape. Others prefer the ease and efficiency of working with wood. Regardless, the first consideration is the availability of material. If the project is above treeline or within terrain with limited sizable trees, native timber may not be an option. Tree size or species may not be suitable for construction. In this case, workers must harvest rock locally or use non-native material. Longevity needs to be balanced with resource availability and the desire to maintain the character of the trail and its environs.

➔ ROCK

Rocks of various sizes are used for trail definition, marking, erosion control, drainage, trail hardening, and other purposes. First, determine the number, size range, and shapes of rocks needed for a project. Second, probe for a quarry site of suitable rock. This can be done with a rock bar and knowledge of the local topography and ecology, which indicate where available rock may be located. The quarry should be out of sight of the trail and uphill, as gravity and slope will aid in moving rock to the work site. Rocks can be found on the surface but in many cases will be partially buried under duff or leaf litter, requiring excavation.

MOVING ROCKS

The most important rule to remember when moving rocks is to not lift anything unnecessarily. Slide or roll them if possible, although when necessary, several people can lift heavier rocks using a carry sling or rock litter. Most rocks used for trail structures are impractical to lift by hand, and rolling or sliding them often requires two people. However, smaller rocks, such as those for scree or cairns, can be carried safely to the trail by one person (see figure 7.1). Remember to lift correctly to protect your back, and be mindful of the terrain.

Larger rocks of the sort needed for steps, water bars, and other similar features will require additional effort. Sometimes one person can maneuver a rock to the trail with a rock bar (see figure 7.2) or with muscle power—rolling, flipping, and sliding the rock along.

However, usually several people will need to work together to move rock, using rock bars and pick mattocks. Two people with rock bars can also move rocks more easily than one over greater distances. This is often called "double barring" and requires extra safety precautions and clear communication. One person places the bar firmly below the rock and holds the bar as parallel to the ground as possible, levers, and lifts as far as the bar placement, safety, and strength allow. The first person communicates with the second person that he or she is ready and has a solid hold on the rock. The second person then positions a bar firmly below the rock at the same level as the first bar. This firm placement is called a "bite." Both people then lift until the first person begins to lose the bite.

Figure 7.1, top. Use good body mechanics when lifting rocks. Don't be afraid to use tools and/or another person.
Figure 7.2, bottom. A rock bar is a great tool for moving rock and can be used in a number of ways.

Figure 7.3. Two people with rock bars can work together to move big rocks with relative ease.

This is where communication is most critical. It is essential that the second person can hold the weight of the rock while the first person gets a better position on the rock and a better bite that will allow further lift. They repeat this process until the rock flips or rolls (see figure 7.3). When using this technique or any other barring work, do not handle the rock with your hands; if one worker's bar loses hold on the rock, the other worker will be in a dangerous position.

In locations with "spongy" areas between rock sources and the trail, crews can make a skidway by placing dead logs side by side and sliding the rock across. Rolling rocks through mud can create strong suction power and be slippery and extremely difficult to negotiate. Carefully coordinate joint efforts to prevent accidents, particularly pinched or crushed fingers. As a general rule, use either tools *or* hands when moving a rock with another person. Moving with both tools and hands can cause fingers to be crushed between steel and rock as objects shift.

7

WORK SMART

- Choose a good route, clear of obstacles.
- Always quarry uphill of the project.
- Never position yourself below the rock or on the downhill side.
- Lift with your legs and do not twist.
- Learn how a particular shape of rock moves.
- Anticipate and prepare each move to save energy.
- Use logs as runners to avoid low spots, muddy sections, or holes along a quarry path.
- Build large, sturdy barricades to avoid losing rocks.
- Always choose the lowest impact route to move materials.

SAFETY

Avoid working below a person moving rocks. Wear a hard hat. Limit the number of people working on a particular slope—it is possible to have too many people and too much activity in one location. In some cases, it is best practice to either close a trail to hikers during construction or to post someone to direct traffic. Hikers sometimes stand in a particularly hazardous location and observe the work in progress, so watch for bystanders, know where your coworkers are, and let everyone know when you are attempting a difficult maneuver. Losing a rock is not only very dangerous but also a waste of effort. If a rock does roll out of control, shout the universal warning of "ROCK!"

Barricades

While working on a steep slope, crews can build simple log-and-debris barricades (see figure 7.4) next to the trail and below where they are quarrying to prevent rocks from rolling down the slope. Spending a lot of time and sweat moving a rock only to see it slip away can be both very frustrating and dangerous. Solid dead logs and/or freshly felled logs stacked between trees or boulders create a backstop that rocks can be rolled into. Sometimes barricades are built just in case a rock is lost when it's being maneuvered to the trail; other times they might be a requirement for the safety of coworkers and hikers. However, barricades should never be relied upon to replace well-planned and safe rock movement.

SHAPING AND BREAKING ROCK

A specialized, advanced technique when working with rock is using hammers and chisels to shape or break it into usable sizes. This can eliminate bumps, protrusions, overhangs, or other irregularities that make a particular rock difficult

Figure 7.4. Use dead and downed wood to build barricades in order to ensure that hard-fought rocks don't get lost. This also adds an element of safety when quarrying and moving rocks.

to work with. For example, you could remove an overhang from a rock that is making it off-balance and therefore difficult to stabilize or set. If a smooth rock would be easier to set, but all you have is one with a bulge, use this technique to remove the bulge.

In deciding where to break the rock, or whether a break in the desired location is even possible, examine it to find places of weakness or fracture planes. Once you locate these, rock shaping can be done with a variety of specialty hammers and chisels, each designed for slightly different applications. Hitting a chisel or swinging a hammer with a blow in the desired spot sends a shock wave through the rock. The energy is released along the path of least resistance. If the strike is along an existing weakness, the energy will travel down this path and weaken the bonds between the particles in the rock. Before picking up a hammer, be sure that all options have been considered and that breaking the rock is the most efficient. As a general rule, if a rock does not break after a few well-aimed, precise blows, reconsider the plan.

Shaping rock can often save time and effort if done by an experienced stoneworker, but for the novice it can be ineffective. Because rocks all break differently, it is very important to be able to "read" a rock and anticipate how it will break to avoid wasting time, energy, and materials. This evaluation takes experience and training. Knowledge about both local and general geology is also very helpful.

SPLITTING ROCK

Sometimes a trail is far from appropriate-sized rocks. If so, bedrock or large boulders can be split into manageable pieces. To improve the chance of a controlled, clear fracture, use a stone hammer and score a line to weaken the rock. As with shaping and breaking rock, the break is more likely to be successful if done along a fracture plane. Be exact and consistent with each swing. If a break is difficult, more scoring may be necessary.

Drilling

Drill a line of holes along the desired score line. This can be done by hand with a tool called a star drill (which you hit with a hammer) or with a pneumatic hammer drill, also known as a rock drill (see figures 7.5 and 7.6). The distance between the holes will vary according to the difficulty of breaking the rock in the desired location, which will depend on the rock type and its fracture planes. Drill holes that are deep enough to insert feathers and wedges properly. Insert a pair of feathers and a wedge in each drill hole, with all of the feathers facing out along the desired line of fracture. With a small sledgehammer, pound the wedges alternately and evenly. To get an even break, hit the wedges until they are all at a uniform height. They can then be left to sit while they slowly split the rock. If this does not happen, repeat the pounding process or drill additional holes and insert wedges until the rock splits (see figure 7.7).

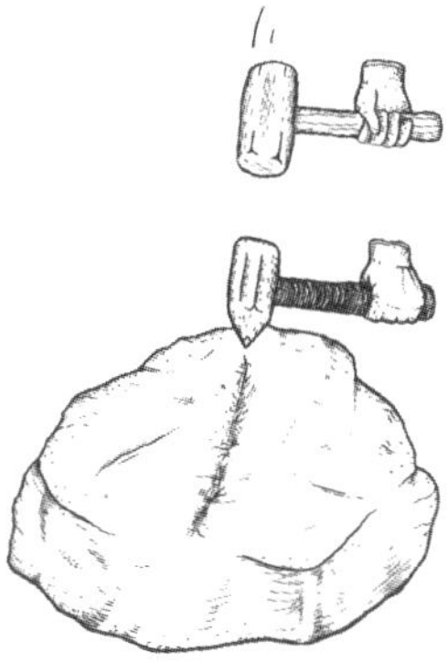

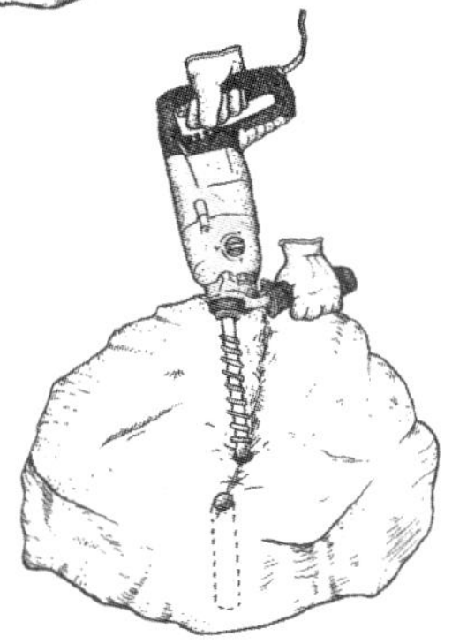

Figure 7.5, above, top. Scoring a rock is the first step in rock splitting.
Figure 7.6, above, bottom. Drill evenly spaced holes along the scored line.
Figure 7.7, below. Add feathers and wedges in the drill holes. Use a hammer to tap the wedges down in a consistent pattern.

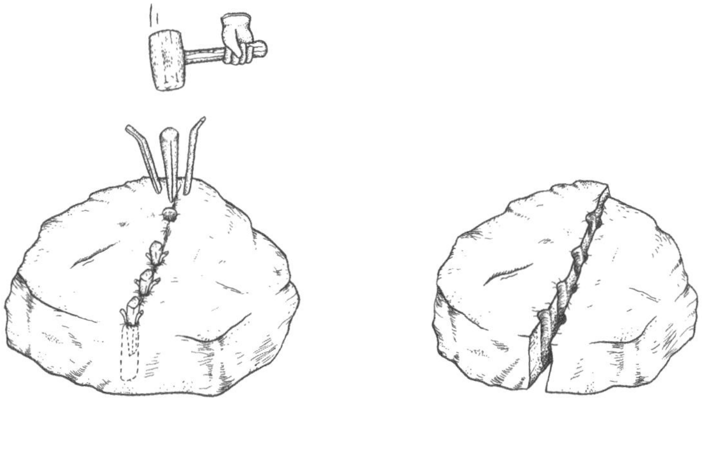

Successfully splitting a rock can be difficult—almost impossible with certain types of rock. It can also be complex, and further training in the process is strongly suggested for success. Even with the advent of powered drills, breaking rock is very time-consuming, and the question of whether to do it should be highly scrutinized.

➔ WOOD

Native wood, cut from trees in the vicinity of the trail, is an essential construction material for stream bridges, bog bridges, ladders, water bars, and cribbing. If a sizable amount of wood is needed, felling trees over a larger area can minimize the impact on the immediate vicinity.

Find trees appropriate in size and length that are uphill and hidden from the trail. Use what is readily available. If there is the luxury of a choice, spruce and hemlock are ideal in the Northeast because they are usually straight, lack large branches, and can be cut and peeled easily. Hardwoods, such as locust and oak, can also be good options, but in the large dimensions required for good water bars, they are difficult to maneuver. Conifers, such as hemlock, spruce, and cedar, are much more resistant to rot than common hardwoods, such as beech or birch. Get to know local tree species and find out which have the best resistance to rot.

Trees should be felled, limbed, peeled, and cut to the appropriate length on-site

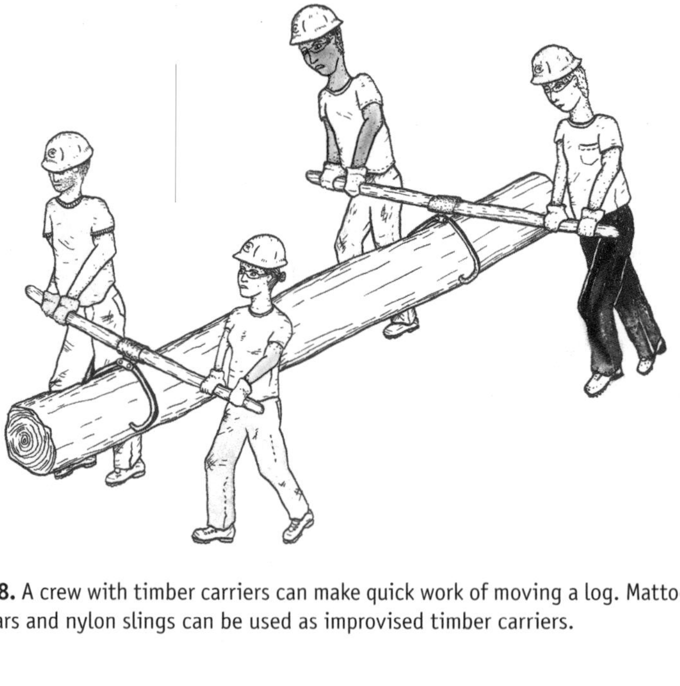

Figure 7.8. A crew with timber carriers can make quick work of moving a log. Mattock handles or rock bars and nylon slings can be used as improvised timber carriers.

(away from the trail) to prevent bark, wood chips, and other waste products from littering the immediate area of the trail. A freshly peeled log can be extremely slippery, so some trail workers peel the log at the trail and remove the debris later or, if time allows, wait for the log to dry before transporting it to the trail.

Once prepared, logs can be carried by hand, dragged, or slid down to the trail by one or more people. Log carriers require a minimum of four people (see figure 7.8). Large and heavy logs can be dragged to the trail or lowered down a steep slope with the aid of a Griphoist or other block-and-tackle systems.

GENERAL TREE-FELLING PROCEDURES

Trail builders can improve their tree felling and cutting techniques even after years of work. It is imperative that the inexperienced sawyer learn under the tutelage of a skilled sawyer. With practice, a novice can graduate to more complex bucking and felling. The directions given in this section are simply an introduction to felling using either a chain saw or crosscut saw and do not contain all the information needed to safely fell a tree, which is learned through training and practice with an experienced sawyer. It is absolutely necessary that anyone interested in felling trees learn safe felling and bucking techniques from a certified trainer.

First, choose a tree that fits the project's needs. As discussed previously, consider proximity to the trail and project site. Then consider the species of tree and the amount of wood the tree could provide. There are various ways to assess tree height and utilization that experienced sawyers can learn and use to ensure that a tree will provide adequate material. Once the tree or trees are chosen, various factors must be considered in assessing the tree and creating a felling plan.

THE RIGHT TOOLS: TREE FELLING

For ax or crosscut saw felling:

- hard hat
- ax or crosscut saw
- plastic wedges
- sledgehammer

For chain saw felling:

- hard hat; ear, eye, and face protection
- chaps
- gloves
- wedges and sledgehammer
- gas mix and bar oil
- chain saw
- scrench, files, and gauges

ASSESSING THE TREE AND SURROUNDINGS

Health of the Tree

Look for signs of rot, insect or animal damage, basal scars, signs of fire weakening, splits, or any other irregularities that may compromise the structural integrity of the tree. Rot can sometimes be evaluated by taking the butt end of an ax and thumping evenly around the tree. Rotted wood often emits a dull thud. (*Note*: It takes considerable experience to adequately assess rot that is not apparent from the outside.) A tree with rot may present significant hazards and will need special consideration in felling. It will also most likely not provide good building material. Never fell a tree that is above your ability. Fellers must know their own abilities and limitations; be prudent and honor them.

Size-Up

Size-up is the evaluation of the tree and the immediate area concerning multiple variables in determining the felling plan and identifying hazards.

Lean is the deviation of the tree from vertical. Often trees have lean in two directions: the dominant head lean and the secondary lean. Both must be taken into consideration. It is easiest to fell a tree in the general direction of its head lean and can usually be done within 45 degrees of the combined lean, granted it has a cleared path to be felled. With advanced felling techniques a tree can sometimes be felled in any direction regardless of lean. However, it's easiest and less complicated to fell a tree with its lean.

In addition to knowing the lean, the feller needs to study the tree carefully to determine how weight of the major limbs, crown, snow and leaf loads, and bends in the trunk affect the balance of the tree. With complex trees, particularly hardwoods, it can be difficult to judge how the limb weight and the overall crown weight is distributed. At this time, it is also important to find and note any dead branches that could be hazardous in the felling process.

A simple way to assess lean and to factor crown and limb weight is to use either a plumb bob, an ax, or any other straight-handled tool. After the initial assessment of the lean, walk far enough away to be able to view the profile of the tree and hang the ax or plumb bob with the heavy end down. Hold up the tool to be used as a plumb line and match the handle to the base (butt) of the tree. Then assess the lean of the entire tree, including the crown, determining how much the tree deviates from vertical. Repeat again from another direction perpendicular to the initial assessment. In complex trees this may have to be done a few times to thoroughly assess the dominant and secondary lean. Also consider wind speed and direction. If a strong wind is present, it may make sense to wait until weather conditions improve before felling. The direction of the wind should be taken into account when determining the felling plan and direction of fall.

Clear the Felling Zone

After choosing the direction for felling, space must be cleared so that the tree can fall completely to the ground. If the tree gets hung up on another tree or some other obstacle—often called a "leaner"—it can be time-consuming, troublesome, or even dangerous to bring it down. It could also potentially damage the needed wood and surrounding trees. Look for potential hazards, such as standing dead trees, debris, rocks, uneven ground, or downed logs in the felling area. Once the tree has been assessed and a safe fall zone has been established, examine the work area. Look for people who could be injured, dead trees or branches that could be disturbed, structures that could be damaged, and other possible issues. The zone of safety for other crew members and the public should be at least two and a half tree lengths away from the stump that will remain.

With the direction and felling zone cleared, the next steps are to establish an escape route and an alternate escape route and to reassess the felling plan. Follow these safety procedures before beginning the cut:

- Clear the area around the base of the tree so the feller will not be restricted or confined or have any disturbance in concentration during cutting.
- Clear an escape route and alternate route, and rehearse exiting several times so the feller can quickly move away from any danger. The escape route should be at a 45-degree angle away from the desired fall and absolutely not directly behind the desired fall. Be sure the route is clear of debris and tripping hazards (see figure 7.9).

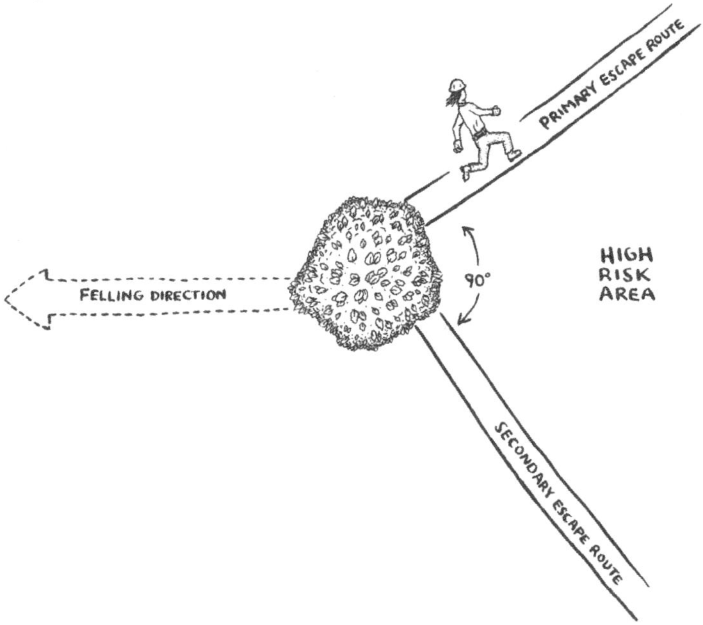

Figure 7.9. Plan and clear out your felling escape route prior to making any cut in the tree.

- Before felling, be sure everyone is two and a half tree lengths away. If the tree could fall near a trail, post one or two people (two and a half tree lengths away) on the trail to halt traffic until the tree is safely down.
- When the tree starts to fall, the feller should move away from the butt of the tree at least 25 feet. Kickback, which happens when the butt end springs back off the stump, is always a potential hazard, regardless of cutting technique.

Chain saws are very common tools for working with wood on trails, though, as ever, adequate training is absolutely necessary. However, main principles used for tree assessment, felling, limbing, and bucking do not change whether using a chain saw or a nonmotorized saw or ax. For the experienced sawyer, different tools offer more options for accurate directional felling techniques. The open-face felling technique is appropriate for all felling tools except axes, but the execution of the back cut is different between chain saws and crosscut saws. This will be discussed in full detail below. The two most widely accepted and respected chain saw certifications are from the Game of Logging and U.S. Forest Service Missoula Technology and Development Center. Courses for these certifications can be found around the United States through the U.S. Forest Service, Park Service, Bureau of Land Management, and many certified agencies and private trainers.

Felling Procedure

Face Cut and Back Cut

The first cut in the felling procedure is the face cut, which is done on the side of the trunk in the direction of the planned fall line. Proper execution of the face cut creates the front of the "hinge" that will guide the fall of the tree in the predicted fall line. The face cut is created by starting a shallow top cut into the tree, cutting 80 percent of the tree's diameter, and matching that with an undercut resulting in a face cut that is between 70 and 90 degrees (see figure 7.10). The proportions of the face cut and back cut are important to get right, as this establishes the hinge that will hold the tree erect until the feller is ready for it to drop. If a tree is 10 inches in diameter, the ideal hinge width will be 10 percent of that diameter, or 1 inch. The front of the hinge, or apex of the face cut, is the result of the top cut and undercut. The apex should be 80 percent of the diameter. So in this example, the apex would be 8 inches in length. It is imperative that all wood is cleared where the top cut and undercut meet, which provides for a safe and controlled fall. If done properly, the fall line will be exactly at a right angle to the face cut.

After completing the face cut, the feller will make the back cut—or bore cut if using a chain saw. Before initiating the back cut, ensure that the face cut is properly directed toward the intended fall. If using a chain saw, complete the hinge with the bore-cut or plunge-cut technique. If using a crosscut saw, make a simple back cut in line with the apex of the face cut. Before beginning, make sure no coworkers are near the fall line; everyone should be two and a half tree lengths away. Check

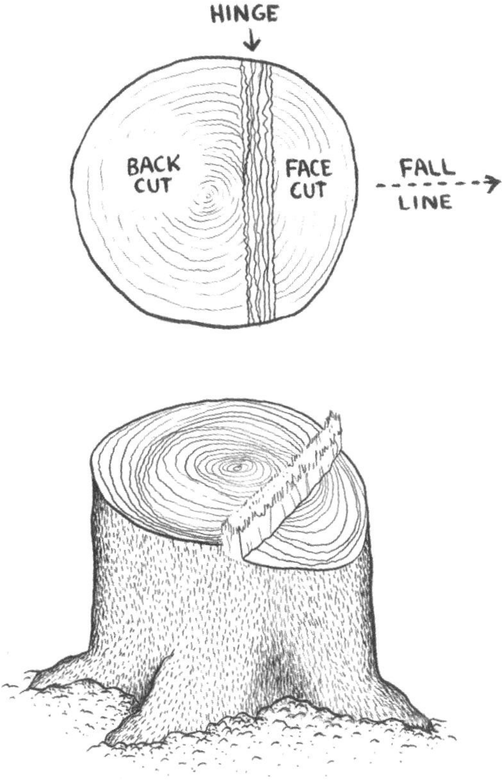

Figure 7.10. Chain saws, axes, and ax-crosscut combination all strive for the same basic felling parameters.

escape routes one final time before proceeding. Make those in the area aware of the progress of the cutting.

The back cut should be in line with where the top cut and undercut (face cut) meet and should be parallel to the ground. If using a chain saw, create a hinge that is 10 percent of the tree's diameter by bore-cutting into the tree parallel to the back of the front cut hinge. Leave a small strip uncut in the back. This is the holding or "trigger" wood. Place a plastic wedge into the back cut oriented in the direction of the fall to ensure that the back cut will not collapse when the remaining wood is cut. At this point the only material holding the tree upright is the trigger wood. When that trigger wood is cut away, the hinge alone can no longer support the weight of the tree, and the tree will fall, closing the face cut as it reaches the ground. As the holding wood is cut, watch for the first, almost imperceptible movement of the tree, and then as soon as the tree begins to fall, quickly and carefully exit the cutting area using the primary escape route.

If felling by crosscut saw, follow the same directions except begin the back cut from the back of the tree before evenly removing wood toward the apex of the face cut to create the hinge as the tree begins to fall. As the saw begins to come near the ideal hinge width, increase speed to reduce "barber chairing"—prematurely splitting up the bole of the tree. Place a wedge behind the saw if space allows. If the tree gets hung up in another and becomes a "leaner," use a rock bar, cant hook, peavey, winch, or rope to roll or twist the tree and free the top. Exercise extreme care when performing these procedures.

Make adjustments to the direction of the fall by using wedges, either behind the saw when cutting or by removing the saw and pounding the wedge. Use wedges after the saw is far enough into the wood that there is room to insert them to assist in levering the tree over.

Bucking and Limbing

Once a tree is down, it must be cut into appropriate pieces (called bucking) and limbed. Since the tree can shift during this work, it can be as dangerous as felling, so be aware of the tension and compression dynamics.

Tension and Compression

Before cutting wood of any length, one must consider the forces being exerted on the wood: tension and compression. Wood fibers are flexible, oriented vertically within a tree, and bend under their own weight. This causes them to be compressed on one side of the tree and stretched under tension on the other side. Before cutting, determine where the tree or wood is compressed and where it is under tension. If the side under compression is sawed into, the saw will most likely become bound as the wood continues to compress. If there is a lot of tension and compression on wood and the tension is released quickly, the saw will not bind, but the cut will not be a controlled cut, making it more likely that the wood will break quickly and split before the cut is complete. Spring poles are the most extreme cases of tension and compression and can be very dangerous. Spring poles are trees that are bent by another tree or object's weight and contain an immense amount of stored potential energy. The best plan of action is to avoid creating such situations by clearing the felling or cutting area to minimize potential hazards .

Be sure to determine tension and compression before making a cut. Assess what will happen in each instance before releasing the tension or compression. Downed trees and logs can be very dangerous if they are not assessed properly. As with felling, determine an escape route and be aware of the tree in relation to your position because it will shift as limbs and wood are cut.

➔ OTHER MATERIALS

Dimensional wood is commonly used in frontcountry trail construction. Even in the backcountry, the ease of installation may make it more cost-efficient to bring in materials rather than shape and process native wood on-site. Pressure-treated wood is also an option. Be sure to use proper safety procedures and gear (particularly gloves and eye protection) when working with this type of wood, which is chemically treated. Always cut treated wood away from open water and wetlands.

MINERAL SOIL AND GRAVEL

Mineral soil and gravel are integral materials for most trail projects. Occasionally a borrow pit must be dug to provide gravel or mineral soil for fill work along the trail. Although such pits can be dug near the trail, they should be out of direct view and when no longer needed should be filled with debris and hidden. Gravel for trail projects needs to be of a type and size that drains well and can be transported to the work site in sacks, buckets, or, if possible, a wheelbarrow. For frontcountry trails, gravel is typically purchased and transported to the project site.

➔ HOISTING AND RIGGING EQUIPMENT

Moving rocks with winches and hoisting equipment can be very dangerous if not done properly. Be sure to get the appropriate training before using any hoists or winch systems. Training can be found through various organizations, including Trail Services, LLC; AMC; the Professional Trail Builders Association; and American Trails.

GRIPHOIST

The Griphoist has become the most commonly used hoisting mechanism for trail work (see figure 7.11). Although come-alongs and other cable winches are readily available, the Griphoist has more safety features and versatility. The number of safety features depends on the model. One such feature is the mechanism by which the Griphoist pulls or releases the wire rope. It has two "grip jaws," one that is always locked around the rope; if one were to fail, the other would hold the system. Many Griphoists also cannot be put into "neutral" while there is tension on the system. Another major safety feature is the inclusion of one or more shear pins that prevent the machine from exceeding its load capacity. (*Note*: Shear pins can break from wear and prolonged use, so be sure to carry extras.)

Moving very heavy or large amounts of rock easily and safely over long distances may be effectively done only with the help of a Griphoist lifting and pulling system. Griphoists control the lowering of rock down a steep slope and are

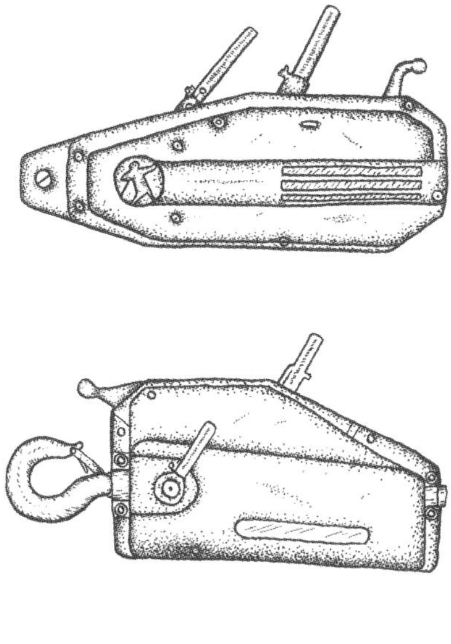

Figure 7.11. Griphoists can be found in working load limits of 1 ton, 2 ton, and 4 ton. Different models may have slight differences in operation and maintenance.

capable of pulling rock uphill or out of a hole. Such equipment can also position, rotate, and flip large rocks.

Trail crews have found that Griphoists with a 1- or 2-ton capacity are the most effective and versatile. The Griphoist is a closed-cased device that grabs and pulls, or releases, a wire rope straight through the mechanism. This has the advantage of ease of operation and the ability to use rope of unlimited length. Chain falls, chain winches, and some winches with enclosed casings do not always work well, because dirt and debris get into the mechanisms. This causes them to jam, compromising integrity and safety and requiring frequent maintenance. Whichever winch or hoist device is used, be sure it is rated for the job. Read and understand operation and maintenance instructions. Follow all safety procedures. Wearing hard hats and leather gloves is mandatory when working with winch or Griphoist systems with wire rope, which may develop very sharp splinters.

Never use "cheater" bars on a winch or Griphoist. Winches and Griphoists have safety handles that are designed to the equipment's specifications and have shear pins that will break after a certain load limit is exceeded. Do not overstrain or shock-load a winch, Griphoist, wire rope, or rigging. Snapping rope and rigging can cause serious injury.

"Donkey" winches powered by chain saws may prove practical for moving rocks or logs in some cases. Horses, oxen, or machinery might be feasible, even necessary at times, to move large volumes of material. Generally, however, these options are not needed and may not be appropriate due to the potential for increased damage to the treadway and its environs.

Be sure to receive adequate training before using a Griphoist system. This chapter covers only the basic facts and does not contain all the information needed to use a Griphoist safely and effectively.

Rigging

A variety of rigging equipment is needed to accompany a Griphoist system. Use equipment that is sized accordingly with the hoist and wire rope rated for the task. To ensure adequate safety, all rigging should be able to bear five times more load than expected; this ratio is called the safety factor. The weight an item can bear is the safety rating, or safe working load (SWL). The SWL of each rigging component will vary depending on how it is set up and used. Inspect rigging regularly for wear and damage; retire equipment that is questionable. The following are common components for Griphoist systems.

Nylon slings

A variety of nylon slings can be used with a Griphoist or rigging system. One common type is the 3-inch-wide, 4- to 10-foot-long eye-and-eye sling, used for Griphoist and skyline anchors, suspension points, and guy lines. Additionally, there are 4- to 12-foot-long slings, referred to as endless loops, for choke-hitching rocks to be lifted, extending anchors, or guy lines. Newer, thinner, lighter slings are available as well. Know the difference in safety ratings for each component. These ratings can be found on the slings, and they change depending on a sling's use and orientation.

Rock basket

A custom-made nylon-webbed device for wrapping large rocks when winching, the rock basket is especially useful for rocks expected to roll and tumble as they're moved (see figure 7.12).

Snatch block

This pulley, usually with a hook, has a side that opens to insert wire rope. The snatch block can redirect rope or double its carrying capacity. Use an appropriately sized block with a sheave sized to the wire rope diameter. Do *not* use "break away" snatch blocks that are usually chosen for small logging and tractor applications.

Shackle

A U-shaped steel piece closed with a heavy pin, the shackle can connect slings, chains, and wire ropes. Smaller shackles often don't have enough space to accept wide slings.

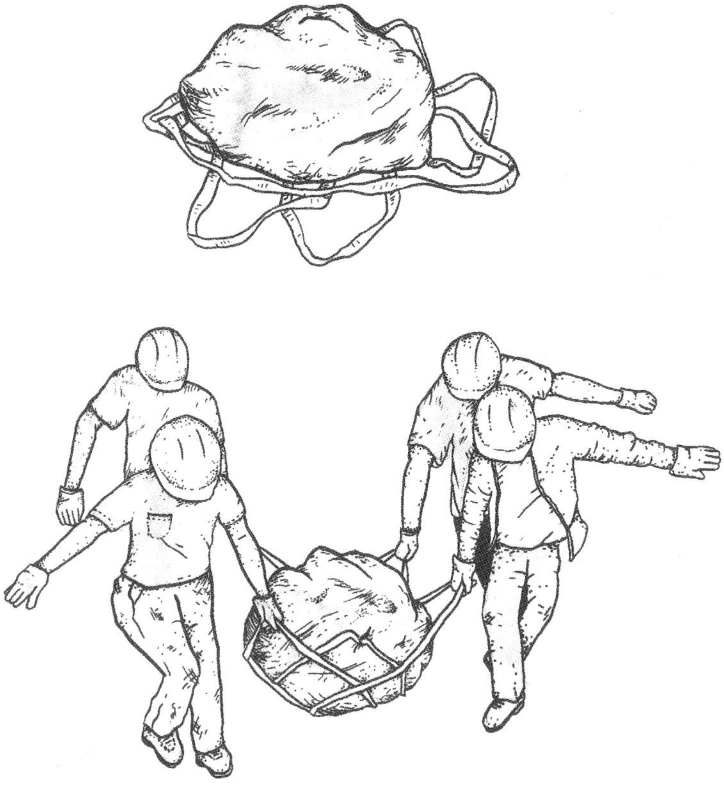

Figure 7.12. Nylon webbing can be stitched together as a basket and hooked to a rigging system. The basket can also be hand-carried by the crew.

Rock box

This is typically a 3-foot-square, 6-inch-deep homemade box for carrying scree and rubble along a skyline.

Tripods (for treeless areas)

Tripods are generally made of 2-inch-square steel tubing with ⅛-inch-thick walls and are attached at the tops with threaded rod. Heights are commonly 8, 10, and 12 feet. Lightweight aluminum tripods are available through rigging manufacturers.

Saurman/Mule Grip

This hardware component creates a point of attachment on the hookless end of a wire rope when used in a high-line or rigging system (see figure 7.13).

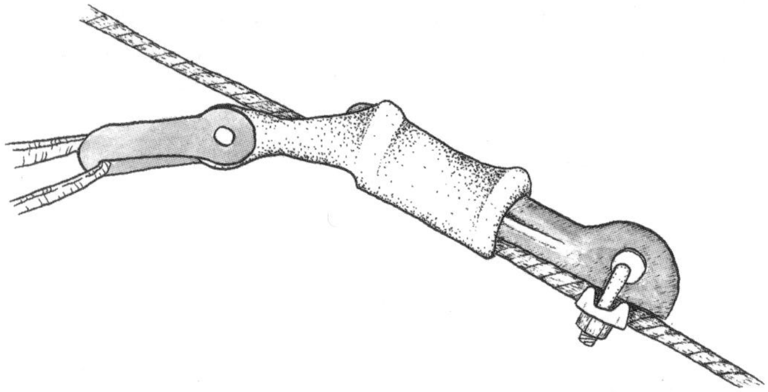

Figure 7.13. The saurman is a steel device used to shorten the length of steel cable.

7

Griphoist Techniques

Basic Single-Line Pull

Griphoists are primarily used to pull or lower a rock by dragging it or controlling its descent down to the work site. Anchor the Griphoist to a large tree by looping a sling around the base of the trunk. A 3-inch-wide eye-and-eye sling looped in basket fashion will help avoid chafing the bark and damaging the tree. Securely wrap the rock to be moved with a 2-inch-wide endless loop sling. Encircle the rock, taking advantage of indentations and projections on its surface. An easy, self-tightening way to secure the rock is to put one end of the loop through the other, creating a girth hitch. A rock bar or mattock is often necessary to lift a rock to slip the sling under and around it. "Wrapping" a rock is a skill that takes time and experience. A rock basket greatly facilitates securing a rock and will hold the rock if it tumbles and rolls.

Always have someone stationed at the Griphoist and at the loading site. When pulling a rock across the ground, never let the Griphoist alone do the work. Have someone lever the leading edge of the rock with a rock bar or mattock to unsnag it when it gets caught or digs into the ground when advancing. On a slope, avoid being below the rock in case it slips from the webbing.

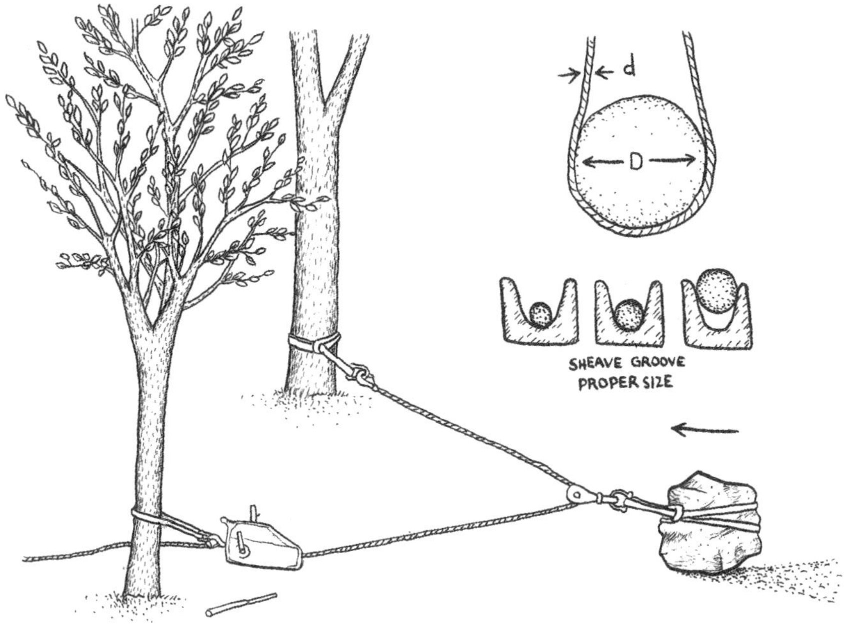

Figure 7.14. Mechanical advantages (that is, 2:1) can be set up to assist with operation. As more advantages (for example, 3:1, 4:1, etc.) are put into the system, the greater the forces that will be felt on the equipment. Make sure all equipment is rated to handle the forces created. D:d ratio applies only to mechanical advantages. Dramatic bend in a wire rope (creating an angle of less than 90 degrees) can put extreme stress on the wire rope and displace strands if the rope is not run through a block with a large enough diameter sheave. Depending on the type of wire rope being used, the diameter of the sheave (D) should be sixteen to twenty times the diameter of the wire rope (d). Smaller diameter blocks may be used when the wire rope does not exceed a 90 degree angle, but the sheave groove must still be the correct size for the diameter of the wire rope. Cable and fiber rope diameter and rigging block sheave groove widths need to match. There is tolerance for plus or minus $1/16$ inch for the cable and ropes. Too small or too big will yield premature failure of the equipment.

A two-to-one mechanical advantage can be employed by hooking a snatch block to the load, running the wire rope through the block, and attaching the end to another anchor near the winch's anchor (see figure 7.14). If doing this, be sure to have the appropriately sized snatch block to correspond with the diameter of wire rope, to pull accordingly and prevent kinks in the rope. In addition, be aware of the excess force that is being exerted on the system.

Skyline System

A skyline or high-line system is a more advanced Griphoist rigging technique that lifts and moves rocks above the ground from a quarry to the work site via a tensioned wire rope (see figure 7.15). The rope is suspended above the ground by trees or, in treeless areas, by steel tripods (see figure 7.16). Rocks can be transported uphill or downhill, across a slope or over a gully, pulled up slight inclines,

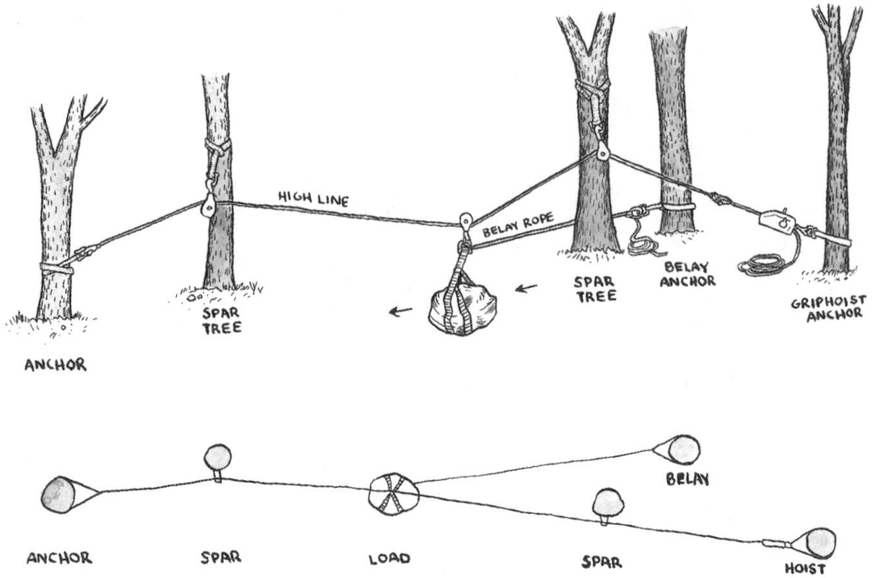

Figure 7.15. These are the essential elements of a skyline, but they can have a lot of variation in a real-world setting. One key element is that the entire system is in as straight of a line from anchor to anchor as possible.

or brought across steep side slopes in a controlled way. A skyline can also transport buckets of soil and gravel or boxes and baskets of small rocks for scree walls. Items can be carried distances of 200 feet or more. Although a skyline requires additional equipment and setup time, it is an efficient way to move large quantities of rock. One of its greatest advantages is that it does not drag rock over the ground, which protects soils, vegetation, and fragile areas, such as alpine environments. It is particularly effective when there is a large quantity of rock in the same area a distance from the trail.

Setup. If trees are in the area, the first step is to find two appropriately placed large trees (called spar trees) and two anchor points, which can be either large trees or boulders. Ideally, the quarry and the project site on the trail should be between and in line with the two spar trees. The two anchor points should also be in line and far enough beyond the trees so that the wire rope is suspended at a 45-degree (or less) angle from the suspension point in the spar trees.

Place the two suspended snatch blocks high enough in the spar trees to prevent the rock from touching the ground when it is hanging from the wire rope. Skillful and safe tree-climbing techniques or a ladder will help to set up this system. (*Note*: Portable tree-stand ladders used for hunting separate into smaller parts and can be assembled to the desired height and secured to the tree using straps.) Choker a sling around the bole of the tree above a limb or bulge to keep it from slipping down. Use a 3-inch-wide, 3- or 4-foot-long eye-and-eye sling, and hook a snatch block to the free

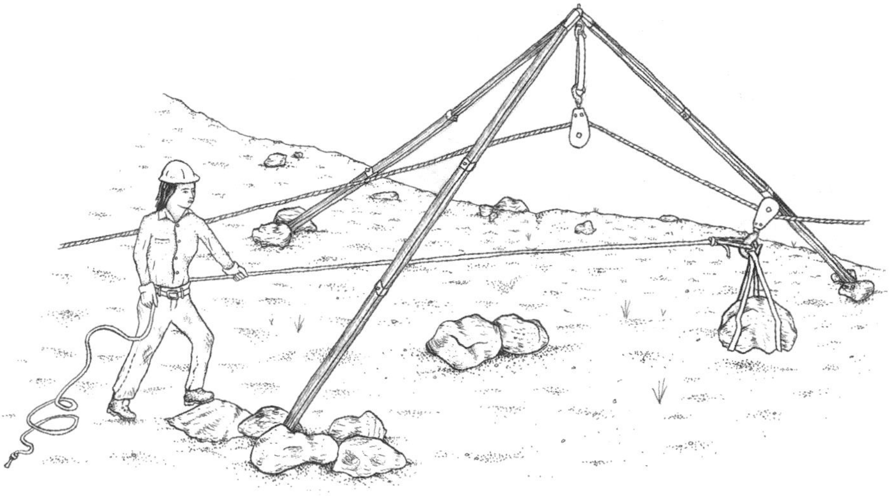

Figure 7.16. Tripods provide height for a skyline system where tall elements can't be found, such as in alpine or open space settings.

eye. Anchor the Griphoist close to the ground so it can easily be operated, and hook the end of the wire rope to the anchor on the far end. Insert the wire rope into the snatch blocks and feed it into the Griphoist, leaving enough slack in the line to reach the load. Put the third (traveling) snatch block on the slack line. Finally, tie a belay rope (one that is long enough to pull, or lower, the load along the skyline) to the third snatch block (see figure 7.17). Fully tension the system and then test it with a small rock to be sure everything stays in place. If the test is successful, the system is ready to lift and move a load.

Sling a rock so it can be lifted straight up and be held securely while suspended. Hook the traveling snatch block to the sling. Keep one person stationed to operate the Griphoist and another near the load to watch and coordinate its progress. The person near the load should be in charge of the entire operation and communicate with the Griphoist operator using simple commands, such as "Tension," "Slack," and "Hold," which mean, respectively, to take wire rope in, let wire rope out, or pause until further instruction.

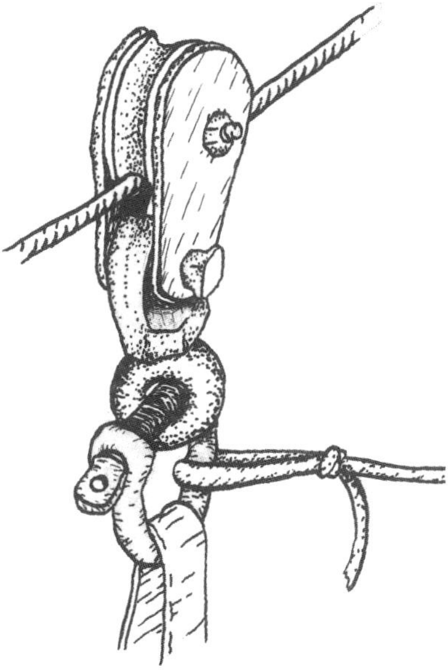

Figure 7.17. Detail of a typical rigging connection of load sling to shackle to travel block. A belay line is also attached.

The Griphoist will increase the tension on the wire rope and lift the rock. As the wire rope approaches horizontal, the tension becomes even greater. Check all equipment and anchors frequently to ensure they are working properly and holding securely. Once the load is suspended from the taut skyline—high enough to clear the ground during transit—it can be pulled, or lowered, to the work site. To aid in pulling the load, anchor one end of the belay rope and run it through a pulley attached to the traveling snatch block to increase the mechanical advantage. To control lowering and avoid damage to the spar tree, belay the load using a port-a-wrap or a z-drag: a series of shackles that the belay rope runs through.

SAFETY TIPS: SKYLINES

- **Beware of the bight (anyplace the wire rope changes direction).**
- **Keep fingers away from the snatch blocks and Griphoist.**
- **Visually inspect the entire system many times a day.**
- **Do not stand under any load or wire rope under tension.**
- **Make sure there is only one person giving directions and that directions are brief and clear.**
- **Always use a belay rope when moving rocks downhill.**
- **Stay uphill of a load at all times.**
- **Wear all appropriate PPE, and limit the number of people around the system.**
- **Be aware of damage to anchors or spars throughout the operation.**
- **Check to see that webbing is in good condition and in the appropriate place.**
- **Make sure all hardware is pulling in line and nothing has shifted throughout the operation.**

Once the rock has arrived at the work site, continue to hold the belay rope or tie it off. Release the tension of the skyline with the Griphoist and lower the rock to the ground. Completely slack the skyline before releasing the load.

A skyline system is quite versatile and adaptable. The setup and operation just described is the most basic and may have limitations due to terrain, availability of convenient trees, and distance between the quarry and project site. To manage these variables it's important to have extra gear on hand. A selection of slings of various lengths and types, shackles, extra rope, and snatch blocks allows for greater flexibility of setups. Overall skyline length can be increased by using a longer wire rope or by having a long auxiliary wire rope for the skyline that is tensioned by the Griphoist and its wire rope. Griphoists can be very helpful, effective, and efficient tools when used safely and wisely. Be sure to get adequate training before operating a Griphoist or any skyline system. Information, training, supplies, and resources can be found through various outdoor organizations.

➔ WORKING IN THE ALPINE ZONE

Working in the alpine zone requires special considerations. The alpine ecosystem is extremely fragile; it is imperative to take extra care to avoid disturbing vegetation and soils. Due to the sensitive nature of alpine areas, materials can be difficult to gather. Therefore, tripods are practically indispensable in alpine zone rock projects. Smaller rock buckets and crates can be helpful, especially when gathering and transporting rocks for scree walls, which are commonly needed on popular trails. When collecting rocks, disturb as little soil as necessary. If possible, remove rocks from the windward side of slopes, where less vegetation grows due to exposure. Most important, consult the land manager and specialist concerning the work area involved.

Also, due to the openness of alpine terrain, space may be available for airlifting non-native materials, if needed and desired. Although the building materials would not be of local origin, they would serve to preserve the existing resources in this fragile zone.

➔ CLEANUP

After quarrying is completed, "brush in" evidence of excavation by filling quarry holes with debris, deadwood, and leaf litter, especially those near and within sight of the trail.

Use debris to fill any spaces where materials were removed. Corridors where materials were transported should be brushed in well. This will likely keep curious hikers from venturing into an area that is revegetating; it should appear natural enough to escape the notice of anyone who is not specifically looking for the disturbance. If brushed in properly, the area should revegetate and blend into the surrounding environment in little time.

CHAPTER 8

TRAIL CONSTRUCTION AND MAINTENANCE

AT-A-GLANCE

By using proper techniques, you will be able to construct and maintain a sustainable trail.

- **Construction:** Cut the trail corridor, remove excess organic material, and create a sustainable treadway.
- **Reconstruction:** Manage treadway problems by fixing old structures and constructing new ones where needed.
- **Erosion control:** Address erosion by building drainages, stabilizers, retainers, and hardeners.
- **Basic maintenance:** Take care of four tasks: clearing drainages and blowdowns, brushing, marking trails, and delineating trails.

Before beginning any project, consider the two main goals of trail work: to reduce human impact to a single path and to strive to make the treadway appealing for hikers, thereby enhancing the hiking experience while upholding the first principle of mitigating natural resource impact. A trail must be stable and supported by structures to prevent erosion to have a treadway that is inviting to hikers while minimally affecting the natural environment. By carefully considering the surrounding resources and recreational use, trail planners can make construction and reconstruction decisions that best enforce both goals.

After designing a trail and learning about tool use and safety, commence trail construction and reconstruction. "Construction" refers to the building of new trails or structures, and "reconstruction" involves repairing and restoring existing ones. Ideally, a well-planned trail, as discussed in Chapter 4 (page 30), reduces the need for major repairs and, in the worst-case scenario, redesign. However, improper placement of trails does occur. In certain situations, relocation may be the best option; in other cases, reconstruction is a feasible choice.

Construction and reconstruction are ongoing processes because a trail is dynamic and changes over time due to wear from foot travel, erosion from water drainage, and destruction from weather events. Once the trail is "worn in" by initial use, it may require the addition of drainage structures or other features.

➔ TRAIL CONSTRUCTION

The initial construction phase is quite simple, composed of three parts: cutting the trail corridor, tread construction, and marking.

CUTTING THE TRAIL CORRIDOR

The very first step of construction is cutting the trail corridor. Employ hazel hoes, saws, and other cutting tools and begin clearing the path. If construction is not occurring in a federally designated Wilderness Area, the most efficient tool is undoubtedly a chain saw operated by an experienced sawyer. Cutting new trail can be dangerous if working in a congested forest, so care should be taken regardless of tree size. Before cutting begins, obtain the required permits or other regulatory approval that may be needed.

Brush and blowdown clearing are nearly identical in the construction phase and the maintenance phase, except that in the former, the process is starting from scratch. (See instructions and information on brush clearing on page 165 later in this chapter.) The width and height of the trail corridor will depend on the specifications with which the trail must align. If constructing to a primitive/backcountry specification, avoid cutting out large trees because the stumps are difficult to remove. Moreover, trees along the side of the path can serve as natural trail definers, demonstrating to hikers where the route lies. They can also add to the aesthetic quality of the trail and serve to stabilize soils. If constructing to a polished and engineered specification, more thorough clearing will most likely be needed to accommodate tread width and clearance as well as bench construction on steeper slopes.

Be sure that the cutting is in accordance with the flagging placed by the person who initially laid out the proposed trail. Either keep the flagging on center or stay to the right or left, as prescribed by the flagger. Have an agreed-on method and stay consistent.

Determine whether trees being cleared are softwoods, such as spruce and fir, which do not sprout from cut stumps, or are hardwoods, which do. Softwoods should be cut flush to the ground or slightly below grade to facilitate rot. With hardwoods, it is important to pull the stump out of the ground to prevent resprouting. To facilitate this, it is often easier to keep the stump about waist height so that the trunk can be used as leverage for the removal of the lower portion. A helpful tool for stump removal is the Pulaski, which can be used to both dig around roots and cut them. Rock bars and a Griphoist can also assist with large stump removal.

After major tree cutting is complete, use loppers to complete final touches of removing branches. See the clearing guidelines mentioned in the "Maintenance" section of this chapter (page 159) for further details.

TREAD CONSTRUCTION

Now that the trail corridor has been cut, work can proceed safely and easily within this zone. Create the treadway by clearing organic materials and soil and shaping the tread into a slightly outsloped walking surface (see figure 8.1).

Figure 8.1. Pin flags can serve as the "final" line for new trail construction. At this point, the initial clearing of the corridor and any line adjustments have been completed.

8

Duffing

When all trees and shrubs have been cleared from the designated area, scrape away any organic materials, such as leaves, needles, roots, bark, and organic soil, to begin construction of the tread. This process is called *duffing*. Excavate down to mineral soil, which does not hold as much water as organic soil and allows percolation. Without removal of the duff layer, organic material will mix with or underlie the mineral soil tread surface. As that organic material decomposes, the tread will sink and slump. The importance of thorough duffing cannot be overstated.

However, on a completely flat trail, there may not be natural drainage features to shed water. If water does not percolate adequately, it may be necessary to build drainage structures. A flat treadway is not ideal because water has nowhere to drain. If the trail must be flat and low initial use is expected, consider leaving the duff and letting hikers compact the existing soil. Another commonly used technique is to import mineral soil from a borrow pit, a source of mineral soil that is dug away from the trail to minimize its impact. Be sure to fill in the pit after use with rocks, soil, and other debris and to disguise it with leaves and branches. For most trails, the amount of use and the type of soil will determine the tread construction needed.

To remove duff, use a hazel hoe, Pulaski, mattock, fire rake, or other digging and scraping tool. To ensure a uniform tread, mark each side of the treadway to the specified width before starting. Begin by scraping and rolling back the duff, including the extent of the upslope and downslope of the trail. Either broadcast the organic material downhill from the trail (beyond the downslope), or reserve it for later use to naturalize areas that were disturbed during the construction process. Chop out the dense mat of fine roots beneath the duff with a fire rake and Pulaski. Use a root ax for bigger roots.

Sidehilling, or Cutting a Bench

After removing the duff to expose mineral soil, shape the treadway. When building a new trail that traverses a slope, you'll need to make a relatively flat surface for the tread. This process is referred to as sidehilling, or cutting a bench. Begin by using a hazel hoe, mattock, or other scraping/digging tool to cut into the bank (see figure 8.2). Here three parts of the trail are created: the upslope, the treadway, and the downslope. The upslope, logically on the uphill side of the trail, should be cut to a grade of 45 degrees or less. If steeper, the soil will not be stable, and vegetation, which helps to retain the soil, will not likely grow. The width varies from 1½ feet

Figure 8.2. Use the natural sweeping motion of the grub hoe to achieve a nice backslope, pulling the mineral soil down and onto the treadway.

to 3 feet depending on the type of trail, topography, and local trail specifications. Although appearing flat, the tread should have an outslope of 4 to 8 percent so that water can drain and not pool on the treadway itself. Remove any piles of debris or soils that collect on the downhill side of the tread to allow water to flow freely. The third part of the trail is the downslope, which, like the upslope, ideally should be 45 degrees or less. Be sure to install proper drainage (discussed below), with the downslope graded to shed water at every outside curve. With the proper grades, curves, and drainage structures, it is less likely that the trail will need reconstruction in the future.

It is very important that the tread, upslope, and downslope are dug down to mineral soil, with all duff moved far enough downslope or away from the construction zone that it does not inhibit drainage. Duff and organic material can be taken from the construction site via wheelbarrow—if allowed—or bucket and dispersed away from the trail or used for revegetation.

Final preparation of the treadway will depend on the specific standards for the trail and the intended use. If the trail is near a road and will be used by many families and small children, consider a smoother tread with many of the roots and rocks removed. However, rocks and roots are seen as part of the backcountry experience and generally should remain, as long as they are stable and will not become ankle-twisting hazards. After the treadway is completed, if additional trail structures are needed, they can be installed any time after the initial construction phase.

→ TRAIL STRUCTURES AND RECONSTRUCTION

Even a well-laid-out and constructed trail will need regular maintenance and potentially additional trail structures as it ages. Because trail structures are time- and labor-intensive, keep them to a minimum in the initial trail design. However, on any trail section where the grade is steep enough to warrant concern about erosion, structures can be installed either preventively or as erosion issues become apparent. Remember that just constructing a trail, which removes vegetation and exposes bare soils, allows minerals and particulates to dislocate downhill into waterways. Poorly built trail structures can inadvertently strip the area beyond the treadway of organic soil, which can prohibit growth of trailside vegetation and cause siltation of local water sources. The goal of trail builders and maintainers is to minimize this impact. Carefully built trail structures, such as bridges (see Chapter 9, page 186), can be creative solutions to address this concern.

Two main factors affect the extent of a trail's reconstruction: number of visitors and the character of the land. More visitors mean more boots, footprints, trekking pole depressions—in short, more impact. Areas that are wet, are on steep slopes, have poor soils, or support fragile vegetation require particularly careful—and sometimes costly—reconstruction efforts.

When reconstructing a trail, minimize the visual impact of the proposed work and avoid undue infringement on the trail's natural and aesthetic qualities. Keep in mind that visitors come to a trail for a specific outdoor experience; often they do not want to visit a highly constructed trail, but rather a wilder area that maintains close contact with the natural surroundings. Overconstruction or excessively regular and obvious construction features can degrade the trail environment and, consequently, the opportunity to experience a sense of wildness.

There are three major steps in the reconstruction planning process. The first is to identify the problem. (If following a trail log, this may already be done.) Often, the immediate problem is merely a symptom of a larger problem, so the second step is to locate the identified problem's source. After this, in the third step, the damage itself can be addressed. For example, when dealing with an unofficial, or bootleg, trail, the problem is the existence of the trail itself. However, simply trying to close the trail generally does not address the source of the problem, which may be a muddy section of the main trail that hikers are avoiding. Draining the muddy main trail is an essential component to solving the bootleg trail problem.

In most situations a combination of techniques is necessary to solve the problem. The most common combination in trail reconstruction is to "drain and retain," since many tread problems come from lack of drainage, which leads to erosion. To fix the source of the problem, install drainage to allow water to flow downhill away from the trail, and install a retention device to stabilize and retain the existing soils.

➔ EROSION-CONTROL STRUCTURES

Erosion due to running water, exacerbated by hiker traffic, causes the greatest damage to a trail. Because of soil compaction, the channeling of water, and other factors, trails can function like intermittent streams. Even a well-built trail with a proper outslope can develop a small trench in the middle of the tread from soil compaction. Without proper drainage, water will continue to erode treadway soil.

Preventing erosion is the most difficult and important part of maintaining trails over steep, mountainous terrain or through wet and fragile areas. Four categories of structures and techniques are used to prevent and/or control erosion:

Drainages are probably the most important ally of trail maintainers. Earthen water bars and swales, for example, can be considered a dynamic form of erosion control. Set across or along the trail, drainages keep or direct water off the tread. Drainage features must be built into every trail. If a trail is properly laid out, constructed, and drained, often no other structures are needed.

Stabilizers, also called retainers, conserve the soil that is already present in the trail, stabilizing the tread. They can fill the treadway and retain soil by reducing the steepness of the slope through the creation of terraces. Rock steps are common stabilizers.

Hardeners are used where a trail crosses wet areas that cannot be effectively drained. By keeping hikers out of the mud, trail hardeners not only make hiking more pleasant but also protect fragile soils and vegetation. Stepping-stones and bog bridges are examples of hardeners.

Definers channel hikers onto the established treadway or hardened surface, preventing trail widening and protecting adjacent vegetation and soil from being trampled. Scree, or edge rock, is often used as a definer.

While erosion-control devices serve specific purposes, they may also achieve other important goals. For example, scree set along the edges of a rock staircase not only defines the trail but also aids in retaining soil along the steps and ensures that hikers do not walk around the structure. Bog bridges can also serve as trail definers while performing their principal duty as hardeners.

→ DRAINAGES

According to almost every trail worker, drainage is the most important feature of any trail. With well-designed and well-constructed drainage, most trails can be very stable. Without adequate drainage, a trail will most likely deteriorate.

GRADE REVERSALS

This is a category of drainage structures and techniques sometimes called grade dips, Cowetta dips, swales, and numerous regional variations of the same premise. They use the basic physics of reversing the grade to keep water moving across the trail and not down it. Well-designed grade reversals can be practically maintenance-free and are favored by bicyclists and other recreational users because they are relatively barrier-free. Generally, the term *grade reversals* is applied to new trail construction, and a variation called a *rolling grade dip* is installed on existing trails.

Grade reversals ensure that water drains thoroughly off the trail at a natural low spot or obstruction, like a large rock or root. They can be incorporated during new trail construction by laying the trail in concert with natural dips and by digging swales into these low points. This will collect and drain any accumulating water.

To construct a grade reversal, dig a shallow depression completely across the treadway in the shape of a fan, with the wide edge on the uphill edge and the narrow on the downhill edge. The sides of the swale should be of a gentle grade. This will allow the low area to drain downhill toward the outflow ditch. The outflow should be dug off the edge of the trail with the same standard as any other outflow ditch. Be sure the sides of the ditch are also gently sloped, creating a flat-bottomed drain (see figure 8.3).

For an existing trail, install a rolling grade dip. This type of reversal works well on steeper sidehill slopes. The dip incorporates a constructed berm reversing the grade with a long and broad outsloped edge uphill to shed water. These structures work best if used frequently to reduce water volume and velocity, controlling erosion (see figure 8.4).

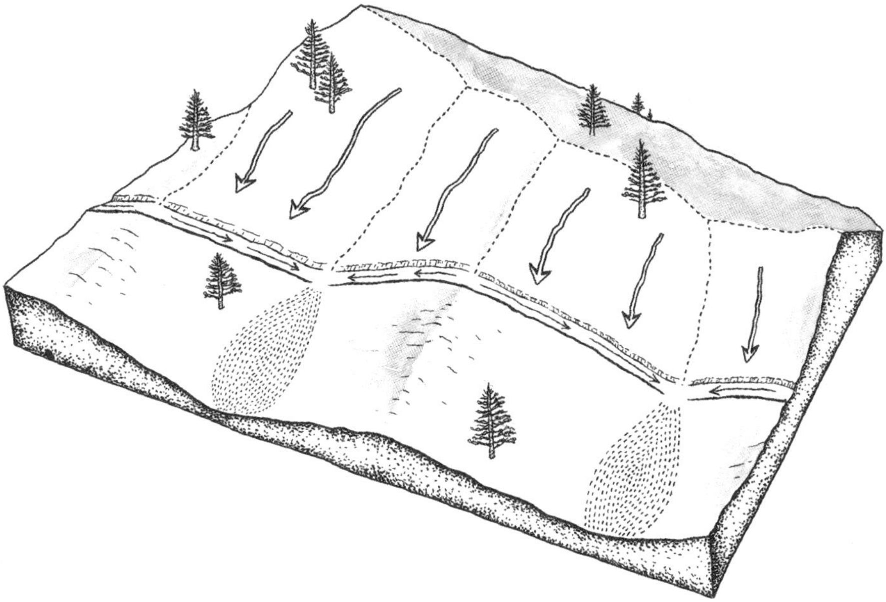

Figure 8.3. Grade reversals use the landscape contours to build in natural drainage points, minimizing water runoff getting caught in the treadway for long stretches.

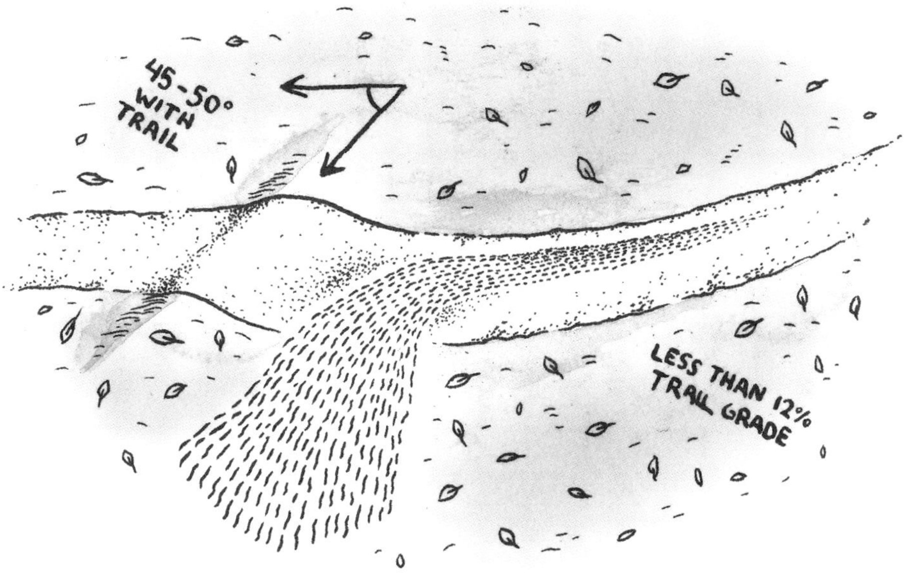

Figure 8.4. Purpose-built angled drainages catch and shed water.

WATER BARS

Where grades are too steep for simple swales or the volume of runoff is too great, install water bars. There are two types of water bars: earthen and reinforced. The latter can be made of either wood or rock.

Effective water bars fit the surrounding topography and trail conditions. On a steep slope where erosion is occurring, water must be removed near the top of the slope, mitigating damage below. Locate the area upslope where water first comes onto the trail or water volume may collect, and find a point on the downslope to remove it efficiently. Look for evidence of seeps or springs or of water movement, such as leaf litter, soil, and debris deposits. Check the trail for erosion damage during or just after a rainstorm to see runoff conditions at their worst. At stream crossings, where there is a possibility of the flow jumping the channel and onto the trail, reinforced water bars might be necessary down the trail to displace flooding waters.

Ideally, water should be channeled from the trail without significantly impeding its flow, thereby preventing it from depositing sediment and clogging the water bar. For this reason, natural turns in the trail can be excellent water bar locations (see figure 8.5). Water will be more easily removed, and the water bar will be somewhat self-cleaning, an important help in annual trail maintenance.

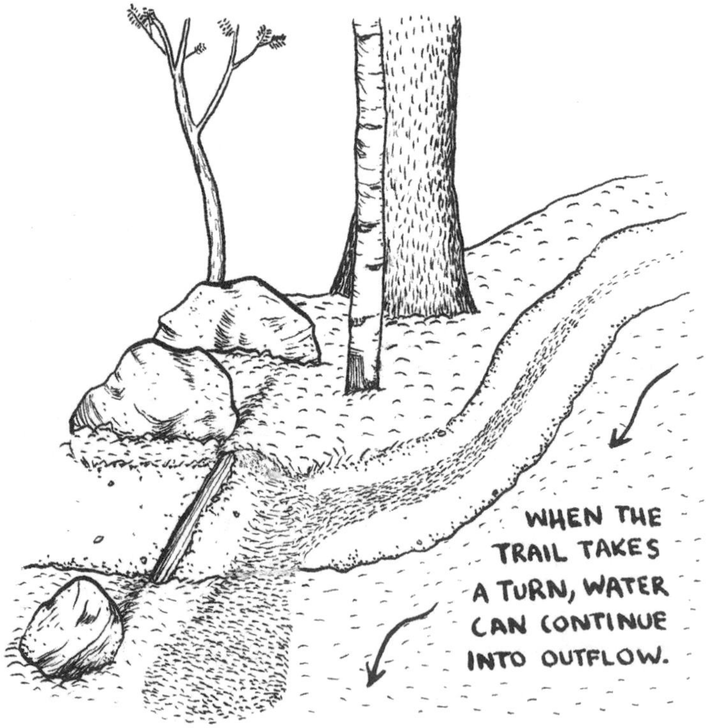

Figure 8.5. Natural turns in the trail can be effective places to shed water.

The spacing of water bars along a trail depends on the steepness of the slope, the amount of runoff, and the availability of places to divert water. Poorly laid-out or gullied sections of a trail may offer few good placement choices. Excavating larger and longer outflow ditches may be necessary to ensure that water exits and stays out of a gully or trail running straight down a slope. However, steep trails, such as one up a fall line, may be practically impossible to drain. On grades of 20 percent or more, every place on the trail that can have a water bar should. On shallower slopes, water bars can be spaced farther apart.

Once a site is chosen, the first step to building a water bar is to dig a trench at an appropriate angle, ideally pointing 30 to 50 degrees downslope relative to the center line of the trail. Too shallow an angle will result in the water slowing down and accumulating soil and debris that will eventually clog the water bar (see figure 8.6). Too wide an angle—anything in excess of 70 degrees—may accelerate runoff, undermining the water bar and increasing erosion potential. In general, the steeper the slope, the greater the angle needed. This ensures that the water will not come to an abrupt stop when it hits the water bar but be redirected off the trail. Soil type must also be considered when deciding the angle of the water bar. In looser, more granular soils, scouring and eroding of the outflow ditch can happen more easily. One solution is to lessen the angle of the drainage. Another solution is to retain the soil in the drainage. This can be done by lining the ditch and outflow with angular rock cobble. However, both of these options can make water bars more difficult to maintain. A third option is to install a check dam or two in the actual drainage, so water will be slowed and soil can be reclaimed, if necessary. Be sure the trench extends off both sides of the treadway. Neither water nor hikers should be attracted to go around either end of the bar; if that happens, channeling and soil compaction will misdirect water and negate the water bar's utility.

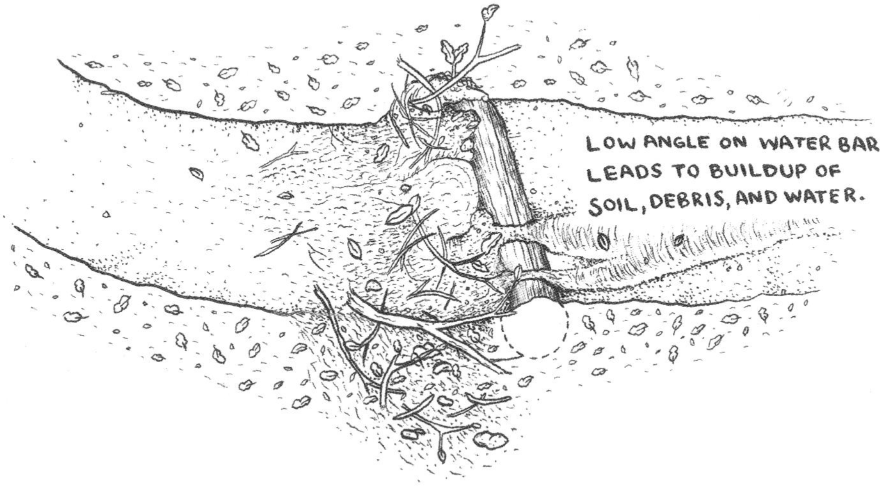

Figure 8.6. A drainage with too shallow an angle will only catch and hold water and debris.

On trails that have steep-sided gullies where removal of water is difficult, steps may be the only reasonable solution for keeping erosion in check. However, every possible exit for water should have a water bar, even if it requires digging through the walls of the gully.

A combination of steps and water bars is often used on steep slopes (see figure 8.7). However, if soils are stable and slopes are shallow, then water bars alone may suffice. Creative placement of water bars and steps in a complementary sequence prevents the water bars from clogging because the steps retain loose soil. Steps are therefore protected by water bars that remove water from the trail and keep the steps from becoming undermined by erosion.

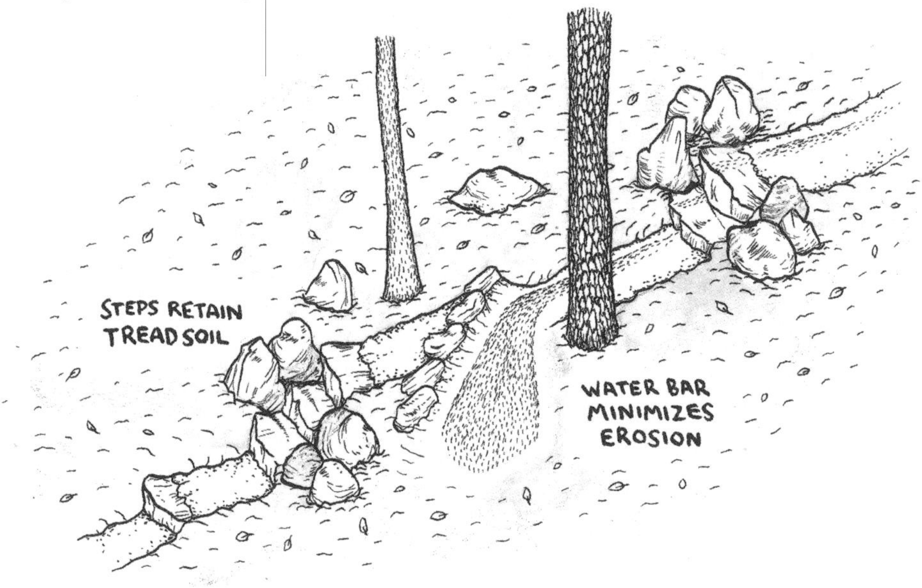

Figure 8.7. Steep sections of trail often require both drainages and steps. A general rule of thumb is to add a drainage at the top and bottom of every set of rock steps.

8

Earthen water bars

Earthen water bars, also called drainage dips (see figure 8.8), are often used on logging roads and are easy to construct. This style of water bar is useful in areas where the grade is less than 12 percent. On grades of more than 12 percent, the downhill side of the water bar must be reinforced by either wood or rock.

To make an earthen water bar, dig a very wide, smooth, U-shaped ditch across the trail at an angle informed by the pitch of the slope, as discussed earlier. Steep sides will collapse under hiker traffic and clog the ditch. Extend the ditch across the entire treadway to capture all runoff. Use the soil excavated from the ditch as backfill to build a substantial mound (up to 1 foot high and 1 foot thick, with a gradual

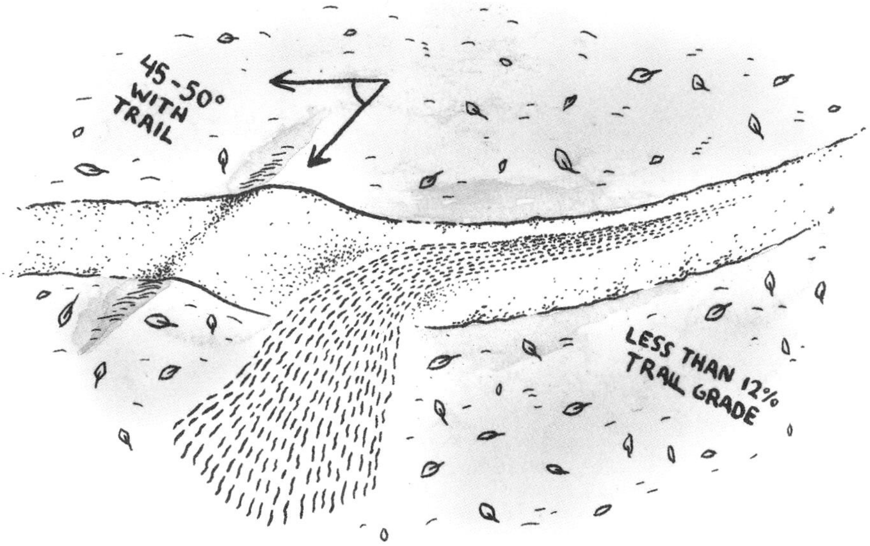

Figure 8.8. Earthen water bars function similarly to a rolling grade dip.

ramp) on the downhill side along the length of the ditch. Dig the ditch at a sharp angle (45 to 50 degrees) to prevent the force of the flowing water from eroding the mound. The mound can easily break down under the forces of water and hiking traffic, so for added strength, use rocks to build its foundation.

The next step is to construct the drain into the earthen bar. Starting 4 to 6 feet uphill of the ditch, shape the treadway so that the trail gradually slopes into the drainage. This should serve to gently collect the water and feed it slowly into the ditch. One of the main goals of a drain is to get the water off the trail in a dispersed, gradual way so that it does not cause any further erosion or deposition.

Add the excavated mineral soil and small rocks to backfill the mound on the downhill side of the ditch. (Do not use any duff, roots, or organic mud.) This needs to be very well packed into a solid, gradual ramp that can extend as far as 4 feet down the trail. The backfill mound should be slightly higher than the bar, gradually sloped, and about 1 foot high. With traffic it will compact and wear down. Once again, for traffic and water to flow through this entire structure without creating excess erosion, the gradient should be very gradual, gently guiding the course of the water.

Finally, dig an outflow ditch off the lower end of the water bar to remove the runoff completely from the trail. The outflow ditch should be broad and flat-bottomed (12 inches wide or more at the bottom), free of roots and obstructing rocks, and with sloped sides. A narrow ditch or one with protruding roots or rocks will clog

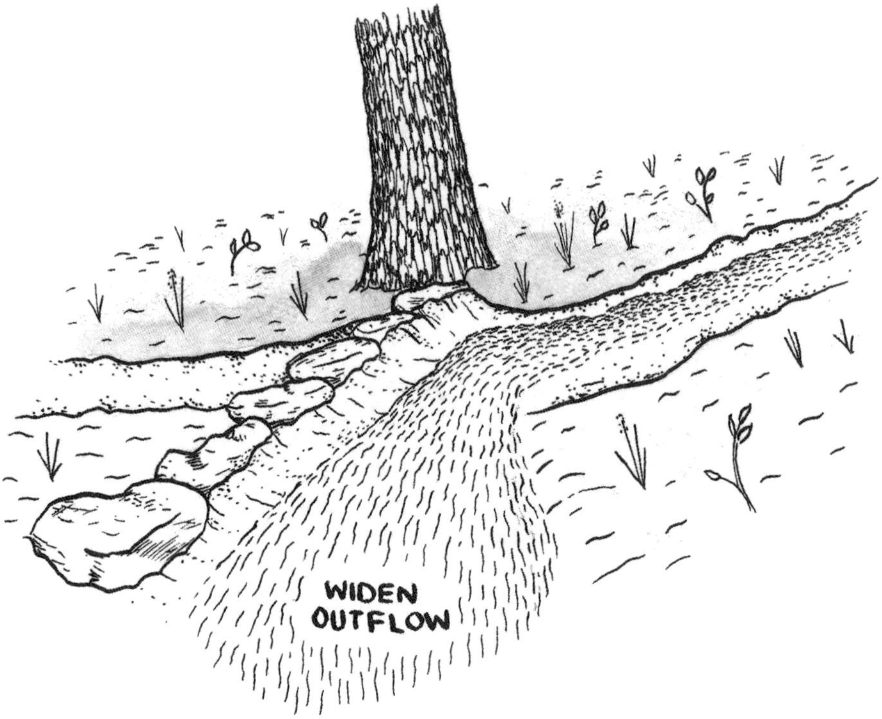

Figure 8.9. The end of the drainage off-trail. The outflow should fan out to broadly disperse water runoff.

easily. The length of the outflow ditch depends on the terrain, but it needs to be long enough to ensure that water will leave and not reenter the trail. Fan out the end of the outflow ditch to allow water to disperse and help prevent it from clogging (see figure 8.9).

If water falls or drops steeply off the edge of the trail, line the outflow ditch with rocks to slow and disperse the water, thus protecting trailside soils from eroding. (This functions much like an object placed at the base of a gutter on a house.) This technique is particularly important in the alpine zone, where plants are small and easily disturbed.

Reinforced water bars

The technique for constructing a reinforced water bar of rock or wood is similar to that of an earthen water bar. Although more time-intensive to build, a well-made, reinforced water bar can last for decades. Of the two types, rock water bars, placed solidly and properly, provide a more durable alternative to wood water bars. They are also more appropriate above treeline, where wood is scarce but rocks are plentiful. The basic details on how to construct a wood water bar are nearly identical to those of a rock water bar.

Rock water bars

There are two traditional ways to construct a rock water bar: the cake method and the toast method. The cake method (see figure 8.10) is preferred as it results in a more rugged structure. Once a site is chosen, the first step is to gather rocks. Look for rocks that are at least 12 inches thick and have at least one flat surface to form the face of the bar (side facing the drainage). Then dig a trench wide enough to hold the rocks, as always using the recommended angle of between 30 and 50 degrees relative to the axis of the trail. Be sure the trench and the rocks extend off both sides of the treadway.

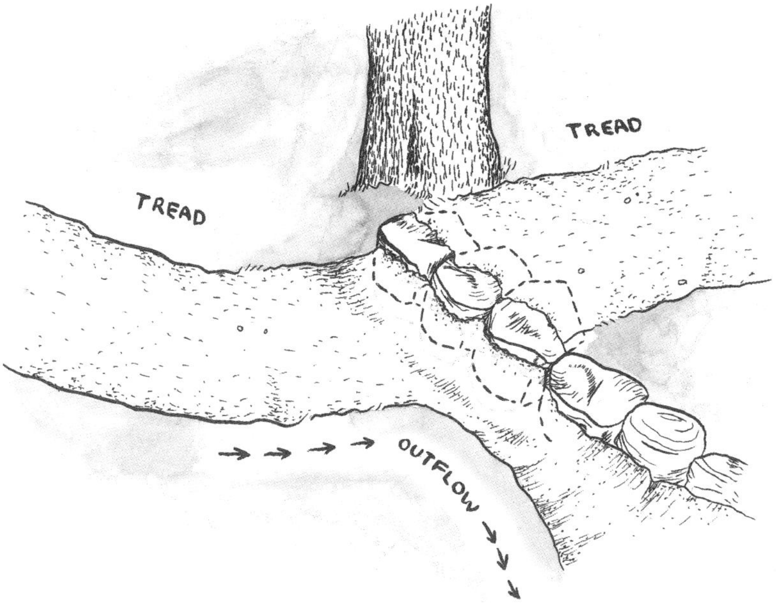

Figure 8.10. Rocks butted together form the skeleton of a rock water bar.

The trench should be deep enough that the top of the rocks will be almost flush with the trail on its downhill side. A trench that's too shallow may leave the water bar sticking up too high and increase the danger of it being undermined. Soil and rock excavated from the trench should be heaped on the trail behind the water bar to be used as backfill later. Leaf litter, organic mud, and roots are not good backfill and should be disposed out of sight of the trail.

Set rocks into the trench one at a time and tightly together, or slightly overlapping each other, starting at the lower end; each rock should be set slightly forward of the one below it, much like shingles on a roof. Water will flow from one rock to the next without seeping between. Be selective in the orientation of the individual rocks and mindful of a good step area to be used by hikers. A good step is not too high off the tread, shaped well, large enough to accommodate foot traffic, and desirable to use. Rock in the treadway should only protrude 4 inches above the ground. Rocks off to the side may be higher, to deter hikers from going around the structure. Water bars are meant to be walked over smoothly. They should never be an obstacle.

It's important to set all rocks securely so that flowing water and foot traffic won't dislodge them. Test the stability by kicking and jumping on set rocks; there should be no movement. If a rock isn't quite set, try to wedge it tighter or reposition it slightly with a rock bar or mattock. Well-packed mineral soil or rock crush around the rock may help and will compact solidly when tamped into place. The extra effort should ensure that the water bar will work properly and last for decades.

The second way to construct a rock water bar is the toast method—setting thin, flat rocks on edge into a deep and narrow trench (see figure 8.11). The toast method should only be employed when the cake method is not possible. Bury the rocks deep enough to be stable and set them so they lean back slightly downhill against the backfill, and overlap them in shingle fashion. This technique works well when only flat, thinner rocks are available, such as in areas with shale or slate. However, a rock on end, especially if not buried completely, has the possibility to give. It can upend when stepped on and act like a lever, weakening the entire structure. To counteract this, deposit fist-sized rocks and crush in the trench and fill with mineral soil to further anchor the structure.

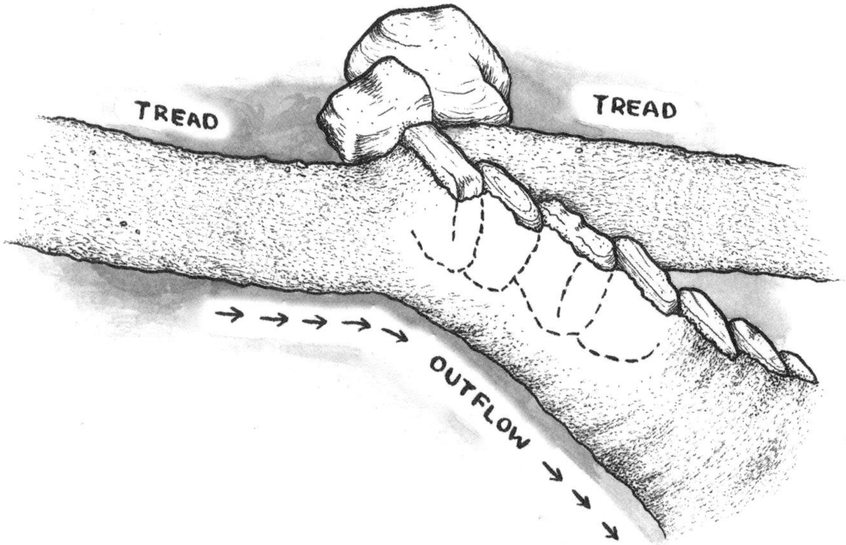

Figure 8.11. Thin, taller rocks overlapping the next form the skeleton of a rock water bar.

Wood water bars

Any rot-resistant type of wood, such as spruce, hemlock, or cedar, can be used for a wood water bar. In general, avoid using hardwoods as most hardwood species are prone to rot quickly. The diameter of a water bar log should be at least 8 inches at the log's small end. The length depends on the width of the trail, which in some cases can be more than 10 feet; water bar logs should extend at least 12 inches past both outside edges of the treadway.

Peel the bark off the logs; if left on, bark can hold water and cause accelerated rot, or it can clog the water bar when it eventually falls off. Be aware that peeling may be very difficult late in the growing season. Peeled logs can be quite slippery to walk on, so consider using an ax to square off the top edge of the logs across the treadway, creating a rough surface for better footing. Remove only a minimal amount of each log to preserve its structural integrity.

Dig a trench an appropriate size to accommodate the log. It should be buried with only a few inches showing, using the same guidelines as those used with a rock water bar. The log should fit snugly in the trench with no high points or voids underneath; when stepped on, they should not roll or lift.

A large pin rock can be placed on each end of a log to help hold it in place (see figure 8.12). Pin rocks will also help prevent hikers from going around the structure. Sometimes, with good planning and skillful use of tools, you can wedge a log between existing boulders.

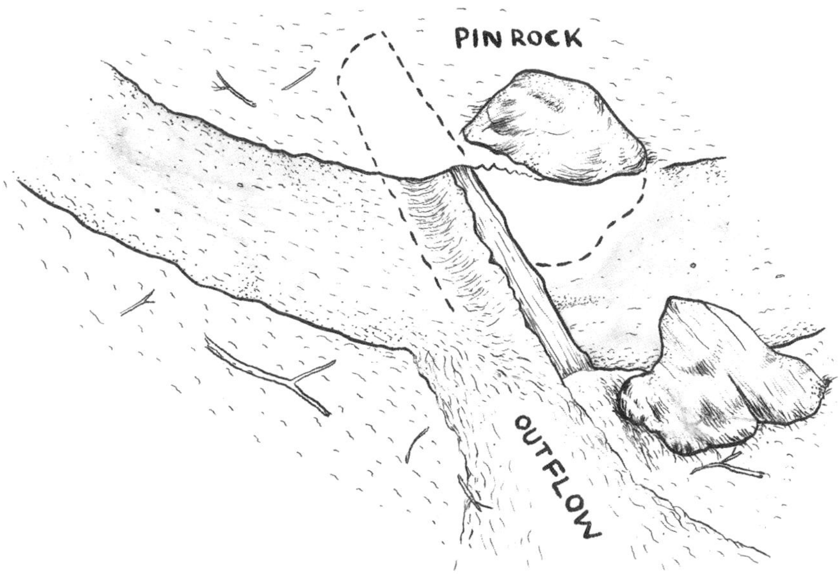

Figure 8.12. A log the length of the treadway plus 1–2 feet extra to bury into either side of the trail.

If pin rocks are scarce or unavailable, use wooden stakes made from similar rot-resistant species as the water bar itself. Stakes should at least be 3 to 4 inches in diameter and a few feet in length, shaped to a point where they will be driven into the ground by an ax or sledge. Place two stakes at each end of a log in the water bar, and drive them into the ground at outward sloping angles. This will effectively wedge the log between the stakes and stabilize its position. Saw off excess height on the stakes as long as there is enough pressure on the log.

When the log is in place, build the drain in the same manner as the other types of water bars. The drain should be large and dispersing; the backfill mound (built from the excavated soil) should be appropriately sized and gradually ramp down from the downhill side of the structure; and the fan above the bar should be dug and shaped to direct water into the channel and off the trail.

CROSS DITCH

A cross ditch ensures that runoff or small streams bisecting a flat section of trail cross cleanly and efficiently, flowing away from the trail (see figure 8.13). Dig a ditch large enough to capture and contain all the runoff from the immediate area in which the ditch will serve. Use soil and rocks excavated from the ditch to build up the banks on both sides. Where flow is high, line the sides of the ditch with rock where the ditch meets the trail, as in the construction of a rock water bar. To prevent hiker traffic from beating down the ditch's banks, set a large stepping-stone into the bank on each side. To help retain the depth of the ditch, "tile" its floor between the stepping-stones with one or more rocks, set flush or below the dirt surface and abutting each stepping-stone. This can be quite effective but is difficult to get right. Refer to the "Stabilizers" section on page 132 and the information about rock stairs for more details on setting rocks. In either case, make sure the natural waterway has an outflow ditch.

8

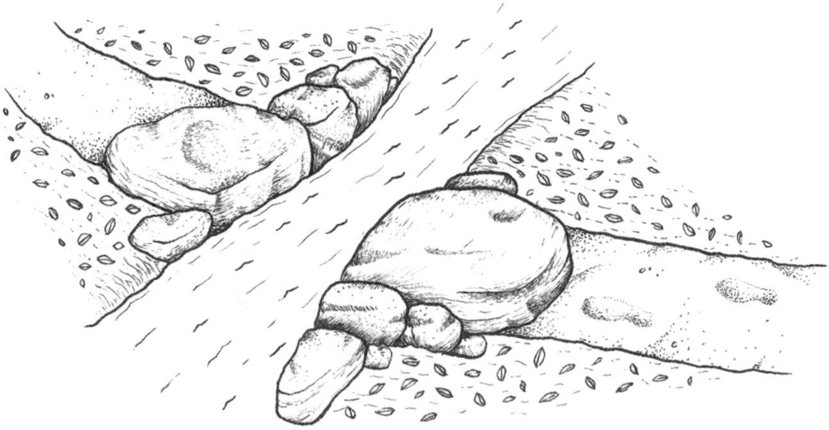

Figure 8.13. A cross ditch is a drainage structure that starts well off one side of the tread to catch water and carries it across to the other side.

SIDE DITCH

A drainage ditch along the side of a trail collects water where heavy seepage, springs, or runoff enters the trail and cannot be immediately removed. As water travels downslope toward a trail, a side ditch constructed on the trail's uphill side can catch it and channel it alongside, but not onto, the treadway. After traversing the length of the ditch, the water can be carried off by an outflow ditch on the same side, if possible, or carried across the trail and off the downhill side via a water bar (see figure 8.14). Although helpful in some locations, this drainage structure often needs continual maintenance, and if it is constructed along the fall line of the slope, it can exacerbate erosion.

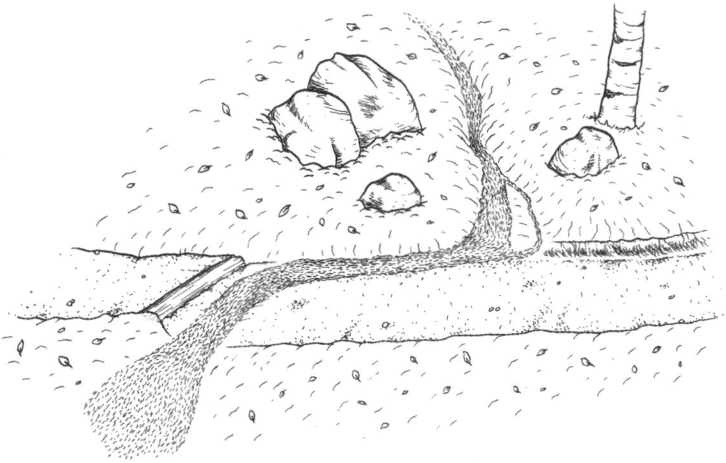

Figure 8.14, above. A side ditch is dug on the uphill side of a trail to catch water, then connects to a cross drain to shed it off the other side.

Figure 8.15, below. Uphill drainages catch water before the turn. Tread below the turn is outsloped or requires a water bar to shed any other water.

SWITCHBACK DRAINAGE

One method of draining a switchback is to direct water along the uphill side of the switchback's upper leg (see figure 8.15). With the use of a side ditch, the water can then be properly and completely drained out, bypassing the next curve in the switchback. In some cases, it may be necessary to drain water off the downhill side of the upper leg of the switchback. In this case, a second water bar on the lower leg of the switchback may be necessary to remove water completely.

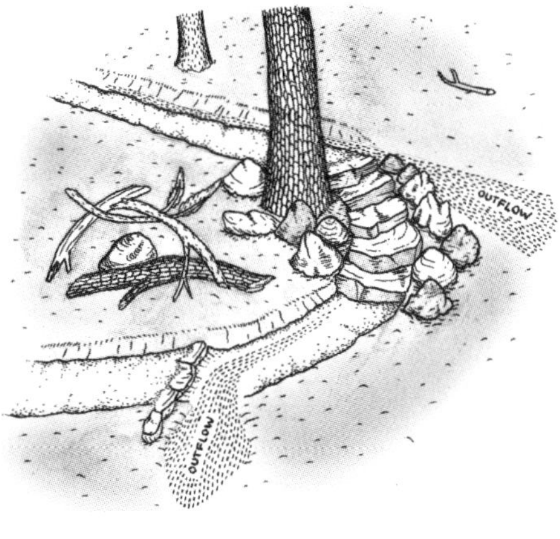

➔ STABILIZERS

STAIRS

Stairs protect from erosion and assist with soil retention on steep trail grades. The basic purpose of stairs is to provide a stable vertical rise on the trail, which slows water and retains soil. Although highly effective stabilizers, stairs are very costly, time-consuming, and labor-intensive to install, and they appear unnatural in the landscape. With proper trail design they can potentially be avoided, but they are often necessary on trails with steep slopes. Stairs are an important technique in reconstruction (although probably less used than drainages) as trail slopes steepen and erosion damage becomes extensive over time (see figure 8.16).

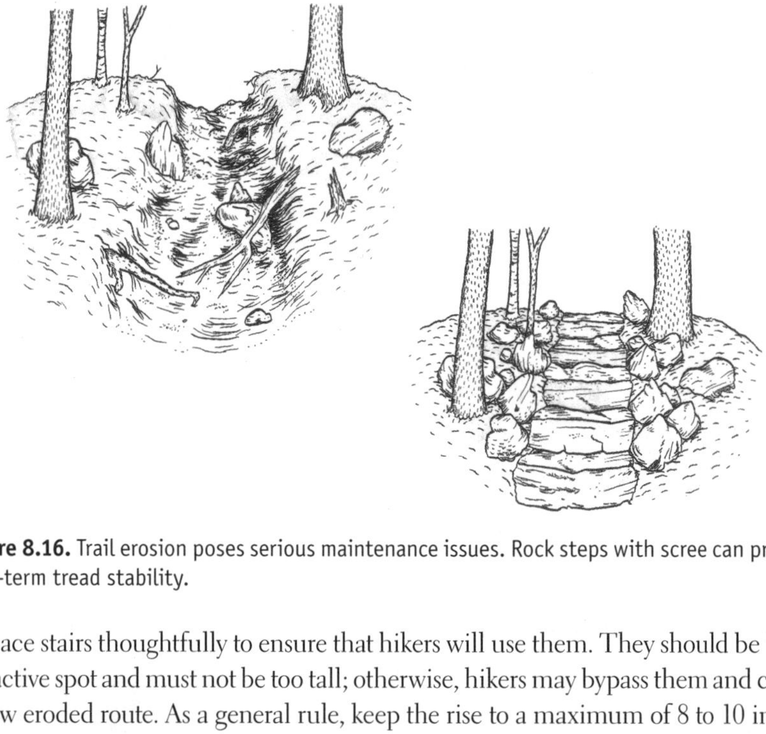

8

Figure 8.16. Trail erosion poses serious maintenance issues. Rock steps with scree can provide long-term tread stability.

Place stairs thoughtfully to ensure that hikers will use them. They should be in an attractive spot and must not be too tall; otherwise, hikers may bypass them and create a new eroded route. As a general rule, keep the rise to a maximum of 8 to 10 inches per step, but standards will vary according to users and the character of the trail.

Some hikers avoid even well-placed steps, particularly if they are tired. To prevent this, edge the sides of the staircase with scree, a method often used on alpine trails. This is especially helpful when steps need to be placed in wide gullies, where it is easy for hikers to bypass them. Scree has the added benefit of supporting and holding the bank soils in place. (Scree will be addressed later in this chapter on page 156.) Brush, logs, and other debris can also be used to prevent bypassing of a stair structure. This practice cannot be emphasized enough. There are many examples of well-made rock steps that are rarely used because nothing deters hikers from going around them.

Rock stairs

Rock stairs are far more desirable than wood stairs because they last longer and can be built to appear more natural and less intrusive. Over time they will begin to look like part of the trail, especially if they are placed artfully. Even where suitable rock is not readily available, rock stairs are so superior to wooden stairs that the additional effort to obtain rock is well worthwhile. Any shape of rock can be used; however, large, flat-surfaced rocks are much easier to work with and make a more usable tread. Rocks should weigh at least 100 to 200 pounds, as smaller rocks are more likely to become loose. However, excessively large rocks can result in a trail that feels overbuilt, with structures that don't fit into its character.

Start by laying out the stairs, determining the ideal rise and run of the steps to be installed to reach the desired location.

Always build a staircase from the bottom up, and situate the foot of the staircase at the very bottom of a steep trail section as opposed to midslope, where the foundation rock could become exposed and undermined. The base step helps determine the best location for each subsequent step, so it should be large and set deep, its top flush with the treadway. Over time, hiker traffic will wear away and compact the soil below the bottom step. If the step is not set deep enough, water will eventually erode the surrounding soil and jeopardize the stability of the staircase. Each subsequent step should be set either resting on the back edge of or sitting behind the step below, depending on the slope. Rock crush, small angular stones made from crushed larger rocks, should be packed and filled around each set rock to aid in stability and setting.

THE RIGHT TOOLS: ROCK STEPS

- 18-pound rock bar
- single-jack and double-jack hammers
- pick mattock
- shovel
- root ax
- dirt bag

INSTALLING ROCK STAIRS

There are a few methods of building rock stairs and their variations. These methods often reflect the site conditions, the region, and an organization's preferences.

The cone method

Locate a rock with a flat stepping surface that is wide enough to fill the treadway. Use the side that has the flattest surface for the step. Dig a cone-shaped hole—narrow at the bottom, wider at the top—so that the bottom edges of the rock will contact the *sides* of the hole, like a scoop of ice cream in a cone (see figure 8.17). If

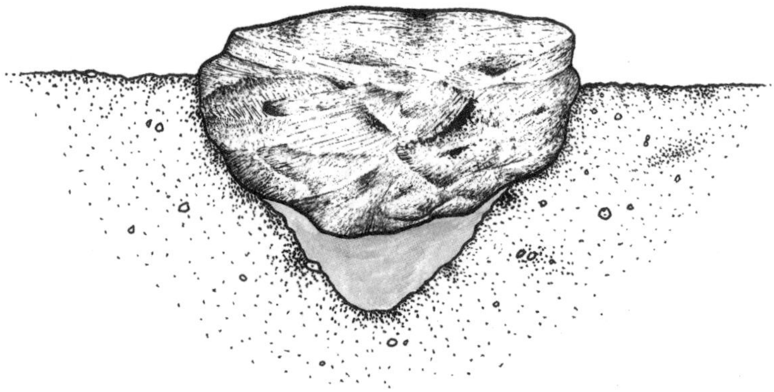

Figure 8.17. The cone method is one way to set a rock as a step stone or as part of a staircase.

the hole has straight sides, the rock will fall to the bottom when placed into it. The hole needs to be deep enough for the top of the rock to be at the desired height. The rock should fit in the hole so its perimeter rests firmly on the sloping sides of the hole or it will move back and forth. Remove all roots and medium or small stones from the hole.

Once the hole is dug, maneuver the rock so it can be lowered, flipped, or slid into the hole. Try to get placement right the first time: once a large rock is dropped into place, it may be very difficult to reset it, especially if the trail is muddy or if the soil is loose or sandy. Three solid and widely spaced points of contact are ideal and will keep the step from rocking. Use brains, ingenuity, pick mattocks, and rock bars to position the rock. Rock steps should not shift at any point, not even slightly. Jump on the step; if it moves at all, try repositioning it. To keep the step in place, tightly pack or tamp good mineral soil or rock crush around it. Do not shim above the ground with rocks; seasonal freezing and thawing can work them loose. "To shim is a shame" is a slogan to remind oneself regarding this practice. Occasionally, a rock can be stabilized by pinning it with a larger adjacent building rock, although both must be solid and unmoving when finished. Sometimes you need to remove a stubborn rock after you've placed it so you can improve the hole or find a better rock to fit in that location. Proper rock stair placement requires skill, experience, hard work, and tremendous patience.

Crush-and-fill method

Another method for building rock stairs involves creating gravel, or crushed rock bed, to set the steps in; this is called gravel setting or crush-and-fill setting. This method is very helpful in places that lack soil or areas that have minimal mineral soil available, or in situations where it is necessary for the steps to gain elevation above the existing mineral soil. The first rock step must be solidly installed and have absolutely no movement or shifting. Behind the first step, lay a bed of gravel or mineral soil, into which you'll set your next rock. This second step may be set behind the first one or rest on its back edge, depending on the rock size and shape. As the steps are installed, add scree or gargoyles on the sides to hold in the gravel. Gargoyles are large rocks set beside the step rocks, which help to define the tread and also support the structure. Solid contact between the step rocks and the gargoyles ensures that crushed rock and soil packed behind the structure will not wash out over time. Rock crush can be used behind the steps and gargoyles to set them in place, but shim rocks should never be used for the front of the structure, as they are prone to fall out.

Dry setting method

Although more difficult than setting steps in soil or crushed rock, secure and attractive footing can be built to help hikers gain a short ledge. However, in ledge areas there is often little or no soil to set the rocks into. This leaves the builder with just two choices: setting the stairs on the exposed bedrock or creating a bed of gravel. Setting rock on top of rock (dry setting) is the most challenging type of stair placement and requires much precision. Hand tools can be used to shape the rock so that it comes into good contact with bedrock and other structure rocks.

For aesthetic reasons, and in some cases to allow for better drainage, it is best not to build perfectly straight staircases. To avoid a manufactured feel, incorporate asymmetry and employ twists and bends (see figure 8.18). Offset some steps rather than keeping them in a direct line, but make sure that the placement doesn't impede a hiker's stride. Understand that each staircase is a lesson in creative problem solving. Rocks and soil types differ from area to area, and each site has its own peculiarities and difficulties.

As with the entire trail, staircases require drainage. Without it, even the largest, most stable steps will eventually work loose as the soil around them erodes. Ice and frost will heave the steps in winter as well. Always build drainage, preferably rock water bars, above a series of steps. Plan for and install rock water bars in the middle of long staircases, taking advantage of turns where possible.

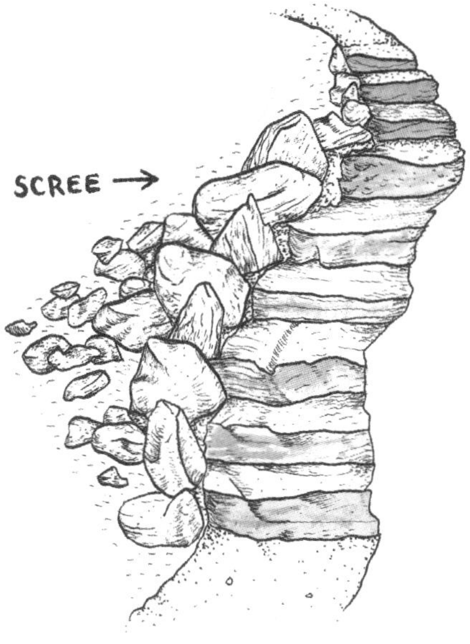

Figure 8.18. A little artistic license can add character to a rock staircase.

8

ROCK STAIRCASE LAYOUT

Supplies

Tape Measure, Line Level, Line (parachute cord or smaller), 2 or 3 people

Step 1: Measure the rise and run.

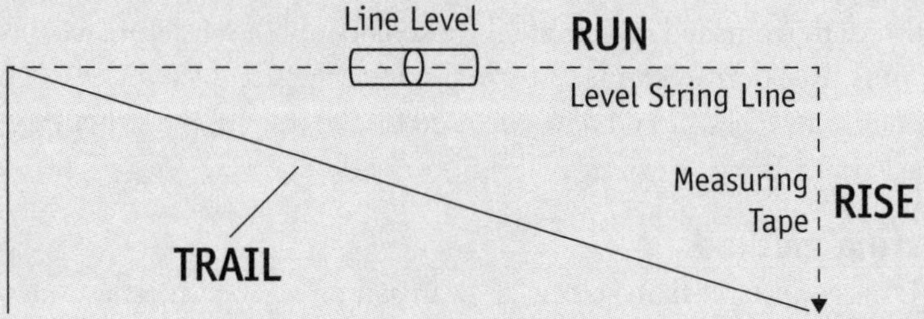

1. With one person at the top of the slope and one at the bottom, run a string line with a level across the top of the project. Be sure to have the top end at grade and the bottom end directly above the proposed site of the base step. Now, make sure the string line is level, with the line level in the middle of the string line. You may need an additional person to look at the level.
2. Now measure the height from the ground (at middle of base step). This is your RISE.
3. Then measure the length of string being used. This is your RUN. Now you have the amount of elevation (rise) you need to gain, as well as the length (run) you have to gain it in.

8

Step 2: Use the measured rise and run of the slope to calculate the rise and run needed for each stair.

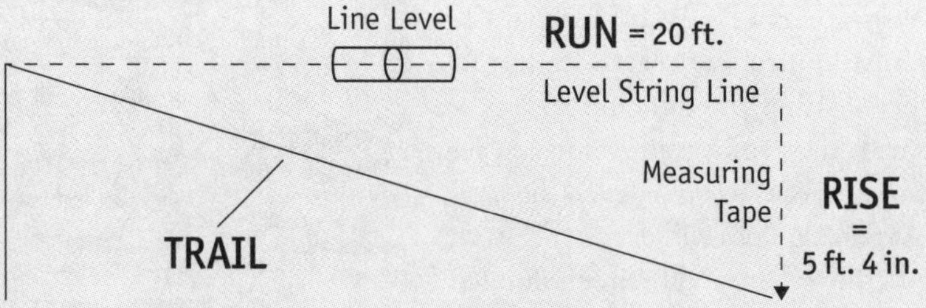

So, in this example, you have 5 feet, 4 inches (64 inches) to gain over 20 feet (240 inches).

The optimal rise of each stair would be between 8 and 10 inches. Using 8 inches as a starting point, then 5 feet, 4 inches (64 inches) broken up into increments of 8 inches would be 8 steps (64/8=8), a nice round number.

If these 8 steps are spread out evenly over the entire 20-foot run, each step would have a 2½-foot run (20/8=2.5).

Step 3: Use this guideline, with 8 inches of rise and 2½ feet of run for each stair as an example, to construct your staircase.

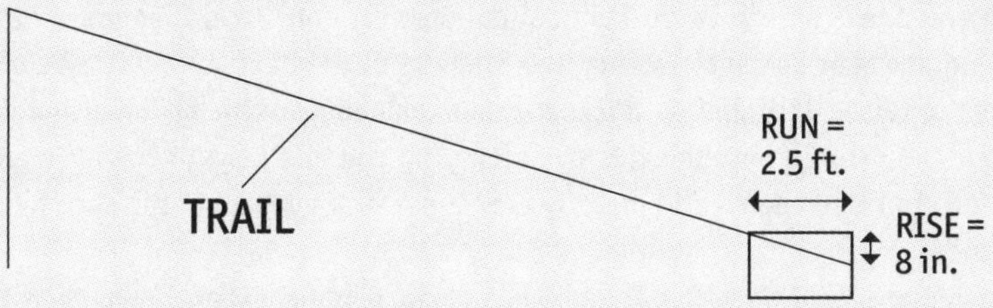

Start with a string line as a guide. Given that equal rise should occur throughout the entire staircase, the outer edge of each rock stair should form an even and consistent slope over the entire staircase.

Setting up the string line involves one line and two people (or one person with anchoring creativity).

1. After placing the first rock for your base step, hold or anchor the bottom end of the string line to the middle of the base step.
2. Stretch the line 8 inches above grade and anchor the opposite end to the top of your slope.
3. Be sure to hold this line taut to get the most exact reading.
4. The outer edge of each stair should touch the string line. This may be difficult to see in the midst of construction, since leaving the string line in place is often not practical. But it's a relatively easy device to set up, so you can check your work as you proceed with the construction. Once again, another pair of eyes can be helpful.

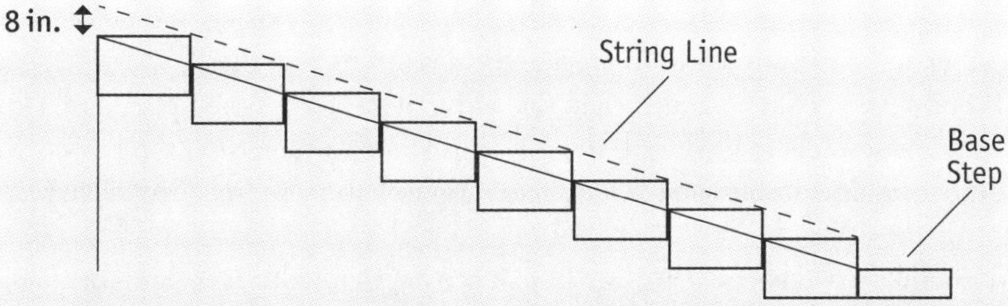

8

This technique is particularly helpful when you have a predetermined amount of rise to gain, such as in a very severely eroded/gullied section of trail. By using the string line and gaining height consistently, you can avoid tunneling into the ground (not getting enough rise), a pier-style staircase (getting too much rise too soon), or inconsistent rise (which is uncomfortable and can be tough on the knees).

A string line is a useful guide to help builders stay on track. If your stair ends up being above or below the string line, the rise of the next stair will have to be lowered or raised accordingly. If this happens, the angle of the string line will be changed. You can get around this by setting up the line next to the other constructed stairs, as opposed to directly over them, and eyeballing the stair height from there.

Yes, you are building with native rock, and no, it is not exact. However, with a little bit of planning, not only can certain disasters be avoided (that is, tearing out work), but the finished product can be functional, professional, and generally good trail work.

WOOD CHECK STEPS

Wood or log check steps are often simpler to construct, but they have a fatal flaw—wood always rots eventually. Log check steps only provide a short-term fix, and their use is discouraged. They act as check dams and retain soil but may encourage continued erosion.

For frontcountry applications, pressure-treated dimensional lumber can be used. Use of pressure-treated wood greatly lengthens the life span of the structure but may diminish the trail aesthetic.

The construction of wood steps is similar to building wood water bars, except that steps are installed perpendicular to the trail, not on an angle. Also, backfill is moved to the uphill side of the logs rather than to the downhill side.

As with wood water bars, spruce, hemlock, and other rot-resistant and resilient woods are the preferred choices. Peel the bark off the logs to increase their longevity.

Log diameters should be between 6 and 12 inches. On steeper slopes a larger diameter log gives more vertical rise. With small-diameter stock, steps must be closer together and more numerous to provide the desired vertical rise.

Wood steps should be longer than the width of the trail. When placed in a gullied-out or severely eroded trail, the log ends should extend into the banks. Too short a step allows water and people to go around and will not adequately retain the soil.

To build a wood check step, dig a trench at a depth roughly one-third the diameter of the log. Save the excavated mineral soil for backfill, and then set the log into the trench and secure it with pin rocks (see figure 8.19).

Once the log step is secure, backfill the uphill side with the excavated soil. When steps are placed in a series, the bottom of the upper log should be just a bit higher

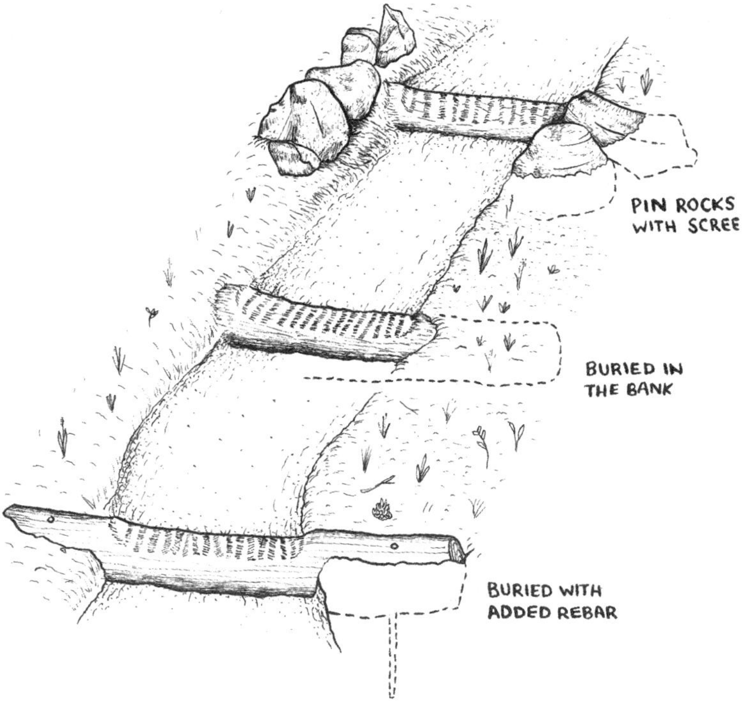

Figure 8.19. Wood check steps can be pinned in various ways. Make sure the logs are wider than the treadway.

than the top of the lower log, with the soil in between sloped slightly downhill (see figure 8.20). This will prevent water pooling behind the steps. Finally, flatten the top of the log slightly with an ax or chain saw to make a firm, flat tread.

A much more stable design for wood stairs involves tying all the steps together with runners. These can be either dimensional or native timber and can be connected using many different types of joining techniques. There can be several variations to this design, but essentially all the wooden steps become platforms of well-drained soil, boxed in on all sides to prevent erosion.

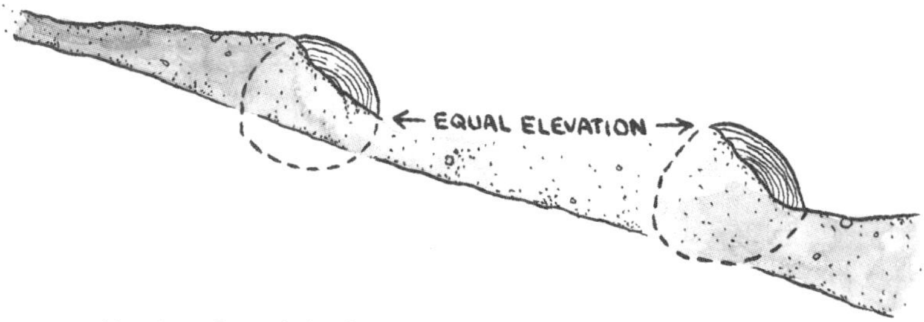

Figure 8.20. Side view of wood check steps.

CRIB STAIRS

Crib stairs are boxes constructed of large rocks or wood, filled with smaller rocks and capped with mineral soil. This type of stair construction works well where livestock are present, and it integrates smoothly with regular rock stairs in areas that are less steep but need further stabilization.

Before building a rock crib staircase, determine the amount of rise and run you need in the given space. Then choose large, heavy rocks to sink into the ground to support the cribs. Dig a hole and set the first front rock step. If there is any possibility of the soil around the sunken rock eroding and undermining the stairs, sink the first rock flush with the ground, as you would for a traditional rock staircase.

Next, set rocks to serve as sides of the first step, ensuring good, high contact points with the front rock. Once these are set, proceed with setting the front rock of the second step. Make sure that more than half of this rock is buried, with the bottom at least one-quarter of its height below the top of the first step; you don't want to have to ramp the soil tread of the first step to adjust for a second step that is too high. If the soil in the first step is properly retained, there is no way the second step can be undermined.

Now fill the area behind the stair with small rocks, decreasing the size of the stones until you end with crushed gravel. Top it off with several inches of well-drained mineral soil. Continue with additional steps until you reach the top of the planned run.

Wood check steps can be made in a similar manner. For more information about working with wood, refer to the Stone Hardeners section and the description on turnpikes on page 150.

SPECIAL TECHNIQUES

Where traditional reconstruction methods fail or are not feasible, such as in very steep locations or on bare ledges, more complex structures, such as log ladders, metal rungs, or pinned steps, may be necessary.

Log Ladder

Log ladders (see figure 8.21) allow hikers to safely and responsibly ascend or descend a difficult ledge. Without a log ladder, hikers risk injury by climbing the ledge itself, or they may damage adjacent soils and vegetation by bypassing the ledge. There are many variations of log ladders to suit the steepness and characteristics of any ledge. A basic design is described below, but the main components of a ladder are two long uprights, known as *stringers*, and steps, known as *rungs* (log rungs are fastened in between the two stringers).

Figure 8.21. Log ladders can be good options in steep terrain with rock slabs.

First, measure the ledge to determine the length of the two stringers. Make sure the stringers are a few feet taller than the ledge so hikers have something to grasp when standing on the top rung. Cut, limb, and peel a matching pair of stringers from straight, sound trees 8 to 12 inches in diameter. Place stringers with the larger butt ends down, leaving 18 to 24 inches between them. If there isn't a good, solid foundation for the butt ends, use a base log to support the stringers. The base log should have a diameter equal to or larger than the diameter of the butts of the stringers, and it should be at least a couple of feet longer than the distance between the outer edges of the stringers. Base logs may be cut longer to fit securely into particular features at the base of the ladder. Set the base log into a trench dug in the earth, or fit it into gaps or cracks in the ledge. Cut shallow notches on top of the base log into which the bottoms of the stringers can be set. Spike the stringers into place. Shave the top of the base log if it doubles as the first step.

Lay out the placement of the notches for the rungs along the inside of the stringers so that spacing from the top of one to the next is the same (12 to 16 inches). The notches should be 4-inch-deep and 4-inch-wide dadoes, or three-side notches, with the top and bottom sides flat, level, and parallel to each other. Be sure the notches on the left are level with those on the right. Saw the top and bottom sides first, and then saw a few relief cuts in between and chisel out the remaining wood. When a pair of notches is complete, cut a rung and shape it to fit.

Cut rungs from 6- to 8-inch-diameter logs and flatten them to provide a stepping surface. Remove no more than one-quarter to one-third of the log. Measure the distance between the insides of the pair of notches and cut the rung to that length. Cut the bottom and top rung ends to form a tongue 4 inches wide and a little more than 4 inches long to fit into the notches. Fine-tune as needed to achieve a good, snug fit. Position the rung in the notches and drive a spike through the outside edge of the stringers and into the ends of the rung. It is best to predrill with a carpenter's brace to ensure the spikes will not bend upon installation. Construct the ladder one rung at a time, starting at the bottom.

THE RIGHT TOOLS: LOG LADDERS

- ax
- crosscut saw, bow saw, or chain saw
- large chisel and mallet
- hatchet (for shaping the log)
- tape measure, small level, lumber crayon
- mattock and shovel
- sledgehammer (for driving spikes)
- 10 12-inch-long, 3/8-inch-diameter spikes

CRIB LADDER

Another stabilizer to consider is the crib ladder (see figure 8.22), which consists of a combination of cribbing and stepping. This structure is useful on very steep slopes or those with thin soil that make it difficult to secure regular steps. To construct a crib ladder, begin by building a log ladder, and then lay it into or up against the slope. Backfill each rung with soil and small rocks to help secure the ladder and the slope. Do not leave gaps behind the rungs, as hikers might inadvertently step into them.

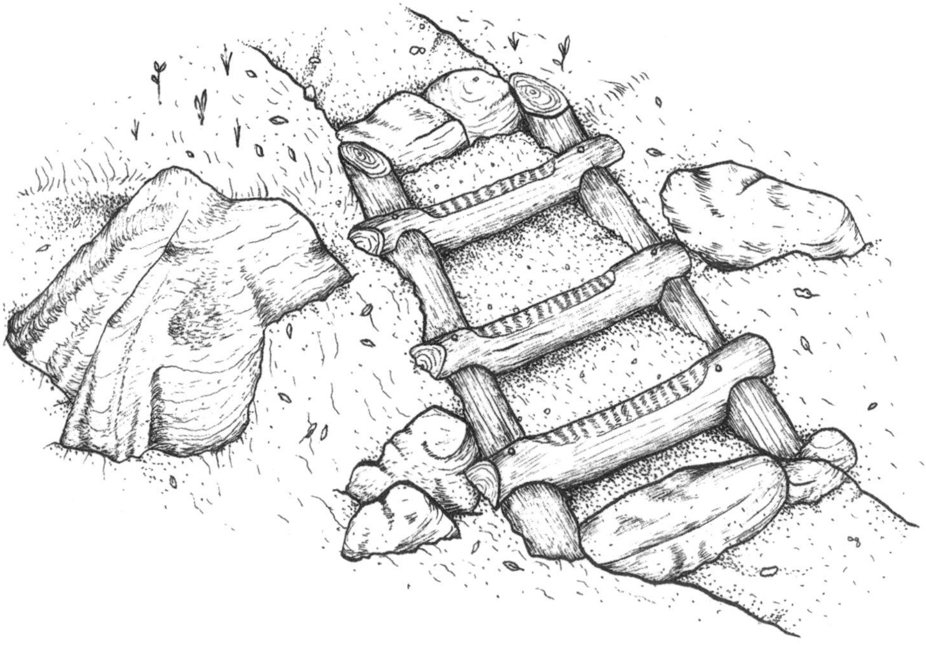

Figure 8.22. A crib ladder is an option for shorter sections of awkward terrain.

PINNED STAIRS

Land managers and trail clubs in the Northeast sometimes use wooden pinned steps (see figure 8.23) to climb and traverse difficult ledges that do not provide adequate footholds and handholds and cannot be avoided through trail relocation. Pressure-treated wooden steps 2 feet long are produced by cutting 6-by-8-inch stock diagonally across the long axis from end to end. They are attached to the ledge with foot-long steel rebar set partially into the rock, using a pneumatic rock drill. A drill can also be used to cut steps into a ledge. Most managers agree that pinned stairs should be used only as a last resort to more conventional work or relocation, due to expense and difficulty as well as aesthetics.

It may also be necessary to use pins when building rock stairs on a ledge. Once again, this is not only difficult but also changes the character of the area itself by introducing a permanent, non-native piece of metal into the ledge. The decision to pin should be taken seriously, as it is a complicated and labor-intensive process. Also, the resulting stairs will be a permanent feature of the trail, one that some people may feel does not fit with a backcountry aesthetic. However, when there are no other options, pinned stairs can create tread where it may seem impossible otherwise.

Proceed cautiously and slowly; mistakes are irreversible and will create a permanent mark on the ledge. Although further training and preparatory practice for this work are necessary, the main steps are as follows.

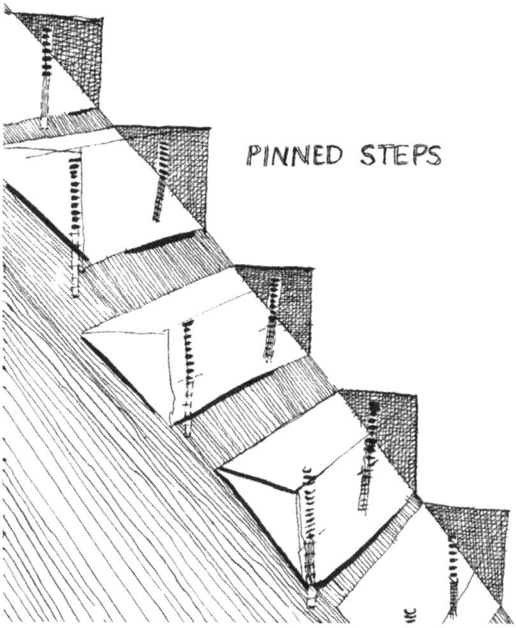

Figure 8.23. Pinned steps are an option to create good footing on slab.

8

Make sure the ledge is clear of organic debris. Place the rock you want to pin exactly where it is to sit. The rock must be of good quality, and its placement must be firm, with two solid contact points below where you will drill the holes. (Pinning does not stabilize the rock; it only keeps it from sliding along the ledge.) Next mark the drilling spots on the bottom of the rock. Then drill holes into the ledge at the desired locations, using necessary precautions and a trained drill operator. Be sure the drill bit is perpendicular to the ledge rock to ensure that the two drilled holes will line up with the marks on the underside of the step rock. Before drilling the step rock, place the pins in the cleaned ledge holes and line them up with the markings on the step rock, a difficult but necessary procedure. After drilling the step holes, thread the steel pins through and seal with either epoxy or tamped lead wool. Your rock has now become a semipermanent feature on the ledge.

STEEL RUNGS AND LADDERS

Steel rungs and ladders are also pinned into the ledge, so the same care should be taken as when building pinned stairs (see figure 8.24). Be sure to get proper training and practice before attempting to construct steel rungs and ladders. As with pinned steps, holes are drilled in the ledge, but in this case, two holes are drilled in such a way as to receive a ½- to ¾-inch staple-shaped metal rung (often galvanized steel, sometimes rebar). Each set of holes must be drilled at the same slight uphill angle to ensure the rungs will fit properly. Drilling the holes slightly wider than the distance between the rung's prongs will ensure a tight fit. Steel rungs are made solid when they are hammered into the holes. About 3 to 4 inches of the rungs should protrude from the ledge to serve as handholds and footholds. This can vary slightly to match the steepness of the terrain, but more protrusion than this can leave a dangerous gap where hikers' toes and children's feet may become stuck. After pounding in the rungs securely, seal the holes with either epoxy or tamped lead wool. Fabricated steel ladders are installed in much the same way.

Figure 8.24. If native trees or lumber are out of the question, steel rungs provide a good option.

CHECK DAMS

Check dams can be effective soil-retaining structures for trails that are severely gullied. A series of check dams can be built to slow down erosion.

Check dams are constructed similarly to water bars, but they are perpendicular to the trail instead of at an angle. Water bars channel water off the trail, and check dams drain water in sheets across the ground surface while retaining soil. These structures are used as stopgap measures; they are not intended to last but to help the gully fill in and hold soil. Therefore, wood is an acceptable material to use.

ROCK AND LOG CRIBBING

Rock and log cribbing, sometimes called retaining walls, are structures that can be used to support a treadway along gullied sections of trail or on steep side slopes (see figure 8.25). They are helpful in work zones that need to be built up to a usable height. Retaining walls are also often necessary when building switchbacks.

Steps and water bars can also help retain soils, but in especially deep and wide gullies that are difficult to drain, erosion may still occur. In this case, it may be better to support the trail with cribbing, which allows for regular drainage. On steep sidehill cuts, cribbing stabilizes the upper or lower slopes along the trail.

Figure 8.25. Build up low areas to keep trail grades consistent. Add deadmen throughout to anchor the structure underneath the tread.

Rock cribbing, the most aesthetically pleasing and durable option, is used to retain the trail or slope or even to create the tread of the trail itself. On steep sidehill locations, the low side of a treadway may need to be built up with a rock retaining wall. Although there are many different kinds of rock retaining walls, they can be split into two broad categories: traditional laid rock retaining walls and rubble retaining walls.

Traditional laid rock retaining walls are perhaps the most difficult rock structures that can be built on a trail. They require intense effort and patience, strong wall-building skills, and many rocks of relatively uniform size and shape. Receiving training before attempting to build one is vital.

This kind of rock wall is built in tiers. The first tier serves as the base of the wall and is laid with an inward lean, with the rocks sunk at least halfway below the grade of the ground. The inslope of the base rocks (face rocks) guides the batter, or overall uphill lean of the rock wall. The greater the batter, the stronger the wall. Each subsequent layer exerts a strong downward force on the layer beneath. Before you begin to build, determine how much batter is needed so you know how far out to lay the first tier. Behind these large face rocks, which are laid first, is the core rock, which provides much of the strength of the wall. It consists of smaller rocks of varying sizes, also laid in tiers, fitting tightly, with all the gaps filled with even smaller rocks. The core rock extends back into the soil. In this fashion the wall is built tier by tier: first the face rocks, slightly insloped, moving into the slope with each tier, backed by a layer of core rock. All of these rocks are set and fitted firmly into place so they have optimal, solid contact and do not create any lever points.

As the tiers progress, it is also very important that the side contact points between the rocks, known as the joints, do *not* line up. Doing this properly is referred to as "breaking the joints" and gives the wall overall stability. Anywhere that joints line up creates a potential instability in the wall. Another factor of stability involves the orientation of the face rocks that form the wall's façade. It is good practice to frequently place headers. These are long rocks with its longest axis perpendicular into the wall so that it extends deep into the structure, tying the face and core rocks together. In addition, place spreaders: rocks that are set horizontally, which cover more area and therefore are more efficient but are not as strong overall. Use a healthy mix of headers and spreaders as face rocks throughout the wall.

The final tier is composed of rocks called cap rocks, which are ideally larger than the face rocks immediately below. Cap rocks require their own mass for stability so it is imperative that they are of significant weight and permanence (see figure 8.26).

To finish the wall, top it with well-crowned or outsloped mineral soil. Separate this soil from the core rock with filter fabric, where possible, to keep the soil from filtering into the wall itself.

Of course, this type of wall is most easily built with uniform rock, although variations can be built with almost any type of rock. This structure is most suitable for larger projects where the trail surface is no longer existent and a bench simply can't be built due to lack of soil.

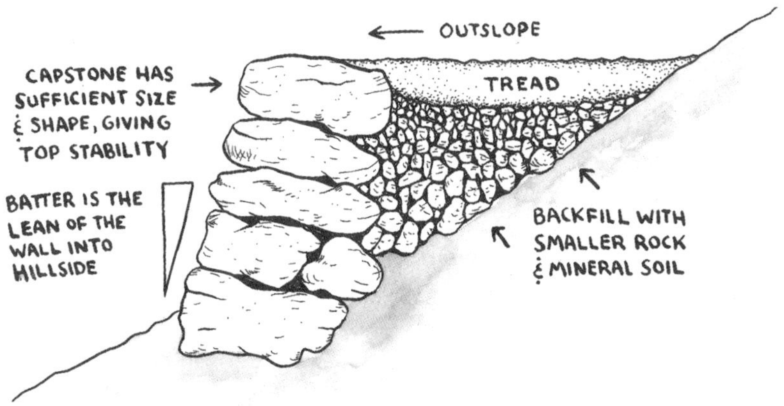

Figure 8.26. Rock retaining walls function similarly to wood but with a different aesthetic. Remember to account for batter when building retaining walls.

One variation is called a rubble wall (see figure 8.27). It is best used for unstable banks where there is still enough soil present for the tread. A rubble wall primarily consists of large rocks set into the bank; make sure they are stable and touching each other to retain the slope. These walls can be either a looser retaining wall without core rock or simply rocks set into the bank. Many variations between a rubble wall and a more labor-intensive rock wall can work in different locations and can stabilize the bank well enough. However, areas with severe erosion or heavier traffic may require more aggressive retainment.

Figure 8.27. Rubble walls can be composed of set stones or loose piles, depending on site and material size.

8

Log cribbing, sometimes referred to as a log or wood retaining wall, has the same applications and follows some of the same building principles as rock retaining walls. The logs should be at least 10 inches in diameter and peeled. Length depends on the project, but generally long, heavy logs are best. The weight helps hold the cribbing in place. The logs should be very secure because they must support large amounts of soil and rock along with the weight of passing hikers. Logs can be secured by large stakes or rocks or butted up against rocks or trees. On multitiered walls, logs are notched together using various wood-joining methods. Breaking the joints, using headers, and knowing the batter of the wall are as important with log walls as with rock walls. Logs set perpendicular to the trail, like a wood step, and notched and spiked into the crib logs can be used as combination steps, spacers, and retainers, as well as acting as headers.

Fill any gaps in the cribbing and build a treadway above it with excavated rock and soil. The treadway should remain gently sloped to the outside or downhill side to ensure drainage. No cribbing should inhibit this drainage. If the treadway is flat or sloped toward the inside or uphill side, water will puddle on or flow along it.

→ HARDENERS

Hikers on trails in flat, low-lying, wet terrain frequently cause destruction of bordering vegetation and soils. When water accumulates on the treadway, many hikers tend to walk to the side of the tread to keep their feet clean and dry. Wet, slippery, muddy areas develop very quickly. This causes a growing problem of soil breakdown and trail widening. Numerous techniques can harden the treadway and keep hikers on the trail, stabilizing soils and allowing trailside vegetation to recover.

Stepping-stones, bog bridges, or built-up treadways are most frequently used in these situations. All are labor-intensive, and their construction affects the environment. Before choosing any of these solutions, first consider drainage and relocation options.

When wet, muddy areas develop on trails it is generally because the treadway is lower than surrounding terrain or the soils are not durable to compaction. Water draining laterally through trail soils becomes trapped on the lower and compacted surfaces of the treadway. Often, what initially appears to be a low, flat section of trail may actually have a very moderate slope, allowing an imperceptible flow of water. Rather than installing a bridge or stepping-stones, a better long-term solution may be to drain the wet area in question—especially if it is small and has a low end that, once ditched, would permit water to flow off the trail. Drain small, flowing, wet areas such as this with water bars and drainage ditches. While installing drainages may not completely dry up the trail, it can reduce the amount of hardening needed.

If an area cannot be drained (or if it should not be drained for environmental reasons) and if relocation is not feasible, then use trail-hardening techniques. These techniques offer dry passage for hikers and funnel traffic onto a hardened surface, allowing adjacent soils and vegetation to reestablish themselves.

STONE HARDENERS

Stepping-stones

Rocks can be set into the mud of wet areas to form a stable, dry, and easily traversed treadway. They can also be used to cross slow-moving streams. Stepping-stones (see figure 8.28) should have a flat surface at least 12 inches across and should be thick enough to sit above the mud. Larger and flatter rocks are easier to set and are less prone to unwanted movement than smaller, rounded ones. Larger stones are also safer and more attractive for hikers. Present the flattest surface for walking by setting the stones in cone-shaped holes, similar to setting rocks for a staircase. Space them in a line along the trail so a hiker with a heavy pack can easily stride from one to the next. Stepping-stones should be stable and must not protrude too high above the ground or be so low as to be inundated with mud and water; otherwise, hikers are likely to avoid them. Even when constructed in a seemingly inviting manner, they are the most circumvented trail structure. For this reason, even though stones last much longer than wood, bog bridges can sometimes be the more effective option when choosing between the two.

Figure 8.28. Use big rocks with good stepping surfaces, similar to rock steps.

Rock treadway (Armoring)

Rock treadway, or "armoring," is simply a more intensive use of rock than stepping-stones. Set stepping-stone-sized rocks side by side, covering the entire treadway, creating a rock-paved section of trail. Fill gaps between rocks with crushed stone to create a continuous walking surface. Be sure to use large rocks to ensure stability, and keep this section level with adjacent rocks. Water from uphill can percolate through the rock treadway and to the other side without inundating it.

Turnpikes

Where an ample supply of good mineral soil is available, fill rock or log boxes with small rocks and then cap them with soil—much like when making crib steps—to create a turnpike (see figure 8.29). When constructing a rock box, be sure the rocks are stable and adequately dug into the ground, with high contact points between them to prevent soil from spilling out. When building a log box using native logs, be sure they are large enough to provide enough height above the ground once they are set into it. Different joining techniques can be used to connect the logs; one of the easiest is a lap joint, which is then spiked into place. Rebar is an alternative to pin the logs to the ground, although holes must be drilled in the logs before they are placed.

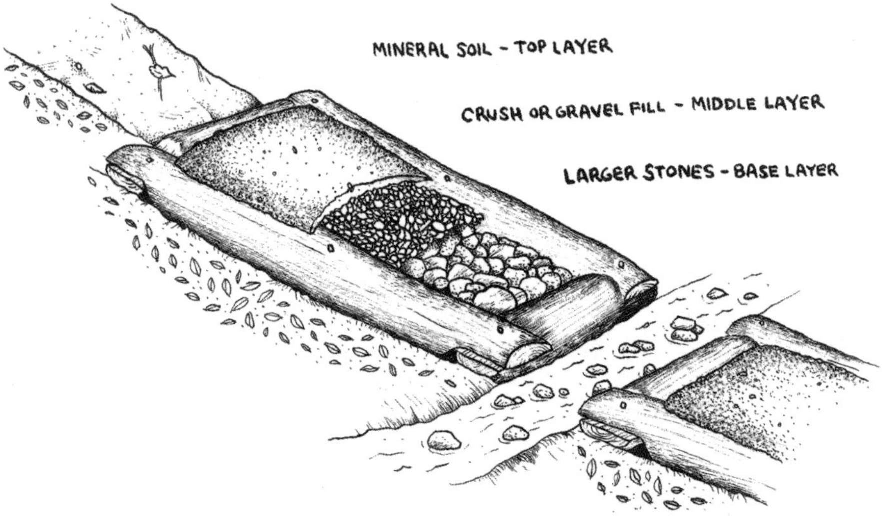

8

Figure 8.29. Turnpikes can be boxed in with wood or rock or—depending on the site—left open on their sides. Fill mostly with rock for better drainage and to reduce soil compaction.

To begin, dig ditches along the perimeter of the wet stretch of treadway. Bury rocks or logs to a depth of at least half their height to ensure stability. When rocks or logs have been secured, fill the interior of the box with rocks of decreasing size, starting with larger, softball-sized rocks at the bottom and working up to gravel. Top this with well-drained mineral soil, crowned in the middle to allow for water run-off to the sides. Turnpikes provide a nice walking surface and last for a long time, even well after the wood box has decomposed, although the construction process is very time-consuming. Long stretches of turnpike can be broken in smaller 10- to 20-foot sections with a cross drain between. In very wet areas it is also wise to dig drainage ditches on one or both sides of the turnpike. Where there is significant muck, geotextile, a durable construction and landscaping fabric, can be laid before application of rocks and mineral fill. This keeps the mucky soils from infiltrating the rock and mineral fill of the turnpike while allowing water percolation.

Bog bridges

In areas where mud is soft and deep, which is often the case in boggy locations, bog bridges, constructed of either milled lumber or native timber, can elevate the tread surface.

These bridges can also be used to ford small streams and drainages. In all cases, they provide a dry, stable treadway. Such bridges usually last 10 to 15 years, although they can last even longer, depending on the species of tree used, the log diameter, the quality of the wood, and bridge's location. Softwoods, such as cedar, hemlock, and spruce, are the easiest to work with and the longest lasting.

A bog bridge is generally made up of two 8- to 12-foot-long flat-topped logs (stringers), which form the walking surface. The stringers are supported near their ends on two base logs securely set into the surface of the mud. The stringers are fitted into notches in the base logs and spiked into place (see figure 8.30).

Native bog bridges are relatively simple to build, requiring only a few tools. However, dimensional bog bridges, which are made of milled 8- or 10-inch-wide stringers and precut base logs, are even easier and faster to install. Getting the materials to the site may be more difficult, however, so factor time and cost of transport into construction considerations. Often, milled stringers can be used with native base logs, reducing the number of trees that need to be cut on-site.

A sharp ax can be invaluable in the construction of a bog bridge, in addition to a crosscut saw or chain saw for efficiency and saving time. A peeler or bark spud can facilitate peeling, and an adze or ax can be used for topping. For driving spikes, a sledgehammer is best, but the back of a root ax will do. Digging tools, such as a mattock, shovel, and root ax, are used for placing base logs.

Figure 8.30. Bog bridges are a good option for long stretches of wet terrain that are hard to drain.

For a basic bog bridge, set two stringers side by side to provide a treadway of adequate width. Stringers should be 8 to 10 inches wide and 8 to 12 feet long; longer boards tend to be springy and may even break under a hiker's weight. The base logs should be 3 to 4 feet long and 8 to 12 inches in diameter. Where the ground is extremely wet and mud is soft and deep, larger and longer base logs or rocks provide stability and better flotation. If the mud and water are particularly deep, a crib box of logs may be needed to make up the height difference and to keep the surface above water; refer to Chapter 9 (page 186) for more information on bridges.

Before beginning construction of a bog bridge, determine the length of the bridge or bridges needed. Often large rocks, roots, and trees will dictate where bridges can be placed and how long they can be. For a series of bridges, divide the entire length of the series so that each bridge averages between 8 and 12 feet. Plan one bridge at a time. When measuring, start at one edge of the muddy area and work your way across to achieve proper spacing and placement. A tape measure works best, but a length of rope or counting ax handle lengths will also suffice.

After measuring the length of the bridge or bridges, the next step is to find appropriate trees. Don't waste wood by using a tree that is too long or large in diameter for a bridge. Trees should be straight, have few branches, and be relatively free of defects. Be sure to cut logs so each pair of stringers closely matches in size and shape. Take the time to find high-quality wood; it will make construction go more quickly and smoothly and result in a better, longer-lasting bridge. Peel logs to retard rot. Cut to length, limb, and peel logs away from the trail so the debris stays out of sight.

To provide a good, safe walking surface, the stringers should be topped flat, leveled, and even with each other, which is most often done using both a saw and an ax. Remove only one-quarter to one-third of the log's diameter; this provides a wide enough walking surface without compromising the log's strength. It is helpful to use a level and to make a mark on the end of each stringer to guide this cut; a chalk line is easiest, but a rope or string can be used along with a lumber crayon. When cutting, brace the stringers between other logs, rocks, or branches to prevent rolling. First, saw relief cuts at 4- to 6-inch intervals with a crosscut saw or chain saw, and then chip out the sections with an ax or adze. Clean up the chips and scatter them off the trail.

If the wood was cut away from the trail, carry the two base logs and pair of stringers to the trail at this time. Position and set the base logs in place. (*Note*: Building a bog bridge is best done in pairs, one person working on each end of the bridge and both helping each other to move the logs.) To gauge the placement of the base logs, lay out one stringer along the center of the treadway on the surface of the mud. Make sure it is at least 6 inches from solid treadway, a stepping-stone, or another bridge. Position the base logs perpendicular to the stringer and so that the stringer overhangs the base logs on their centers by no more than 6 inches. Too much overhang can break off the end of the stringer or tip up the bridge when it is stepped on.

Move the stringer aside and dig trenches to fit the base logs. The trenches should be as wide and long as the base logs and about as deep as one-half their diameter. The base logs must be level and secure; check this by stomping on both ends. It may be necessary to remove roots and small rocks to properly place the base logs. Make sure that they do not rock from side to side; a slight rocking back and forth in the direction of the stringers will be remedied when the bridge is secured.

The next step is to lay out the two stringers on the base logs. Alternate the thicker butt ends to achieve a uniform bridge width. For greater strength, rotate the stringers so any slight crown or curve faces up, higher in the center than on the ends. Position the pair so they fit close together along their entire length but with a small gap between them for drainage. This gap should be no more than 1 to 2 inches so that a hiker's foot cannot slip between the stringers.

With the stringers in position, mark the placement of the notches in the base logs using the stringers as guides. Draw lines with a log scribe, pencil, lumber crayon, or ax on the top of the base log parallel to and straight down along both sides of the stringers. Move the stringers to the side and chop or saw out 90-degree, V-shaped notches between the lines. Be careful not to make the notches too large at first; they can always be enlarged. Check the fit and fine-tune as needed. The sides of the stringers should fit neatly along the sides of the notches and not rest on the bottom. To get the tops of the stringers at the same level, widen the notch of the higher or larger stringer to set it lower. The stringers should not rock when walked on. There may be some small movements at this point, but they will disappear when the stringers are secured to the base logs with nails.

When constructing a dimensional bog bridge (see figure 8.31), set the base logs as described above. The difference is that the lumbered stringers can sit flush upon the base logs. You may need to slightly flatten the tops of the base logs with an ax to remove irregularities and knots.

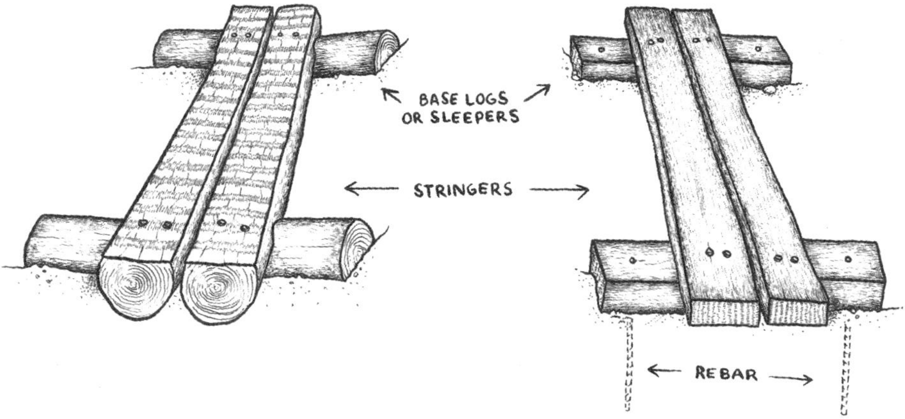

Figure 8.31. A couple of options for building bog bridges.

The final step is to spike the stringers to the base logs (see figure 8.32) using 10- to 12-inch-long, ⅜-inch-diameter spikes. Ten-inch spikes are best for dimensional lumber stringers, but 12-inch spikes are recommended for native material. Drive spikes with a sledgehammer or the back side of a root ax, and strike them squarely. A bent spike is extremely difficult to remove. To reduce chances of bending a spike, predrill with a carpenter's brace, which allows the spike to be driven with relative ease. Slightly angle the drill holes so they pass through the stringers and into the sides of the notches; do so in opposite directions at each end, providing tension to hold the stringers more securely.

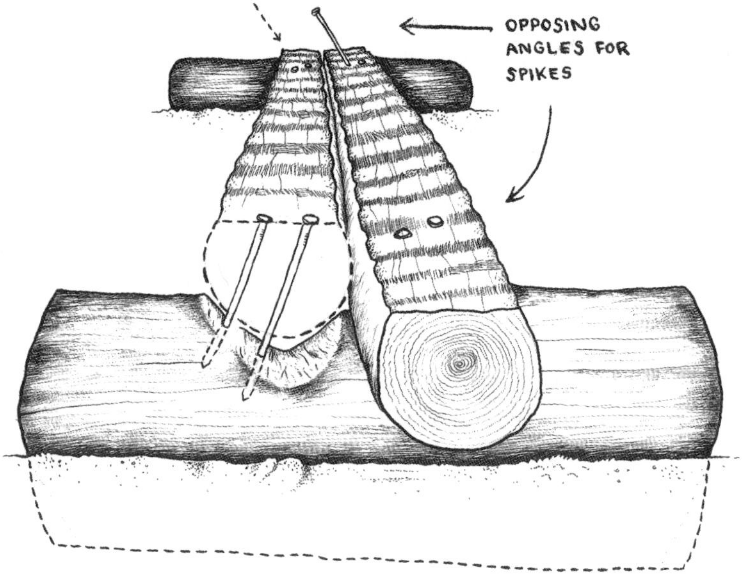

Figure 8.32. Make sure spikes go at least one inch into the base log.

THE RIGHT TOOLS: BOG BRIDGES

- 18-pound rock bar
- pick mattock
- shovel
- root ax
- bark spud
- ax
- chain saw or crosscut saw
- sledgehammer
- 10- or 12-inch spikes, four per stringer for native logs

Bog Bridge Construction Reminders

- For a bog bridge to be effective, make sure that the treadway width is sufficient to make walking on it easy. In the case of particularly thin logs, three stringers in parallel may be used. Along longer stretches of bog bridges, three stringers are used every four or six bridges as a passing area for hikers.
- The treadway should not be tilted or angled to one side, nor should the bridge be unstable, rocking, or very springy. For stringers that are more than 8 to 10 feet long or that are very springy, use three or more base logs for support, with the third equidistant between the two end base logs. It is best to keep bridges short and therefore stable. Shorter bridges are also easier to work with.
- The bridge surface should not be higher than 8 to 10 inches from the ground. It's hard to step up onto or down off a high bridge, and it can be difficult to traverse for those uncomfortable with heights. Dig in the base logs if the unit is too high or if it is unstable.
- At the end of a bridge, hikers should find stable, rocky, or dry soil or a stepping-stone, not mud or slippery roots. When bridges are placed end to end, they should be separated by a space of no more than 6 inches. A stepping-stone can be used at the end of a bog bridge or between adjacent bridges to span a large gap.
- Use caution when building bridges on pond shores or in any areas that are prone to flooding in wet seasons. If water levels rise substantially, bridges will float and drift off the trail. This might happen, for instance, along a pond shore that has beaver activity. In these situations it might be better to relocate the trail than to bridge it. If relocation is not possible, it may be necessary to place large rocks on the bridge's base logs or to pin them down to help prevent rising or floating.

➔ DEFINERS

To save time and effort, hikers will sometimes cut corners at switchbacks, walk on a smooth carpet of alpine vegetation, or go around rock steps. Even a well-marked and -maintained trail may need further defining to curb this tendency. Hikers who stray off a trail in sensitive areas can quickly trample vegetation, compact soils, and hasten trailside erosion. Place definers to make walking off-trail difficult, thus containing traffic to a single, stabilized treadway.

In many ways, a number of previously mentioned structures serve as definers. If people see the best option for foot travel, such as a bog bridge, they will often choose that option as the obviously intended route. However, there are certain structures that serve the sole purpose of defining the trail.

SCREE WALLS

Low, simple rows of small rocks, called scree walls, lining the edges of a trail clearly demarcate boundaries and act as an impediment to straying hikers (see figure 8.33). Scree walls are often needed alongside heavily used trails in open alpine zones. Always line rock steps with scree walls; bypassed edges of steps soon erode and threaten the stability of the steps and the entire slope. Scree also helps block shortcutting at switchbacks and can keep hikers from going around water bars or into drainage ditches.

Use small- to medium-sized rocks that can be carried by one person. Set scree so it can't be kicked or knocked away by someone walking on it. Toppled walls and loose rocks in the trail are hazards, not a help. Securely set scree is particularly important along rock steps because scree also serves to stabilize the soil. Scree walls should only be as large as they need to be because they can greatly infringe on the primitive qualities of the trail environment. Nevertheless, large scree walls may be necessary in locations where hikers regularly stray off the trail. No matter the size, always strive to blend scree walls into the environment.

Figure 8.33. Scree walls protect important natural resources and serve as trail definition.

RUBBLE

To help widened sections of trail outside the scree wall recover from damage, scatter rubble over those sections. Walking on a jumble of small, loose stones is not enjoyable and should keep hikers on the trail. Rubble is also an effective way to close a bootleg trail.

BRUSH

In scrubby and wooded areas, dead brush and logs are useful for narrowing trails, protecting switchbacks, and closing unwanted trails. This brush will eventually rot away, but it will allow time for plants and trees to start growing.

➔ SWITCHBACKS AND CLIMBING TURNS

Even on a very well-laid-out trail, switchbacks or climbing turns must often be constructed to gain elevation. They introduce turns in the trail, allowing it to climb the slope gradually, and serve the dual function of making the hiker's trek easier while protecting steep slopes.

Climbing turns are simply sweeping turns in the trail and can be used effectively on grades of 7 to 10 percent (see figure 8.34). They can still be used with steeper grades, but on the short sections that inevitably run with the fall line, a rock treadway or rock stairs must be installed to stabilize the tread. Therefore, in this case, a switchback is preferable. Like climbing turns, switchbacks allow for a complete change in direction while traversing a slope and gaining elevation; however, they make a much more drastic change in direction than climbing turns and can be used on steeper grades. Basically, a switchback turn creates a well-drained transition zone, or platform, between two climbing ramps, which allows for a complete change in direction. Some form of retaining wall must be installed to support the

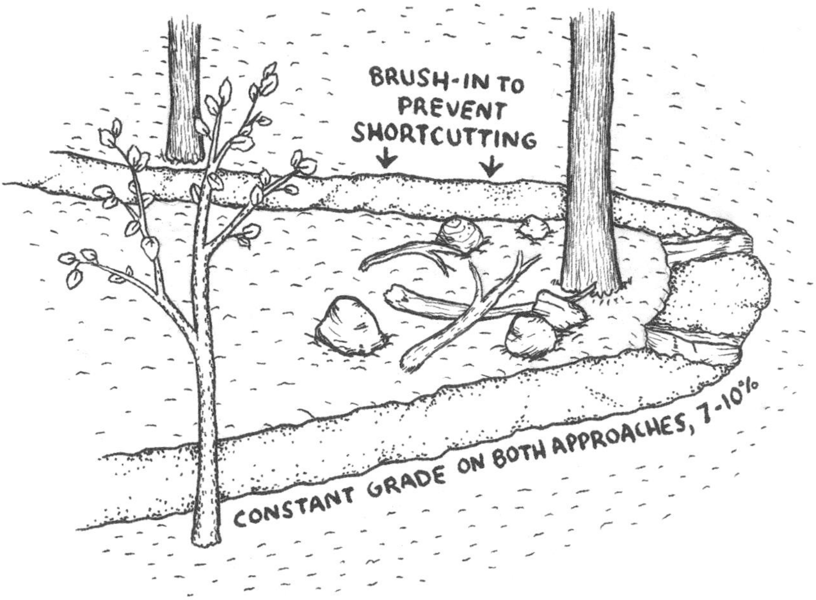

Figure 8.34. Prevent users shortcutting trails by adding brush on the inside corners of turns.

lower edge of this platform and keep it from sloughing off below. The base of the platform above the retaining wall and the uphill ramp above the platform are gently insloped to allow water to collect on the inside of the trail. This feeds the water above the turning platform, which drains off the side before it has a chance to cut down the trail. (Chapter 4, page 34, discusses switchbacks in more depth.)

➔ CLEANUP

After trail work is completed, it is important to make the area look as natural and untouched as possible. The land will repair itself over time, and a thorough cleanup can assist this process. Many heavily worked trails look muddy or raw immediately after construction but will wear in over the course of a year or two. In this respect, rock work has an advantage over wood, since well-constructed rock work fits into the landscape.

Cover raw, worked soil with leaf litter and other organic material. This aids revegetation by mulching the soil, providing native seeds the right conditions for germination. Place brush alongside the trail to close in the clearing and to hold down the leaf litter. Fill in and naturalize quarry holes and borrow pits where excavated rocks and soil were sourced. Ideally, when construction is complete, trail work should be practically invisible to passing hikers.

➔ WHEN TO RELOCATE OR REPAIR A DAMAGED TRAIL

Carefully examine heavily damaged trail sections when deciding whether to reconstruct the old path or to relocate the section entirely. Eroded gullies, difficult ledges, or wide mucky areas on trails can be circumnavigated with a relocated section of trail, or they can be hardened and stabilized. Consider the following in making a decision:

- Will the new section of trail have the same kind of terrain as the damaged section? If so, it is often better to repair the current trail than to build a new trail that will deteriorate in the same fashion. However, if a bypass can cross the same terrain in a less damaging way—for example, if the new trail will cross a slope rather than climb directly up it—then the relocation is worth considering.
- Will the current section of trail be too difficult to close and restore? If the section under consideration is the most obvious route in a given landscape (for example, on a pond shore or on a pronounced ridge), hikers will naturally tend to use the trail even after a relocation is built and the damaged section has been closed. In this case, it is best to stick to the current location. Sometimes a relocation can actually hasten environmental degradation when hikers confuse it with the old location and begin using both interchangeably. This can cause problems on both routes. Unplanned crossover trails can also develop because of hikers' confusion.

Long relocations should be used only when they result in a substantial improvement in the overall environmental conditions. Short relocations around a wet area or eroded section may be appropriate, but the best solution is usually either to close and relocate a long trail section or to reconstruct it. Depending on terrain and management of the area, reconstruction is often the best alternative. Even short relocations may require land manager approval.

➔ TRAIL MAINTENANCE

All trails require regular maintenance. If maintenance is ignored, issues will arise that over time can develop into serious problems. Just as a failure to clean the gutters on a house can lead to expensive water damage, failure to maintain drainages on a trail can lead to severe erosion (see figure 8.35). In both cases, the initial investment (in money and time) has been wasted. Constructing a drainage requires considerable time and effort: rocks must be located, excavated, moved, and installed; trees must be felled, limbed, peeled, bucked, moved, and buried. Cleaning drainages helps ensure a good return on a trail crew's initial investment in building a trail.

Basic maintenance helps keep a trail usable, minimizes deterioration, and prevents damage to the surroundings. The objectives of maintenance are to concentrate impact on the trail corridor and to direct water off the trail. With these goals properly addressed, preventable damage to the resources and the trail can be eliminated.

Figure 8.35. Trail erosion several feet deep because issues weren't dealt with over time.

→ CLEANING DRAINAGES

Clean drainages prevent large-scale soil erosion and the costly reconstruction that could follow, because soil cannot be easily replaced. Clearing blowdowns, brushing, and marking the trail do protect resources, but the main purpose of these maintenance duties is to allow hiker passage and keep a physical trail corridor open. Maintainers can always return to blaze or cut brush, but if they do not clean a trail's drainage in timely fashion, the results could be cumulatively disastrous.

If not familiar with the various aspects of drainage, see page 120 in Chapter 8, which examines drainage and its construction in greater detail. This section describes only the cleaning and maintenance of existing drainage structures.

The physics involved in drainages are simple. Trails, unfortunately, provide the perfect structure for water to travel on its endless journey downhill. Water seeks the path of least resistance, and a trail on a slope in the woods provides less resistance than the slope itself. On a trail there is less duff and fewer roots and rocks to impede water's path, so water will follow a trail unless the terrain or a well-constructed drainage directs it off.

As water travels down a trail it accelerates, and more water joins from the side. Soon a destructive torrent forms, eroding soil from the path. Erosion can be just as devastating over many years of gradual flowing water as it can be during a flash flood. Thorough trail maintenance involves continual cleaning, maintenance, and protection of all drainage structures. In fact, the best time to clean drainages is during or after a rain event to find out exactly where water travels.

Drainages that have not been cleaned regularly will often be difficult to locate. The accumulation of topsoil, rocks, and leaf litter can obscure them from sight. However, these "lost" drainages can be recovered, particularly if they are water bars constructed of rock or earthen drainage dips. Log water bars buried for long periods of time may be rotten and in need of replacement. Search for lost drainages by looking for pin rocks, outflow ditches off the trail, or even the tops of rocks or logs protruding in a telltale diagonal line.

A problem in the East, with its large amount of annual leaf litter and high precipitation, is that drainages become clogged with organic debris. Drainages must receive proper maintenance to be consistently effective. Once a drainage has been located, clean it and restore it to optimal working condition. Do not simply kick the leaves or dirt out of the drainage (a task often recommended to hikers by land managers). Kicking away loose debris works well enough for assessing the state of the drainage, but tools will be needed thereafter.

One effective type of drainage is a wide, flat-bottomed ditch, 12 to 18 inches wide and 6 to 8 inches deep. Adequate width is critical because small twigs and a few leaves will clog a narrow ditch very quickly. The ditch's sides should slope gently up and out; vertical walls can crumble or slough off into the drainage, decrease overall width, and contribute to clogging.

8

Begin cleaning at the uphill edge of the drainage ditch and work down. Typically, this is done with a hazel hoe, fire rake, or pick mattock (see figure 8.36). Scatter all organic matter pulled from the ditch (leaves, roots, and organic soil) well off-trail and downslope, where it won't wash back into the drainage. Use mineral soil pulled from the ditch as backfill on the downhill trail section of a water bar or drainage dip. Continue to move down the ditch, clipping and removing any roots and digging out all rocks. Smooth and pack the sides and bottom of the ditch, and tamp excess mineral soil onto the downhill slope with a shovel or by foot. An ideal drainage has a U-shaped cross section and, when used in conjunction with a rock or wood water bar, rises above and behind this downhill structure to protect it. A properly made drainage is the first defense in diverting water off the trail; the actual water bar serves to reinforce the trail and hold back soil.

Simply clearing the loose debris and breaking up compacted sediment in the drainage is not sufficient; clean the outflow ditch as well. Consider the outflow ditch—which typically extends 4 feet or more off the trail—and the drainage ditch one unit. Therefore, debris, rocks, and roots should be removed from the entire structure. However, the outflow often will be the most clogged section of a drainage and will likely need more work to clear. The outflow ditch permanently removes water from the trail and assures it won't find its way back. This section of the drainage is critical, and it is often much longer than the portion that crosses the trail. Length will vary depending upon trail alignment. A trail moving straight

Figure 8.36. Start at the top and work your way down through the outflow.

down a very gradual or almost imperceptible slope requires an outflow ditch of at least 15 feet because water can easily find its way back onto the trail. A trail that follows a contour on steep slopes needs only a 3- or 4-foot outflow.

Drainage will not be fully effective unless the outflow ditch is wide and clear. The ditch should be constructed straight and allow water to flow far from the treadway to be absorbed by the environment. Widen the outflow ditch gradually as it moves away from the trail so it ends in a flat flare, allowing water to disperse and saturate the ground rather than create an erosive, consolidated stream.

It usually takes several different drainage methods to assure proper water removal on a section of trail. Side ditches, rock crossovers, grade reversals, and other styles of drainage will require cleaning as well. In addition, contour trails need deberming when the tread becomes cupped in the middle and water can't flow off and across the trail because of a berm along the outside edge of the trail. Situations like this may be good opportunities to install a rolling grade dip or an appropriate drainage structure. For further details, see Chapter 8, page 120.

Once the standards described above have been met, move on to the next drainage with confidence, knowing that the one you just finished will effectively protect the treadway and the trail for years to come.

THE RIGHT TOOLS: DRAINAGE

The tools needed to clean a drainage depend on the type of soil and the extent of debris:

- **Use shovels, grub hoes, or fire rakes for final shaping or for drainages that just need light cleaning.**
- **Use a pick mattock or a grub hoe for a drainage that is heavily clogged or in rocky soil.**
- **For fully clogged drainages, use a pair of loppers to cut small, tough roots that have grown in.**
- **For woefully neglected drainages, use a root ax.**
- **Use clippers or loppers to remove adjacent vegetation that is growing or leaning into a drainage.**

➔ CLEARING BLOWDOWNS

Patrolling trails to clear blowdowns—trees or large branches that have fallen onto or across trails—is one of a trail maintainer's first springtime tasks. While blowdowns are more common in winter due to heavy snow, ice, and wind, downed woody debris can be a problem at any time of the year.

Clearing blowdowns:

- Eases passage for hikers;
- Protects resources, because hikers tend to create bootleg trails around uncleared blowdowns;
- Opens trails for early season hiking use; and
- Offers an opportunity to assess the upcoming season's work needs.

AMC's crews complete a report after each patrol, detailing the conditions found on the trail (see Chapter 3, page 25). In addition to axes, patrollers should carry bow saws, crosscut or chain saws, and a hazel hoe, Pulaski, or small mattock to clean water bars and other drainage. For clearing blowdowns, AMC's staff trail crew prefers the ax for its light weight, ready availability, low cost, and ease of maintenance. Also, many maintainers find an ax easier to use because its blade cannot get pinched as a saw's blade can (see figure 8.37). If handled with proper training and practice, an ax can be effective and safe. Some maintainers prefer one of the variety of pruning saws available for clearing. For information on tool training and safety, see Chapter 6, page 53.

Patrollers clearing trails should work in pairs, leapfrogging each other when clearing blowdowns and cleaning drainage. This allows patrollers to cover significant distances in a day—anywhere from 5 to 10 miles, depending on the number of blowdowns encountered, the number of drainages to be cleaned, and the difficulty of the terrain. Pairing up also provides a measure of safety in case of accidents or other issues. Remember to stay far away from your partner's swinging ax or other cutting tool!

Figure 8.37. An ax can be an effective tool in removing blowdowns.

Trees sometimes fall entirely across the trail or their tops break off and hang down onto the trail. Removing these blowdowns is time-consuming and best done with a partner—the tree has to be cut into manageable pieces that can be rolled or carried away. Take a minute to assess the situation to conserve energy and to prevent unnecessary cutting. It might be possible to simply lift or drag the tree off the trail. If the tree or limb is too heavy or complicated to drag and has a small diameter, you can probably make one cut and completely remove the top section of the tree from the trail. If the tree is larger, it may require two cuts—one on each side of the trail (see figure 8.38). Remove the center piece and discard it off the trail. When moving large sections of tree, bend your knees and lift your head to ensure a straight back. Enlist the help of a partner if needed. Move all debris off the trail. Do not place debris in a drainage structure or natural drainage feature.

Leaning or hanging trees are sometimes called "widow makers" because their limbs or tops can snap off without warning and potentially injure or kill anyone underneath. Exercise extreme care when dealing with these trees. Treat them just as seriously as felling a standing tree, and follow the same protocol and safety standards (see Chapter 7, page 99). If a tree is not impeding a passage or in the trail corridor, leave it alone. If it is a leaner or hanger impeding a passage, consider very carefully the danger involved in cutting it. Leaving the tree is always an option. Eventually natural circumstances will bring down the tree or its branches safely in the next windstorm or significant weather event.

Spring poles are another hazard caused by blowdowns. Spring poles are small trees or branches that have been bent into an arch or bow by a blowdown or some heavy object exerting downward pressure. The spring pole, therefore, is under a

8

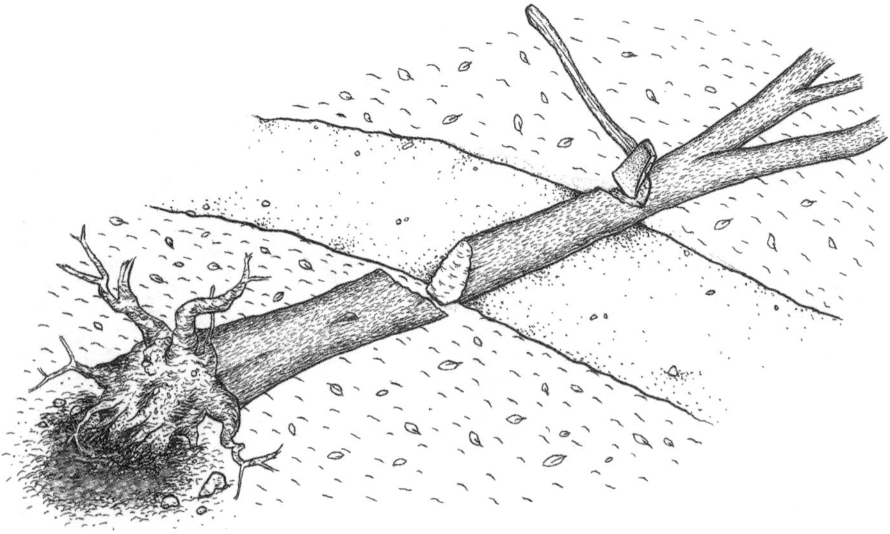

Figure 8.38. Plan chops so that the entire treadway is clear.

great deal of tension and, if handled improperly, can spring back with immense force when released, possibly causing serious injury. One way to relieve stress on a spring pole is to make small cuts on the inside of the bend, allowing the tree or branch to slowly release pressure. Exercise the same caution for tree butts with roots still anchored in the soil; depending on a tree butt's age, there may be considerable forces stored that could cause it to forcibly snap back to a vertical position when cut.

If a very large blowdown crosses the treadway, cutting a notch or steps into the tree to allow passage may be adequate. Some blowdowns may provide the advantage of serving as barriers to unwanted vehicle traffic, as long as there is passage over or around them. Land management areas or management agencies may have particular regulations or guidelines concerning trail clearing maintenance; contact the land manager for specific regulations regarding blowdown removal.

➔ BRUSHING

A well-brushed trail is one in which a hiker with a big pack can walk without touching limbs, trees, or brush. Footing is clear, and the route is easy to follow. Line of sight is open and unobstructed. Branches of trailside vegetation, even if weighed down by rain or snow, do not obscure the trail.

Brushing, sometimes called brushing out or standardizing, means clearing vegetation from established trails. Without regular brushing, even frequently used trails can become overgrown in just two to three years. Brushing *in*, on the other hand, occurs when a decommissioned trail, visitor-created trail or campsite (also known as bootlegs), or wide section of trail needs to be closed to traffic or made smaller. Downed branches and small trees are installed haphazardly on the trail, thus closing it to hikers while attempting to mimic the natural state of the environment.

THE RIGHT TOOLS: BRUSHING

- loppers
- bow saw/handsaw
- hand pruners
- pole saw (for ski trails)

THE DOOR TECHNIQUE

The recommended method for brushing a trail is called the door technique (see figure 8.39). While hiking down the trail with clippers in hand, imagine carrying a door vertically, like a shield. The door's outline marks the trail standard for brushing, although width and height will vary with the terrain. Everything that falls within the door's outline should be removed.

Using this framework, cut limbs or branches flush with the tree or stem. Stubs are unsightly and can create bothersome and sometimes dangerous snags for packs

Figure 8.39. A doorway for a sheet of plywood is a good visual to use when clearing the trail corridor.

and clothing. If all branches along one side of a small tree need to be removed, it is advisable to remove the entire tree instead. Low shrubs and young trees should be cut as close to the ground as possible for aesthetic reasons, to avoid tripping, and to keep the stumps from sprouting. Do not leave pointed stumps. Remove low growth back to the outside edge of the cleared trail.

Where there is heavy growth on a long section of trail, a gasoline-powered brush cutter or saw may be more efficient. Mechanized saws are not allowed in every area, however, so check local regulations before proceeding. Be certain that the operator of a mechanical brush cutter is trained and knows how to use the equipment properly. Safety is the paramount concern. Keep all other workers a safe distance from power equipment when it is in use.

Leave annual growth of grasses, herbaceous plants, and ferns. If this growth is particularly thick and aggravating, use a swizzle stick to cut. Handle swizzle sticks with caution and an acute awareness of your foot placement and the location of other people. When cutting vegetation, think ahead. Remove entire branches of plants that, if left unattended, will continue to grow into the trail in subsequent years.

Pay special attention to small softwoods and the lateral branches of larger softwoods extending into the trail passage.

WIDTH OF TRAIL

The proper width for a cleared trail varies with terrain, vegetation, and management objectives. A 4- to 6-foot clearance is adequate in most situations. In thick growth or in very remote areas, a 3-foot clearance may be more practical and even desirable, if it adds to a feeling of wildness. In high-use areas and on steep slopes with thin, unstable soils, a narrow trail may be needed to limit hiker impact on the surrounding terrain and vegetation. The nearby roots of trailside trees, shrubs, and other plants stabilize soils. However, a narrow trail is not always the solution; heavy user pressure on steep, sloping trails will cause unstable soils to deteriorate regardless of trail width. The best solution may be to reroute the trail and close the existing section.

CLEARANCE HEIGHT

Normally a trail is cleared to a minimum height of 8 feet, or as high as one can reach (see figure 8.40). On slopes, stand uphill to reach higher branches more easily. If tree branches are higher than 8 feet, consider leaving this canopy over the trail to shade outgrowth of shrubs, weeds, and grasses. Conversely, if more trailside vegetation is desired, encourage the growth of wildflowers, grasses, and shrubs by clearing back the canopy to let in sunlight. Be deliberate to avoid a scorched-earth effect, making the trail look like an interstate roadway. Leave some of the most attractive trees and shrubs standing.

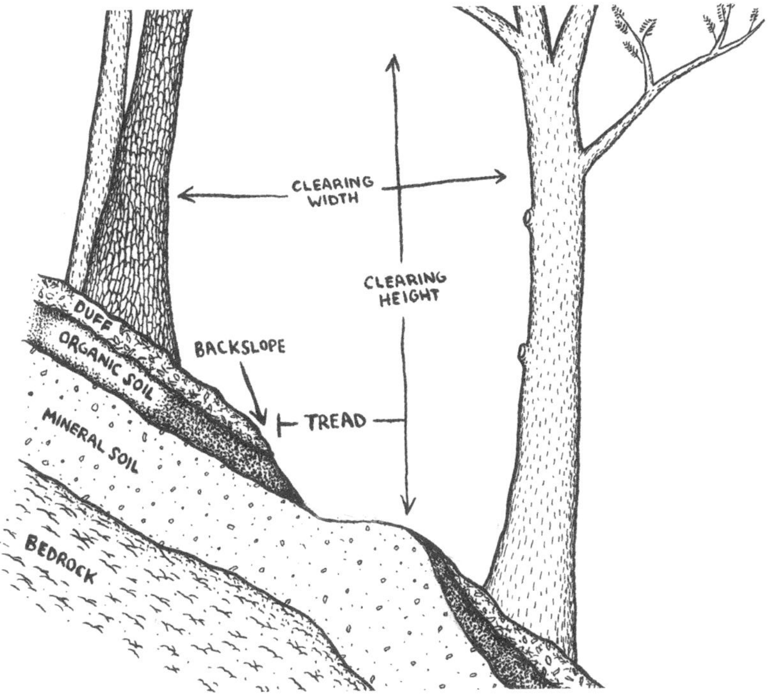

Figure 8.40. Maximum height that the trail corridor will be cleared to.

8

If a trail is popular in winter, clear it to 12 feet high to enable easier travel when snow depths reach 3 or 4 feet. Do this high clearing at any time of year. However, standing on several feet of packed snow will help in reaching higher branches. Use tools such as a pole pruner or a pole saw for hard-to-reach branches.

CLEANUP

Brushing is not complete until all trees, branches, and debris have been picked up and scattered off the trail. Avoid making piles—they are noticeable and a potential fire hazard. In some cases, use a lawn rake to ensure complete cleanup and unobstructed footing. To conceal downed trees, drag them away butt-first until the tops are completely off the trail. Large limbs and small trees can be thrown clear of the trail, but be sure they do not hang in the branches of nearby shrubs and trees or stick up butt-first. Most important, remember to clear all drainages and their outflow ditches.

➔ TRAIL-MARKING SYSTEMS

Good trail markers guide the hiker effortlessly along the route without intruding on the experience. The marks must be easily understandable, systematic, and vandal-resistant. The most popular types of marking include paint blazes; metal or plastic markers; signs; and, for treeless areas, posts or cairns. Tailor marking to specific trail types. For example, a short trail within a state park that is heavily used by inexperienced hikers might be extensively marked. On the other hand, a trail through private land in an urban area may be sparsely marked to prevent heavy or undesirable use. Light marking in remote backcountry locations preserves the wild character of the areas. (*Note*: Standards for markings in federally designated Wilderness Areas may be more stringent or not allowed at all.)

INSTALLING A MARKING SYSTEM

When installing a new trail system or freshly marking an older trail, develop some standards. Carefully think through color, frequency, placement, and form of markings *before* installation. Plot out the color scheme of your marking system on a map of the area, especially if there are a lot of loop trails close together. Blue, red, yellow, white, and orange are good choices; they are visible yet not garish. Natural colors like brown, gray, and green blend into the surroundings and are therefore not good options. Think carefully about how the trail will be used and choose colors accordingly. For example, white is a poor choice for a ski trail. You could employ one color for the main trail in a system and mark all side trails with a second color, as with the Appalachian Trail, where the main route is marked in white and side paths in blue. Use care when the trail is next to boundary lines; property boundaries are usually marked with paint, and if the trail blazes are the same color, confusion can result.

Figure 8.41. Trail markers are important features of any trail system.

Place markers in both forward and rearward directions to indicate the route both ways. Markers should be on trees that are plainly visible along the trail (see figure 8.41). Large trees are preferable, and a marker on a live tree will likely last longer than one on a dead tree. If using a light-colored marker, search out darker-colored trees—and vice versa—to increase contrast.

To ensure adequate and consistent spacing, paint blazes in one direction at a time. Where possible, avoid placing blazes on both sides of the same tree; otherwise, the loss of one tree will result in a twofold loss of marking.

To determine the best place to locate the next blaze, look ahead down the trail. Quickly note a tree that stands out at a suitable distance. Walk to it, and if it is alongside the trail, place the next marker on it. On a straight, wide, or well-cleared trail this may be a far distance. Do not limit yourself to marking only one side of the trail. If there are a lot of turns or curves, the side with the best visibility or sight line will vary. Put the marker at an easily visible height. The usual height for marking is 5 to 6 feet, which is at or just above eye level for many hikers. If a trail is to be used primarily or exclusively in winter, the markers should be slightly higher than this.

The frequency of markers will be determined by the character of the trail and its management objectives. A good rule of thumb is that a hiker should be able to walk more than a hundred paces and still be able to see a marker in either direction. On narrow woods trails with an obvious tread and little opportunity for the hiker to be misled, markers can be widely spaced, perhaps every 100 to 200 feet. On the other hand, a trail without an obvious treadway through an open hardwood forest should be closely marked, possibly every 30 to 50 feet. This is especially appropriate if the trail is used in winter. Where trails follow well-worn roads, markers may be spread farther apart. However, if there are many opportunities for the hiker to turn off the road onto other roads or trails, marking should be more frequent. At trail junctions and crossings mark all the trails as much as needed to ensure a hiker's confidence of remaining on the desired trail.

Do not fail to mark the trail because you think no one could possibly get lost in that area. New trail or road construction, timber harvesting, or blowdowns resulting from storms may unexpectedly change conditions. Bear in mind that trail marking is for the benefit of those who are unfamiliar with the trail and terrain. New or inexperienced hikers rely on blazes for guidance. Marking or blazing should be consistent along a trail's entire length. Interrupting or changing frequency of blazes may confuse hikers.

Immediately beyond any road crossing, brook, or trail, there must be a trail marker, even though there may also be a direction sign. Place a second marker nearby, perhaps 20 to 50 feet from the crossing, in case the first marker disappears or the hiker doesn't see it.

At important changes in the route, such as the trail becoming less well defined or taking a sharp turn, some maintainers and clubs use a double blaze or marker, consisting of two disconnected blazes or markers of the prescribed size, one 2 inches above the other. Doubling serves as a warning to the hiker: "Stop. Pay attention!" Some trail maintainers use offset double markers to indicate direction at turns, the top marker being slightly offset in the direction of the turn.

When a trail is relocated, all blazes or markers on the abandoned section should be obliterated or removed. It is not sufficient to eliminate those at each end, since people may stray onto the old route, see the markers in between, and assume they are on the correct trail. This could cause them to become confused and lost.

Paint Blazes

Durability, universal availability, low cost, and ease of application make paint the most practical solution for marking most trails. Modern water-based paints such as latex are the easiest to handle and apply, and they dry quickly. Oil-based enamels, paints, or inks developed especially for boundary marking last long, but they are toxic and their use is discouraged. Blazes should be neat and well placed (see figure 8.42).

The standard blaze on the Appalachian Trail is a white 2-by-6-inch paint blaze placed on trees. For more than half a century, the shape and color of this blaze—approximately the size of a dollar bill—has proven to be visible and effective.

As with any paint job, preparation of the surface is paramount. On trees with smooth, thin bark, a wire brush or nylon scrub pad works well to scrape off dirt and lichen. On trees with rough bark, such as hemlock or oak, use a paint scraper to create a flat, fairly smooth surface the size of a paint blaze. Do not scrape *through* the bark on any tree, as it will cause resin to ooze out and discolor the blaze. Avoid blazing during rainy or damp weather, as the paint may run or fail to adhere to the surface.

Figure 8.42. When painting blazes, keep size and color consistent and be patient.

When painting a blaze, keep the edges neat, and don't let the paint drip on the ground or the tree. Use a 2-inch brush, which can also serve as a size guide.

A plastic pail is a convenient way to keep blazing supplies within easy reach. You can make carrying the pail more comfortable by taping the handle or splitting open a segment of old garden hose lengthwise and wrapping it around the handle. Pouring small quantities of paint into a paper cup makes painting easier and will not make a huge mess if spilled. You can also apply paint to the brush with a squeezable container, such as a condiment bottle, or with a forester-type paint gun with the nozzle portion removed. To aid in getting the correct size, make a 2-by-6-inch stencil out of hose, rubber inner tube, or similar material.

A paintbrush can be reused within a short time frame by tightly wrapping the brush in plastic, not allowing the paint to dry. Brushes that have been used with oil-based paint can also be wrapped in tight plastic and stored in the freezer. They then can be reused with the same paint color at a later date.

Occasionally it is necessary to remove paint blazes, such as when relocating a section of trail or standardizing a trail section that has been improperly marked. When renewing blazes, remove portions of old blazes that have been widened by tree growth. To eliminate all or a portion of a blaze, scrape it off the tree with a paint scraper or wire brush, or use a brown, gray, or custom-mixed paint matched to the surface being covered.

THE RIGHT TOOLS: BLAZING

- pint or quart of paint
- rag for spills or runs
- small quantity of paint thinner to clean brushes
- several paper cups
- nylon scrub pad or wire brush
- one or two 2-inch paintbrushes
- 2- to 2½-inch paint scraper
- container to carry the equipment

Plastic or Metal Markers

Plastic and metal markers nailed to trees and posts are also effective for guiding hikers. One benefit of these markers is that they are helpful when a directional marker is needed or when a marker requires text or a logo to identify or publicize the trail (see figure 8.43). Options range from simple, unpainted tin-can tops to custom-designed-and-manufactured plastic or aluminum markers that come in various shapes, colors, and sizes. While these markers are easy to install, they also can be removed by souvenir seekers and other vandals. They tend to be expensive, and color and lettering may fade after several years, necessitating replacement.

Markers must be carefully installed for longevity. Nails should be made of soft metal, like aluminum, so they will not damage a chain saw should the tree need to be cut. Drive the nail into both the marker and the tree, leaving an inch between the marker and the head of the nail (see figure 8.44). This allows the tree to grow out along the nail without bending or growing around the marker.

Figure 8.43, left. Non-wood markers are lightweight and have good longevity.
Figure 8.44, right. Plan for tree growth and leave a gap.

➔ MAKING TRAIL SIGNS

Signs are an essential component of any trail; they are usually located at trailheads, junctions, road crossings, and trail features. They can indicate the trail name, direction, highlights, facilities, and distances (see figure 8.45). Some have a symbol or identification of the land manager and maintaining organization(s). In addition to signs, some trails have markers that refer to a special designation or point out that the trail is part of a specific system. These markers are usually placed at trailheads or at intervals along the route.

Figure 8.45. Plastic, metal, and wood trail signs.

ROUTED SIGNS

The most common trail signs are made of wood, with the lettering cut into the sign using a router. Because the lettering is actually incised into the wood, the sign will be legible even after the weather has worn off all paint or stain.

Type of Wood

Consider workability, durability, and strength, as well as availability and cost. The best choices are clear heartwood from ponderosa pine, yellow pine, white pine, western fir, redwood, or basswood. In the southeastern United States, cypress and locust are often used. Use high-quality stock, straight and free of knots, checks, and warps. Also consider what is abundant and available locally—standard kiln-dried spruce and fir work well. Plywood is strongly discouraged and may cause irreparable damage to the router bit because of the hard glue used to join layers of plywood.

High-Density Polyethylene Plastic Signboards

High-density polyethylene signboards have become popular, especially in the front-country. These signs are typically two colors, one on the exterior and one on the interior, so when the sign is routed, the interior color is revealed to highlight the lettering. Therefore, there is no need for painting, finishing, and sealing. Signs can be ordered with the desired routed text or routed with the techniques described below. However, damage repair and "in-house" fixing of these signs may be difficult because of their construction. Before using this type of signage, consider the aesthetics of the area.

Size of Signboard

Smoothly planed boards 1½ inches thick are appropriate for most routed wooden signs. At trailheads, where large descriptive signs are needed, 2-inch or larger stock may be best. The length and width of a sign varies with the length of the message, the size of letters, and the sign's importance. For most sign needs, consider using standard dimensional lumber that is readily available. This tends to be more cost-effective and speeds up production time. Because hikers stand directly in front of trail signs, it is not necessary to make them large, except for those located roadside. Signs along the trail can be made from standard 2-by-6-inch to 2-by-12-inch milled lumber. Roadside trailhead signs may be as large as 2 by 3 feet. Large signs can be made from several boards joined together with biscuit joints, dowels and glue, threaded rods, cleats, or similar equipment (see figure 8.46).

8

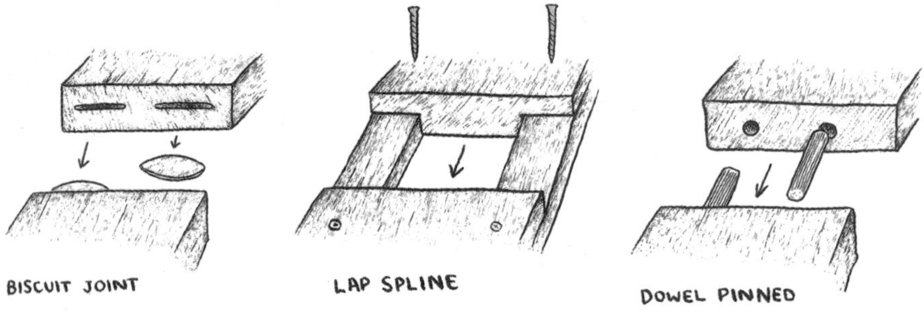

Figure 8.46. Various ways to join one piece of wood to another.

Size of Lettering

Most trail signs will not need lettering larger than 1½ inches in height. Larger lettering can be used for the name of a trail so it will stand out. In general, lettering should be 1 inch or ¾ inch in height.

Routing

A few different routing tools and techniques can be used when lettering signs. A sharp, high-quality bit is essential. A dull bit will burn the wood and leave feathers that make painting difficult and must be sanded out. Use a U-shaped or V-shaped carbide-tipped veining or grooving bit. Carbide steel, although more expensive than plain steel, is extremely hard, lasts much longer, and does a better job if used properly. For 1¼- to 1-inch-tall letters, use a ¼-inch bit, and for ¾-inch letters use a ⅛-inch bit. Larger letters will require a larger bit. Set the depth of the bit based on the desired look of the letters. It is advisable to test out different depth settings on scrap wood to see how the letters will look. When routing letters taller than 2 inches, first set the router to cut half the depth of the letter, and then go over it again, cutting at full depth; this saves wear and tear on the router. Repair mistakes with small amounts of plastic wood filler. This information about routing and bit size applies to routing by hand as well as using a commercial sign machine.

Freehand Routing

Because routing machines are expensive and bulky, some people prefer to hand-rout their signs (see figure 8.47). While this can be a time-consuming process that requires skill and patience, a person can make professional-looking signs with a small hand router and other proper equipment. Use letter stencils to lay out the text (see figure 8.48). Letter style should be simple and all capitals. Many stationery or art supply stores sell various sizes of inexpensive paper or plastic stencils for tracing letters. Higher-quality plastic or metal stencils can be obtained from a sign manufacturer but will likely be more expensive. Some trail maintainers, rather than lay out letters again and again, lay out the text on high-quality drafting paper. This can be placed over the signboard with carbon paper in between. When the text is traced, it produces a carbon outline on the signboard. The drafting paper can then be filed away for future use. Such reusable texts can also save time when making multiple copies of one sign or where certain words, such as *trail* and *path*, or lines of text are repeated. Before routing text laid out on a sign, practice on scrap wood.

Figure 8.47. With a little practice, hand-routing trail signs can be very effective.

Figure 8.48. Stenciling a sign before using a router.

Considerable skill is needed to achieve professional results. Use a relaxed, smooth, and steady motion while following the stenciled letters with the router.

Machine Routing

Several types of commercial sign machines with letter templates are available but are expensive (see figure 8.49). However, the efficiency of production and exactness of the routing can be worth the initial expense.

New technology has been developed in recent years. CNC (computer numerical control) machines, for example, use computer software to program text, logos, and designs. The operator sets up the board on the router table and starts the program, which then routs as instructed. Several styles of these machines are commercially available. One common design has a router mounted on a movable arm. The arm is attached to the machine's work surface, which accepts a range of lumber sizes and letter templates. A pin at the operator end tracks the letter templates up the arm of the machine. This system allows the sign maker to lay out text several lines at a time, all with proper spacing and alignment. The only limitation is the inability to accept larger signs for trailheads.

The machine router's letter templates are different from those used for hand routing and are available in a variety of sizes and fonts. While they are designed to track the pin of the sign machine, moving the router across the sign, a steady and careful hand is still needed to create clean letters. Logos and designs are also easily transferred to sign machine templates, allowing the sign maker to place logos consistently on signs.

Following the same guidelines outlined in the routing section, a variety of signs can be made with ease and consistency. A sign machine can be particularly useful if there is a need to make a large number of signs each year or to make signs with four to six lines of text.

Figure 8.49. Software-based machine router.

Painting and Staining

Many signs are not painted or stained at all. For instance, signs in federally designated Wilderness Areas must be unpainted to retain a more rustic appearance. However, many signs should be painted or stained. Two colors are generally used: one for the background and one for the lettering. Some sign makers simply stain the entire sign or treat it with a clear wood preservative. Others stain first and then paint the lettering with enamel. The entire sign can also be painted, with the background in one color and the lettering in another. For contrast and better visibility, use a light-colored background with dark letters or vice versa. Use a good-quality enamel or latex paint over a compatible primer coat. After the background paint dries, paint the letters. Use a small brush, squeeze bottle, or syringe to patiently and neatly fill the routed letters with paint. Then, with a small brush, nail, or painted stick, direct the paint so it covers the entire inside surface of the routed letters. Wipe away any mistakes before they dry and touch up as needed.

Here's a trick to facilitate letter painting while hand routing: Stencil the sign text on the prepainted board, cover the face of the sign with contact paper, and then rout through it. Quickly brush paint into the lettering and pull off the contact paper. Generally, some touch-up will be needed, and the contact paper and paint do tend to dull the router bit more quickly.

HANGING THE SIGN

The most attractive and effective method of hanging signs is to use a post. Signs can also be hung on trees, but that causes damage, and trees are not always available or in the right location. It's best to use a 6- to 10-inch-diameter post, sunk to a depth of 3 feet. To make a natural signpost, use a rot-resistant wood, such as cedar, locust, or hemlock. Peel off the bark to discourage insects and to prevent moisture retention. If a natural post is not feasible, use a dimensional pressure-treated post.

Bolt the sign to a flattened edge of the post. Bevel the upper end of the post with an ax or saw to shed rain and to create a more rustic appearance. To prevent turning or removal of the post, drive either one length or two crossed lengths of threaded rod, rebar, or large metal spike through the bottom of the post before it is buried. Alternatively, nail one or two pieces of wood to the bottom of the post. Above treeline or on a ledge, use the lengths of rebar or wood to anchor posts inside stone cairns.

Hang signs securely to protect them from vandals. Maintainers use many different techniques to prevent vandalism and theft. Signs that are likely to be stolen, especially those in high-profile popular areas, can be mounted using special nuts and bolts, such as Vandlgard or Tufnut brands, or using countersink bolts covered with wooden plugs or wood putty. If possible, place the signs high enough to be out of reach. Fixing the signs to a post or tree with two lag bolts works particularly well for signs thicker than 1 inch, although such bolts tend to crack thinner signs.

Another potential vandal-resistant (but more expensive) technique is to mount ¾-inch-thick signs on a backboard of the same size cut from 1½-inch stock. First, use lag bolts to attach the backboard to a post or tree through at least two predrilled and countersunk holes. Then bolt the sign to the backboard. Fasten small signs to the backboard with two bolts. These bolts should be offset in opposite corners so as not to split the sign along the grain. Larger signs need four bolts. Using a backboard provides more secure mounting and, if bolted to a tree, also helps protect the sign from splitting due to tree growth. All bolts, washers, and nails should be galvanized or at least zinc plated. Standard ones will rust, leaving an unsightly stain on the sign. Be careful not to overtighten the bolts. This can cause the sign to crack and the paint to chip, allowing water to degrade the sign more quickly.

MASTER SIGN LIST

Develop a master sign list for the trail system to document each sign's location, text, and condition and the date and time the sign was last checked. The list facilitates maintenance, repair, and replacement. Number signs and key them to the master list.

TEMPORARY SIGNS

If a permanent sign is not ready when a trail is to be opened, or if an important sign is stolen, you will need a temporary sign (see figure 8.50). Decent temporary signs can be made by writing on heavy posterboard with permanent, weatherproof ink, such as that of a Sharpie. Use a dark-colored ink; red and light colors tend to fade quickly. Laminate the temporary sign to weatherproof it, staple and glue it to plywood, and hang it on a post or tree. A painted piece of plywood marked with a Sharpie will also work. While not ideal, such signs should last one to two years. Check them for defacing and animal damage if they must serve longer.

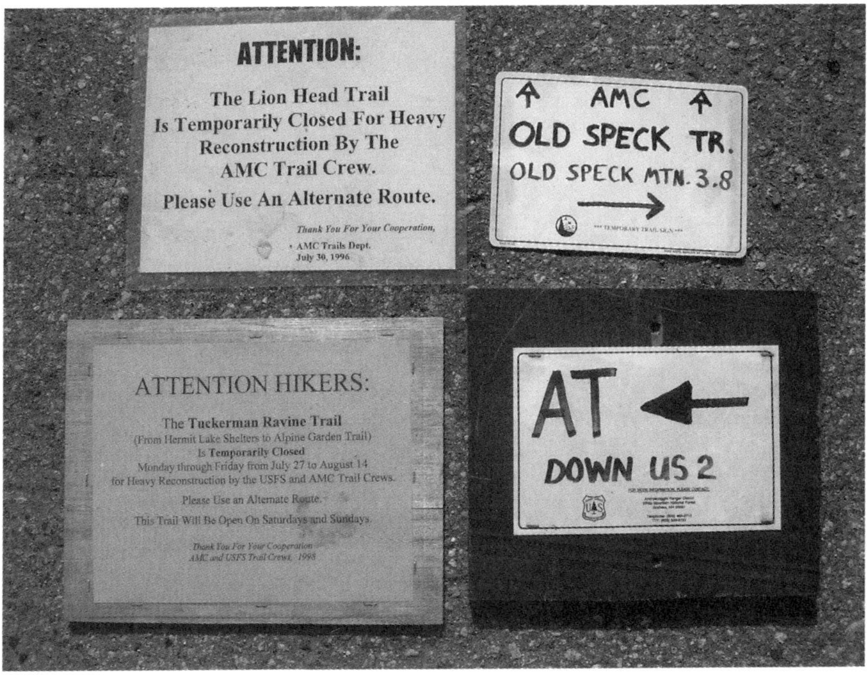

Figure 8.50, above. Temporary signs are far better for hikers than no signs.
Figure 8.51, below. Sign with painted-only text.

OTHER SIGNS

Some maintainers make signs by using a stencil and painting outlined letters on a board (see figure 8.51). This can be tedious, and these signs have a shorter lifespan when left out in the woods; the text may become illegible as weather wears away the paint. Some signs are fashioned from plate steel. The letters are made with a bead of brazing or stenciled and cut out with a torch. This technique is costly, and such signs are generally not aesthetically pleasing in a backwoods setting. However, they may be desirable for vandal-prone areas. Some maintainers use the posts themselves as signs; text is vertically routed or cast into wooden or concrete posts (see figure 8.52). Since these can be securely installed and tend to be very long and heavy, theft is less of a problem.

Figure 8.52. Sign text routed into a post.

RETIRED SIGNS

As part of annual trail maintenance, assess the condition of every trail sign. Each year several signs will need to be replaced due to damage from animals, fallen trees, or weathering. The life span of a trail sign depends greatly on the materials used, weatherproofing, and the location of the sign. When you replace an old sign, don't discard it. Trail signs can have a life beyond the trail.

Give retired trail signs as recognition to individuals who have helped in the construction or maintenance of that trail—they're wonderful gifts. Retired trail signs can be auctioned off to help fund future trail maintenance efforts. Before giving away retired signs, consider assigning them a unique identification number, different from the standard location identification number on a master sign list. This number will prove that a sign was legally acquired rather than stolen.

➔ ALPINE TRAIL MAINTENANCE

Different techniques of trail maintenance should be used if the treadway passes through sensitive environments, such as boreal forest, desert, slab rock, or alpine areas. In northern New England, numerous trails are classified as "alpine," which describes high-elevation ecosystems—above treeline—that are defined by short growing seasons and long, harsh winters. The alpine environment is home to a variety of unique and rare plants, many of which are endemic to that environment. Alpine trails are typically rocky and exposed.

DRAINAGE CLEANING IN ALPINE ZONES

Erosion control is the trail maintainer's primary task in alpine zones, as in lower elevation trails. The loose soils of alpine trails are easily eroded by the lack of drainage structures or poorly maintained ones. In this environment, drainages quickly clog up with loose sand and gravel. Removing this material and reshaping the drainages can be a lot of work. In some instances, heavier tools, such as pick mattocks, may be needed to loosen and remove compacted soils.

Even though digging in the soils above treeline may seem counterintuitive to protecting this fragile ecosystem, a trail without proper water drainage can cause much more damage through erosion. A well-maintained and flared outflow is as important as a well-maintained drainage ditch in the alpine zone—just as it is in other environments. Once the water is carried off the trail, it is important to prevent further erosion in the outflow of the drainage.

BRUSHING IN ALPINE ZONES

Trails through alpine areas require special treatment when it comes to brushing. Use judgment and temperance when clearing trails near or above treeline, where the climate is severe and growth is slow. Krummholz accounts for the majority of woody vegetation in the alpine zone. Krummholz is composed of old and dense dwarf trees that have been contorted from years of exposure to the elements; trees 3 to 4 feet tall can be 60 or 70 years old. Removing one tree in a patch of krummholz can jeopardize the other trees in the patch because they join roots and branches in protection against wind and cold. Trees below treeline grow mostly vertically, but krummholz grow horizontally and close to ground level to adapt to the high winds and weather. At lower elevations, the standard clearing for a hiking trail should be 4 feet wide by 8 feet high. However, trails in the alpine zone that travel through krummholz do not need to be as wide. Krummholz are very slow growers and need only minimal cutting to maintain an open passage for several years. Making proper cuts, as described in the "Brushing" section on page 165 earlier in this chapter, is very important to foster quick healing. In the alpine zone, maintain a cleared passage that is passable through krummholz while minimizing any cutting, and keep up on brushing. Krummholz can slowly but insidiously spread across the ground, obscuring the treadway, and force hikers onto adjacent fragile vegetation. Widening of the tread can be difficult to repair, and damage to the adjacent alpine vegetation may become almost irreparable. Extreme care and consideration are needed when working in this ecosystem.

TRAIL DEFINITION IN ALPINE ZONES

As trails pass through alpine environments, trail definition is critical to the stewardship of the ecosystem. A successful technique used to define treadway through alpine zones is the use of scree walls. Scree walls concentrate hikers onto a single-track through open terrain and provide a physical barrier to the alpine ecosystem (see figure 8.53). These walls can be small and sporadic, providing a reminder of the treadway, or can be large and consistent, lining both sides of the trail for long distances. The degree of trail use, community type, and way a trail is used will determine the size of scree wall needed.

Scree walls also serve to stabilize soils along the sides of the trail that may have been loosened by visitors and erosion. In areas where the trail has become very wide and has begun to affect the alpine vegetation, use scree walls to narrow the treadway. In addition to scree walls, install rubble (see figure 8.54), a collection of smaller rocks and rock fragments, placed in impacted areas to discourage hikers from walking in the area, which helps stabilize soils and encourage revegetation. Take care when constructing scree walls to only choose rocks that are not already protecting alpine vegetation or holding back soil.

Figure 8.53. Scree walls define the treadway and protect important natural resources.

Figure 8.54. A combination of scree walls and rubble can help keep users on the trail.

TRAIL MARKING IN ALPINE ZONES

In treeless areas, trails are marked with conspicuous rock piles known as cairns. (In the absence of rock, posts are used.) Cairns make attractive trail markers and are effective year-round because of their visibility even in snowy and icy conditions. Well-placed and well-built cairns also help protect the fragile soils of alpine areas by guiding hikers on a single trail (see figure 8.55). Cairns are especially important at times of poor visibility or in a storm.

Cairns should be laid out along trails in a fairly direct fashion. Hikers tend to shortcut sharp turns; therefore, it is best to keep the trail curving with the land in gentle undulations. The easiest route is the most likely choice of travel for the average hiker.

Figure 8.55. Cairns can be critical when visibility is poor.

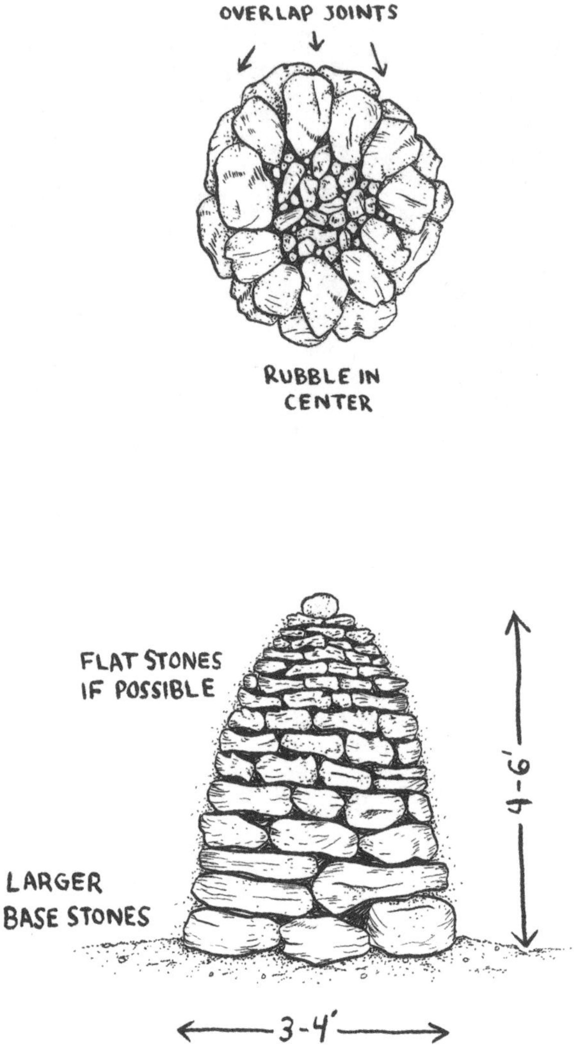

Figure 8.56. It takes a lot of time and effort to build one cairn.

For maximum visibility in marginal conditions, place cairns between 50 and 100 feet apart at conspicuous locations: a knoll is obviously better than a hollow. A cairn has greater visibility if placed on a ledge or mound. If possible, use a light-colored rock, such as a chunk of quartzite, for the top of the cairn, making it more visible (see figure 8.56). Some maintainers paint the uppermost rock. Painted blazes are also used in conjunction with cairns to mark the route, especially in areas where rock for building cairns is scarce or where the blaze's color is needed to identify the trail. If necessary, paint blazes on visible rocks to mark the trail—but this is not recommended. Be aware that any blaze near the ground may be covered with snow and/or ice in winter.

For all alpine trail maintenance needs, be sure to collect rocks that are well away from the trail and not stuck in the soil or serving to retain soil. Look for rocks that are sitting on top of other rocks or that are wedged between other rocks. Trail maintainers must work toward preserving all soil in the alpine environment, and careful rock selection plays a critical role in this effort.

Basic maintenance is crucial to the hardiness of any trail, but there is one last thing to remember: maintain drainages first. Before building cairns, marking or re-marking, or clearing the brush on that last quarter-mile of trail, be sure the drainages are clear, wide, and free. Soil, especially in the alpine areas, is critical and limited in availability; conservation of this resource is paramount.

CHAPTER 9
BRIDGES

AT-A-GLANCE

When a trail crosses a body of water, trail builders must determine the best course of action for getting hikers across. Almost all trails cross one or more waterways somewhere along the route.

- ➔ **Bridge necessity:** Consider the likely users of the trail, location, and alternative routes before you conclude that a bridge is necessary.
- ➔ **Bridge architecture:** Design a bridge based on aesthetics, required span and size, and the experience of the designer and builders.
- ➔ **Bridge construction:** Use lumber of appropriate size and strength based on the bridge design; build supports if necessary.

Proper recreation and natural resource management planning plays an important role in stewardship of the ecosystem and trail users' behavior and experience. On frontcountry trails, users often expect to have safe and dry passage across water. On such trails, even minor stream crossings may need to be bridged. Conversely, in a federally designated Wilderness Area, users are explicitly warned that safe and dry passage over water is extremely limited or nonexistent. On backcountry trails, bridges are usually constructed to prevent resource damage or if there is a probable hazard to hikers. Therefore, as part of trail planning and resource management, it is important to decide whether bridging is needed. If it is, the next step is to determine proper placement and then begin construction while preparing and planning for eventual maintenance.

With the reality of climate change and its likelihood to bring extreme weather events with more frequency and power, long-term planning is necessary to ensure suitable and durable bridge construction. Therefore, intelligent trail layout and well-considered crossing locations are essential to the longevity of trail and bridge infrastructure.

➔ IS A BRIDGE NEEDED?

Urban, frontcountry, and interpretive trails customarily have bridges installed over waterways for user convenience and safety. These trail types demand easy accessibility with as few challenges as possible because they are typically used by individuals with little or no hiking experience. During the design phase it is recommended, and in some cases required, to consider constructing bridges to broad accessibility standards.

On the other hand, backcountry trails are often managed in a way that maintains challenging conditions and provides a wilder experience. The decision to install a bridge usually depends on a variety of environmental considerations and management objectives. Think about the environmental sensitivity of the area, its durability to disturbance, and the projected amount of use. Is it important to preserve the natural look of a river? What are the potential impacts of bridge construction? Should the site be limited to a seasonal crossing to increase off-season challenges and to maintain a more natural feel on a low-use trail? Management sometimes allows for a bridge to be installed only if it is determined that there is an absolute need. Examples include spanning a watercourse that cannot be easily forded or allowing passage across a steep or hazardous natural feature, such as canyon walls. Conduct careful planning and site reconnaissance to explore all options before a bridge is deemed necessary and the design and construction phases begin. Often, by changing a trail's trajectory, the need for a bridge can be eliminated, potentially lowering costs and environmental impact. Avoidance and mitigation are key goals to keep in mind. For instance, carefully choosing a site along a stream that allows for a natural crossing, such as a rock hop, avoids a bridge altogether. Depending on location, land ownership, and site review, permits for bridge and wetland crossings may be required.

Knowing the characteristics of a stream and watershed and the area's use patterns helps to determine the need for a bridge. Consider bridge width and design requirements for both summer and winter use—they are generally different. For example, a stream that is easily crossed in dry summertime conditions may be nearly impossible or, at best, dangerous to cross during spring runoff or in high water situations.

When a bridge is necessary, determine the ideal location and alignment of the bridge in relation to the trail. In general, bridge alignment should be perpendicular to the watercourse or stream channel. Bridge placement should not create an abrupt or awkward entrance onto the structure that could be difficult to maneuver or potentially cause injury. Avoid sharp turns in the approach to the bridge, especially on a multiuse trail or one that allows wheeled or motorized vehicles.

For small stream crossings of 10 to 15 feet, a simple log puncheon or bog bridge (see Chapter 8, page 151) may suffice. A bridge with double stringers (long, heavy horizontal timbers used as supports or connectors) provides better footing. Build a handrail for bridges 3 feet or higher above the stream or for any bridges over a fast current.

➔ AESTHETICS

Consider aesthetics in bridge design; it is important for the structure to complement the landscape and its intended use. For example, a bridge in a remote wilderness would best suited with a more rustic construction and design. However, it may not always be possible to use native or natural-looking materials. A bridge's intended purpose may require stronger and longer-lasting materials that exclude a rustic and native design. Often, a bridge may define the character of a trail due to its appearance and setting. Bridges are places where users, especially in frontcountry locations, pause to reflect or to enjoy the surrounding scenery. However, don't forget to balance aesthetics with the environmental concerns and the structural needs of the project.

➔ DESIGN AND CONSTRUCTION CONSIDERATIONS

Bridges with long spans (typically more than 35 feet) or those over challenging terrain or unstable soils require professional engineering. Professional engineers will evaluate flood-level data and load-bearing capacity of soils, prepare and submit permits, estimate project costs, and design a bridge that meets the objectives and aesthetics of the project. Large bridges often require heavy equipment for construction; therefore, means of access must be anticipated and secured. Modern lightweight composite materials can be used in place of standard wood or steel components. Composite bridges (see figure 9.1) are excellent choices when access is difficult.

Figure 9.1. A fiberglass bridge.

Even when not employing the design services of a professional, it is necessary to determine annual flood levels and regional weather events to establish bridge specifications. This data is available through land management offices and state and federal agencies, notably the U.S. Geological Service (USGS). Smaller or less costly bridges may only necessitate examining evidence of the high-water mark, using such indicators as scraped bark on trees lining the bank or deposits of debris that may indicate seasonal high water. It may be possible to obtain hydrological data from local, state, or federal government agencies to determine flood levels for a particular stream. Local individuals who have knowledge of the waterway, its watershed, and its dynamics can also provide valuable information.

PERMITS

Depending on a number of factors, bridges in certain locations, or of certain lengths or heights, may require a permit. Indeed, most activities within wetland jurisdiction, which is often considered from top of bank to top of bank, need a permit. Projects involving soil disturbance in a streambed or along a stream's banks almost always must have wetland permits as well. Check with local and state agencies before starting any project.

➔ BUILDING SINGLE-SPAN STRINGER BRIDGES

Single-span wooden bridges of native materials or milled timber are the most common bridges on hiking trails (see figure 9.2). If both stream embankments are tall enough to keep stringers well above high water, extensive support may not be necessary. If support is needed midspan, a crib box can be built. A crib box is a boxlike structure, typically made of timber, filled with rocks that acts as an elevated base for stringers while allowing controlled water drainage. It may be needed when the watercourse is subject to drastic changes in seasonal levels.

Secure the stringers to a single base log, sill (a flat stone or ledge), or crib box on each end, using 10- or 12-inch spikes or large bolts. (*Note*: Place the base log on a sill to prevent rot; the base log should not directly contact soil if possible.) Use drift pins to hold the base log in place on the rock if the weight of the bridge itself is not sufficient. In some situations, crib boxes will need to be placed directly in the water. Keep in mind that this will reduce the overall longevity of the bridge. See the "Crib Boxes" section on page 191 for more information on building crib boxes.

Figure 9.2. A native single-span bridge with handrail.

Milled pressure-treated lumber can be used to build simple and durable triple-laminated bridge stringers. Spans up to 12 feet long can be bridged using 2-by-10-inch lumber lengths. For spans between 12 and 24 feet, create laminated stringers by joining sections of 2-by-12-inch lumber together in three layers to form one solid beam. Before laminating, check each 2-by-12-inch section for bows; bowed sections should be positioned crown up to take advantage of the bow's strength. Laminate the 2-by-12s together using both galvanized nails (see figure 9.3) and construction adhesive for maximum strength. Joints between laminated sections should never be closer than 2 feet apart.

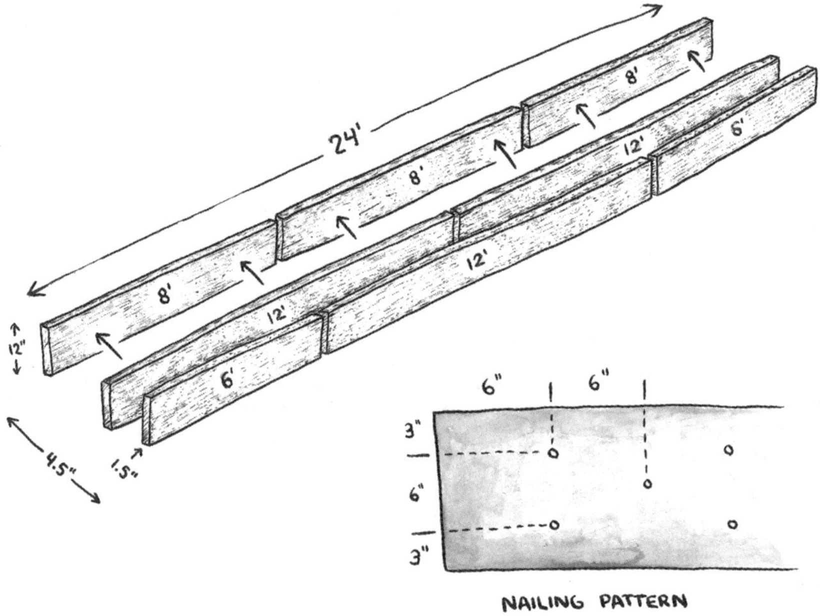

Figure 9.3. Using dimensional lumber in this fashion reduces costs in special orders from the lumberyard.

9

For bridges made of native materials, use rot-resistant wood, such as hemlock, locust, spruce, larch, or Douglas fir, for the stringers and for the base or sill logs. Remove all bark to retard rot. If the bridge project requires treated material, use pressure-treated wood or treat the native wood with borax. Apply liquid wood treatments with extreme caution; while they can lengthen the life of the bridge, the ingredients are often toxic and will leach into the stream or groundwater. If cutting pressure-treated wood on-site, avoid cutting above open water or within the wetland to reduce groundwater contamination. If using a preservative treatment, dry the logs first and apply the treatment on dry ground to keep the liquid out of the water. Try to eliminate contamination of groundwater by limiting cutting and treatment to one area that is dry and easy to clean up. Pack out all refuse.

Where access is easy and the use of non-native material is appropriate (for example, on a high-use trail close to a road), pressure-treated telephone poles are

Figure 9.4. Typical cribbing design for bridge abutments and supports.

good options as stringers. However, keep in mind that the chemicals used to treat the lumber may be hazardous to the environment, especially water bodies. It is no longer recommended to use creosote timber for bridging because of eventual groundwater contamination over its lifetime.

CRIB BOXES

When one stream embankment is lower than the other, a crib box can be used to elevate the low end of the bridge and to level the span. Sometimes crib boxes (see figure 9.4) may be necessary at both ends. Another method of elevation is to construct piers, upright supports of wood or stone. Stone is more durable than wood, but building stone piers requires considerable effort and skill. Gabions, wire cages filled with stones, can be used instead of piers but are not aesthetically appealing. Abutments (see figure 9.5), usually made of large square stones, also serve to elevate

Figure 9.5. Old stone abutments still provide strength and support.

the ends or to secure the center of a bridge. Of these options, log crib boxes are most common. It is very likely that a permit is needed for any crib box, pier, gabion, or abutment as these structures are typically built within wetland jurisdictions.

To make log crib boxes, cut 8- to 10-inch-diameter logs to the length needed, depending on the bridge width. For example, a small 16-inch-wide bog bridge will need only a 3-foot-wide crib box; a wider bridge will require a bigger box. Construct the boxes by laying two logs parallel to each other to form the base of two sides of the box. Then overlay two logs perpendicular to these to form the other two box sides, as in log cabin construction. Cut notches with an ax or chain saw on the underside of each log to help them fit together. Use drift pins or 10- to 12-inch-long, ⅜-inch-diameter spikes to secure the logs together. Add as many layers of wood to the box as needed to elevate the bridge.

To add mass and strength, fill the crib box with rocks gathered nearby. During the planning process it may be tempting to decide to use rocks from the stream channel, but this is not a best practice or legal in many jurisdictions. If it is determined that rocks from the stream must be used, however, this needs to be applied for in the wetland permit for the project. Push or pull larger rocks to either side of the stream and place them along the bases of the cribs, particularly on the upstream side, for added protection during high-water events. Use a taut string, squared-off milled lumber, and a builder's level to get the adjacent cribs the same height. (In a pinch, a half-filled water bottle can be used to determine levelness.)

After the crib has been built high enough, secure the stringers using large spikes or galvanized bolts. The size of each stringer will depend on the type of wood and length of the span.

Due to their length and weight, stringers are hard to carry and maneuver into position. Timber carriers, hand winches with extra lengths of cable or chain, and rock bars can greatly facilitate placement. Put small lengths of log underneath stringers to act as rollers. Use horses or small tractors in easily accessible locations. When the stringers are at the site, place them across the stream, with the ends beside each sill or crib, and then lift them into place. Ramps made of logs and placed against the side of a crib can help get the stringers into position. Again, check the bridge's length and width with the carpenter's level.

DECKING

Two or more stringers, flattened on the top with an ax or adze for good footing, can provide an adequate treadway if the stringers are close together. However, decking is generally best. Install decking, made from small-diameter (4- to 6-inch) logs, larger logs split in half, or rough-cut timber 2 inches thick, after placing the bridge stringers (see figure 9.6). Leave small spaces, ¼ to ¾ inches wide, between deck pieces to allow for drainage. Before installing the decking, consider rolling tar paper or aluminum flashing over the top of the stringers for drainage and to retard

Figure 9.6. Decking provides the best footing.

rot. If the bridge crosses a fast current or is 3 or more feet above the stream, add a secure railing to one or both sides. In some cases, steps or a small ladder might be needed on each end due to the height of the cribs. Pressure-treated lumber can be used for decking and railings. However, avoid pressure-treated wood for a foot surface on sloped bridges or in areas that stay damp—it is extremely slippery when wet. If there is no alternative, use a surface treatment, such as anti-slip paint or wire mesh lath, to enhance traction.

To prevent the complete loss of the bridge during floods, cable one end of the stringers to a large tree, boulder, or natural anchor upstream. If the stringers are washed loose, one end will float free, and the bridge will most likely be pinned against the stream bank, hopefully more or less intact. Later, the bridge can be reinstalled or taken apart and reassembled in place. If both ends are secured with cabling, the bridge will probably stay in place but may collect debris and eventually succumb completely to the forces of high water or flooding. In short, do not underestimate the power of water!

➔ OTHER DESIGNS

The load capacity of fixed stringers generally limits bridge spans to 40 feet or less. A longer distance can be bridged using a midstream center crib with two spans on either side. This is recommended only where flood levels are low and flow is slow; otherwise, the center crib may be destroyed.

Most stream crossings of 40 feet or more require specially designed bridges, such as a laminated timber bridge (10 to 60 feet), a prefabricated steel bridge (20 to 168 feet), a web joist bridge (about 100 feet), or a timber suspension bridge (up to 200 feet). (See figure 9.7.) These are all extremely expensive, ranging from $20,000 to $150,000, and require the expertise of engineers and experienced builders.

Where stream crossings are wide and unavoidable, requiring an expensive bridge, check to see if a nearby trail or road bridge is a good alternative. Sometimes it is best to consider relocating a trail rather than creating a large impact with a new bridge.

Figure 9.7. Three steel I-beams provide the support for this long-span bridge.

➔ SPECIAL STREAM-CROSSING DEVICES

Where large bodies of water must be crossed, bridges on pilings may be the answer. Floating bridges, much like life rafts and docks, can be built using foam blocks or floats, although this may not be practical for winter conditions. Place anchor cables to keep such bridges stable and in position. Use rot-resistant wood and make sure all hardware is galvanized or plated. Consult a local dock builder for advice on pilings and specialized float systems.

One design that has gained popularity is a dock-like boardwalk system to navigate wide wetland areas (see figure 9.8). This design uses dock hardware and dimensional lumber to create an adaptable and adjustable bridge that minimizes environmental impact, increases structural longevity, eases maintenance, and is extremely versatile. Unlike boat docks of a straight utilitarian design, these bridges navigate wetlands on interpretative trails adapting to the topography and hydrology of the ecosystem. The bridge system uses dock pier hardware that is driven into the wetland substrate at set intervals. These dock sections are joined with bracketing hardware that connects the stringers and piers together. Each section in this system is adjustable in height, which offers an advantage if the structure settles throughout its lifetime. The wooden components are also easy to replace, making repair and maintenance access simple.

Figure 9.8. Boardwalks are used in places where water levels fluctuate throughout the year.

→ PLANNING FOR OTHER USES

If the trail is for pedestrians only, build bridges to prevent prohibited uses, such as motorized vehicles. Make bridges narrow, or place barricades, gates, or stiles at either end of a bridge to prevent undesirable access. These additions are particularly effective for keeping out farm animals in agricultural areas (see figure 9.9).

Figure 9.9. Gates can block unwanted use but allow passage when maintenance needs arise.

If a bridge is to be open to motor vehicles or animals or will provide access to any periodic maintenance of a facility, plan the load-bearing capacity of the bridge and its structure accordingly.

Suspension bridges or other high-profile bridge systems that are easily accessible or near the roadside need extra considerations, given their visibility and the increased potential for vandalism or mischief. For example, groups of children might jump on or hang from the bridge to try to make it flex up and down or from side to side. Anti-sway cables attached to each side will make the bridge more stable.

➔ ASSISTANCE

The U.S. Forest Service has extensive experience and information regarding various trail bridge designs. The National Park Service and state park departments may also be able to provide advice and technical assistance. Local engineers, contractors, and utility companies may offer guidance on how to acquire hardware, cable, and other specialty equipment. National Guard units are sometimes willing to take on public service projects and can offer labor and technical help. Check with trail clubs and trail bike and snowmobile organizations for information and contacts. The Professional Trailbuilders Association has information on their website (trailbuilders.org) about locating and working with trail bridge designers and fabricators. American Trails (americantrails.org) provides links to consultants and contractors as well as private and governmental funding sources for trail projects.

➔ INSPECTION AND MAINTENANCE

Inspect bridges and stream crossings annually. Perform regular maintenance and replace materials as necessary. Check wood for soundness, paint or treat with preservative if needed (while taking particular care to protect the water), and fix loose decking and railings. Have a qualified engineer conduct annual inspections of suspension or engineered bridges or any bridge that would likely cause serious injury should it fail. Paint any cables, steel beams, or hardware with rust-resistant paint. Keep a blueprint and photos of each structure on file to aid repair work and documentation. Inspect bridges after flood events and before and after high traffic periods. At these times, take special note of changes to the riverbanks adjacent to the bridge abutments. Examine modifications in the river and evaluate riverbank stability and loss of soil, stone, and vegetation. Sometimes, bridges and water crossings may need to be relocated due to unforeseen bank erosion or other situations that may compromise structural integrity.

CHAPTER 10
SKI TRAILS

AT-A-GLANCE

➔ **Planning ski trails:** Base trail design on good information, including potential users, topography, and target user levels.

➔ **Designing ski trails:** Note striking features and drainage patterns and keep the route interesting.

➔ **Building ski trails:** Construct trails specific to winter use with an option for grooming machinery.

Cross-country skiing, or ski touring, is a fun and increasingly popular sport that provides great exercise (see figure 10.1). Many people consider cross-country skiing a life sport—an activity enjoyed for different reasons at different points throughout one's life. Private cross-country ski areas still attract a significant number of visitors seeking classical skiing on molded tracks and skate-skiing on firm, smooth surfaces. Backcountry skiing (skiing on ungroomed trails or in areas without trails) appeals to those looking for more strenuous activity in wilder environs. Opportunities for ski touring are widespread and exist at all degrees of difficulty—from a jaunt through a neighborhood park to journeys into remote wildlands; from family picnic outings at a local land trust property to multiday cabin-to-cabin excursions.

As skiers and ski technology have become more sophisticated through the years, trail maintainers have improved ski trails and tailored them to specific types of skiing. In the past, adapting existing timber harvest trails, hiking trails, or roads into ski trails was the norm. However, this often resulted in awkward junctions, vast windblown openings, endless climbs, and nearly uncontrollable descents. Trails that are effectively

Figure 10.1. Ski trails provide good recreational opportunities.

designed for skiing are safe and enjoyable and are easily adaptable for other activities, including snowshoeing, cross-country running, mountain biking, and hiking.

Ski touring trails need lots of snow or a smooth pre-snow surface. In most of the United States, the average snowfall has declined over the last 25 years. Winters are generally warmer, and most locations expect later snows, significant thaws, and earlier springs. The ski community has tried to mitigate this weather trend by preparing trails to higher standards. Trail surfaces have become much smoother and often incorporate extensive drainage plans. These surfaces allow skiing with minimal snow and have proved to be relatively maintenance-free. The snow usually retains less water and dries faster, preserving the surface integrity for a longer time. These high-quality trails have become very popular destinations, sometimes because of a lack of snow elsewhere, but often because the combination of dependable skiing surface and varied terrain attracts the interest of skiers.

New cross-country trails are being built throughout the northern United States. Land trusts, schools, and municipal and state parks, as well as clubs, ski teams, companies, and individuals are responding to requests for accessible and reliable outdoor winter recreation. Good ski trails are no longer only available at ski resorts; demand for skiing is bringing trails into local communities.

AMC maintains backcountry ski touring trails in New Hampshire's White Mountains and has constructed ski trails in Maine. It also helps maintain other trails in New Hampshire, Massachusetts, and New Jersey, supporting ski touring as part of a spectrum of outdoor experiences.

➔ PLANNING AND DESIGN

Development of a cross-country ski trail system begins with a determination of need, an evaluation of the expected skiers' experience level, and a projection of user numbers. A critical assessment of the topography and the users' expectations is essential. Refer to Chapters 1 (page 1) and 4 (page 30) for an overview of the applicable elements of trail design.

Maintaining organizations should decide if they want to cater to one type of ski touring experience and expertise level or all types and levels. Topography plays a significant role in this decision. For instance, rough or extremely steep terrain will probably eliminate the possibility of novice trails; flat terrain may not attract more experienced backcountry skiers.

Determination of a standard degree-of-difficulty rating for trails can be somewhat subjective, taking into account many varied factors, including gradient, trail alignment, width, curve radius, and even the visual density of the trailside. Using suggested ski industry standards will aid in this development. The Cross Country Ski Areas Association (ccsaa.org) can be a resource regarding standards and safety. Ideally, a ski touring trail system should contain approximately 50 percent novice trails, 30 percent intermediate, and 20 percent expert. Trail location, terrain, and land management goals will affect this final ratio.

Assess other ski touring opportunities in the region to see if there is a niche to fill, and investigate the potential of connecting with existing trails to establish a larger network. Evaluate other recreational activities and land management practices in the area. Watch for potential conflicts, and mitigate these problems through trail layout and design. One common conflict is the interaction of snowmobiling and cross-country skiing. These two activities may need to be separated for reasons of aesthetics or safety. Timber management may also be a factor affecting winter trail use.

Early in the development process, assess opportunities for expansion and possibilities for future changes in operations. Planning and construction should allow for operational changes and trail expansion. For instance, if considering grooming in the future, design the trail system to allow grooming in loops and, ideally, without traveling over any trail section more than once.

A WORD ON TRACKS

Whether molded by machinery or set by skiers, tracks (smooth parallel grooves) are a precious commodity on ski trails, especially on ungroomed routes with little or no grade. Tracks help keep skis straight, and they offer a firm, stable surface so classic skiers can propel themselves forward easily. Tracks are fragile. Snowmobiles, dogs, sleds, fat bikes, snowshoes, hikers, or discourteous skiers can easily destroy them. After a new snow, tracks that are "skied in" or mechanically made will need an hour for the snow crystals to set before providing firmness and durability. If not on skis or other permitted mode of travel, stay off the tracks!

Well-groomed ski trails.

→ TRAIL LAYOUT

The best time to lay out any ski trail is in the late fall or winter, when leaves are off the trees and visibility is good. As with hiking trails, consult topographic maps and aerial photos to understand the lay of the land and locations of crossings, junctions, and features. Consider the general trail layout process outlined in Chapters 3 (page 24) and 4 (page 30) and the factors specific to ski touring described in this chapter. Traveling a layout on skis or snowshoes in winter is an effective way to evaluate the proposed trails. Flag each route traveled and adjust as needed. This is a great opportunity to check approaches to scenic features and to assure these areas are accessible when covered with snow. Winter layout also helps in identifying how existing drainage affects snow quality to determine construction and maintenance plans.

Best practice is to lay out the trail in a curvilinear route or one that drifts slightly across the terrain and limits long sight lines. Trails that use the existing terrain tend to minimize environmental impact and to save construction and maintenance expenses. Gentle curves and lines add a sense of visual allure without breaking the flow or rhythm of skiing. Watch out for monotony—prolonged uniformity brings boredom. A route should traverse forest and fields, light and dark areas, flats and rolling hills. Break up long climbs and descents with small flats to allow skiers to rest tired muscles or check their speed. Avoid abrupt changes in direction. Use gentle turns to get around obstacles. Watch for overly sinuous trails that break rhythm, as well as long, flat, straight sections. Be willing to rethink and adjust the layout; small changes that ease tight turns and evade difficult ground can lead to significant differences in the construction phase. Walk or ski the route in both directions to assess its suitability. Look for opportunities to add fun stretches, a few challenges, and views of attractive features along the route.

The best formats for ski touring incorporate loops—single loops, stacked loops, or interconnected and compound loops (see figure 10.2). These configurations allow skiers to travel over several trail sections, cover variable distances, and return to the same starting point. A series of loops with various levels of difficulty serves a wide range of abilities.

Consider allowing only one-way traffic on steep trails, places where collisions are likely, or heavily used loops. One-way traffic reduces congestion and provides a greater sense of solitude for the skier.

Point-to-point trails take skiers to a specific place, such as an outlook, and they must then backtrack to the starting point. Although this configuration is common for climbing mountain summits, it is less common (and less welcome) for ski trails. Point-to-point trails are acceptable when connecting two systems or a series of remote cabins. They are also useful if terrain or landowner limitations prevent development of loop trails.

Figure 10.2. Ski trail system design.

➔ SPECIFIC LAYOUT CONSIDERATIONS

Ski touring trails require reliable snow cover. A smooth ground surface enables skiing on minimal snowpack; uneven terrain must have a deeper snow base to provide consistent coverage. Most newly constructed ski trails have much higher standards than trails built even as recently as ten years ago. Newer trails often have extensive drainage plans that include ditches, culverts, grade dips, and broad water bars so the snow surface can endure through thaws or rain events. Siting trails on well-drained ground not only saves construction efforts but also maintains good-quality snow for longer periods.

10

Trails built on smooth and flat surfaces need the least amount of snowfall to open. Old logging roads or naturally occurring benches (flat terrace-like areas) often provide an excellent grade for a trail. Avoid rough terrain that will require a lot of snow cover and significant work. Build terraces or benches on sidehill traverses to provide a flat, stable ski surface. Grooming is often difficult, if not impossible, on unterraced sidehills. Do not include steep sidehills in the initial layout—they are difficult and time-consuming to build. Terracing steep slopes usually demands downslope retaining walls requiring significant work and extensive excavation. Aspect—the direction a hillside faces—and type of vegetation are important factors in siting ski trails. South- and west-facing slopes usually receive the most sun; therefore, snow melts faster, resulting in poor snow retention. In addition, snow and ice crusts form more frequently, and trails with such aspects may demand extra maintenance to keep them safe and usable. Conifers that shade the trail often mitigate effects from the sun, but these dense softwood stands also intercept much of the falling snow before it reaches the ground. The snow in the branches is exposed to the sun and warm temperatures, which causes it to melt and drop water onto the trail, creating potential crusty or icy conditions while not adding to the snowpack. When siting ski touring trails, favor the cooler north- and east-facing slopes and areas of denser vegetation in hardwood or mixed stands.

Recently, in response to unpredictable snowfalls, trail designers have begun to expand openings in the tree canopy to allow more snow to reach the ground. (*Note*: It is good practice to establish trailside openings that receive and store snow to cover bare or icy spots when snow is scarce.)

As important as it is to know where to build ski touring trails, it is equally important to know where *not* to build them. Avoid areas of known avalanche danger, hazardous crossings of waterways, and busy roads. Eliminate or minimize conflicts with other winter recreation, such as snowmobiles, by separating uses and providing adequate visual and sound buffers. It is best practice to keep a distance from roads, as traffic can be distracting and noisy. Look for alternative routes to water crossings. Bogs, ponds, and lakes are often windblown and icy, and they can be dangerous when the ice is thin or wet. Remember, one section of impassable trail can restrict access to the entire trail or a portion of the network.

➔ CONSTRUCTION

Many of the techniques and tools used in constructing hiking trails transfer to ski touring trails. However, there are some specialized trail standards and construction methods specific to cross-country ski trails. Modern trail construction often employs heavy equipment, such as excavators, to establish the tread. These machines—even small, relatively inexpensive models—can pull stumps, move rocks, grade uneven ground, and accomplish a large amount of work quickly. Choose the equipment based on trail width, ground conditions (a tracked machine versus a wheeled one), and the desired finished character of the trail. This choice is often determined by availability. Mini excavators can usually be leased locally, and there is also the possibility that friendly organizations or businesses might donate equipment time.

TRAIL WIDTH

Cross-country ski trails can be any width that balances the aesthetic nature of the trail with skiers' needs. Commercial ski areas build trails wide enough to accommodate visitors who skate and who classic ski. International guidelines for nordic racing suggest widths of a little less than 20 feet. To accommodate snow grooming machinery, plan to size groomed trails generally at least 2 feet wider than the grooming equipment. Be attentive to equipment specifications in the early stages of trail planning if you intend to groom trails.

The width of ski touring trails also depends on difficulty level, type and volume of use, slope, and layout. Easier trails often have a minimum tread width of 10 to 12 feet. Trails designated "more difficult" can range from 8 to 10 feet wide, and "most difficult" trails can be as narrow as 5 to 6 feet. Because skiers may need to snowplow while going down steep grades or herringbone while climbing, trails need to be wide enough to accommodate these techniques. Curves also need to be wider to allow for turning and snowplowing. Generally, increase the trail width 25 percent for two-way traffic, and an additional 25 percent for grades higher than 10 percent or sections where travel may exceed 15 miles per hour.

HEIGHT

Remove branches to a height of 10 to 12 feet above the expected level of snow cover (see figure 10.3). Prune conifer limbs to 14 to 16 feet above the average snow level, as they tend to hold snow and droop under the weight. Hemlock stands often keep snow from reaching the ground, and it is best to prune these to 16 to 18 feet.

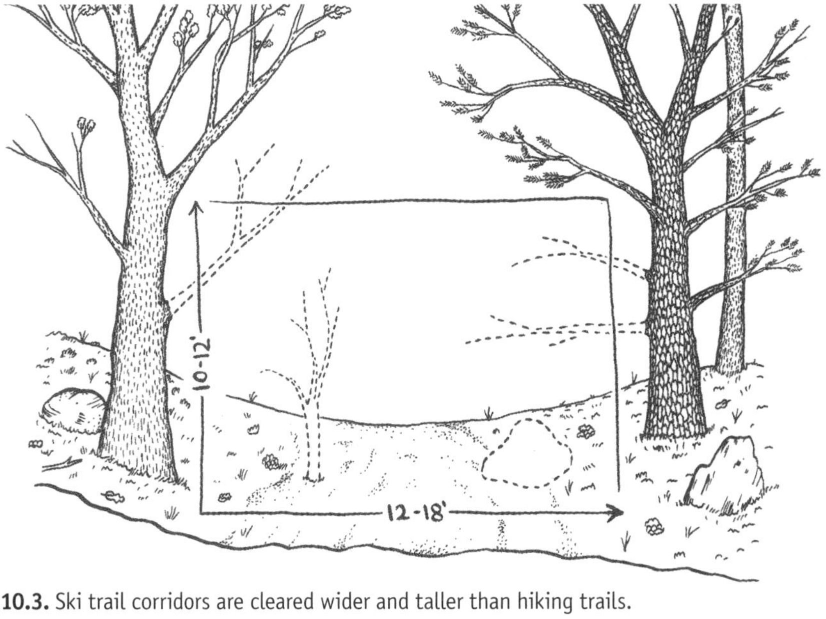

Figure 10.3. Ski trail corridors are cleared wider and taller than hiking trails.

TRAIL TREAD

As noted earlier, the smoother the treadway, the earlier the trail can be used and the longer the skiing season that can be expected. On the trail surface, maintain the natural sod or establish a vegetative covering. This plays a critical role in reducing erosion and catching and retaining the snow cover, especially on slopes. Remove rocks, logs, and other debris. Cut woody vegetation on the treadway flush with the ground. Avoid sandy soils on steep slopes because they are more susceptible to erosion and tend not to hold snow.

Ski touring trails are often built to permit other recreational activities during the snow-free seasons. These trails are built on stable, well-drained soils, and they are generally smooth and slightly crowned to allow surface drainage. Drainage devices, such as ditches, culverts, water bars, and grade dips, are all employed, and the trail surface is sometimes capped with a layer of wood chips, shredded bark, or gravel. Because machinery is often used to create these trails, the initial costs are relatively high, but a very durable, stable, and low-maintenance tread is the result. Skiing can start with very little snow cover, and in summer, hikers, joggers, mountain bikers, and horseback riders can enjoy the trails.

During construction, use seed or mulch to stabilize soils on sidehills and steeper gradients where the tread construction has disturbed the native ground cover. Generally, wood chip and turf surfaces allow skiers to slide more safely across bare spots. Be sure that no obstacle—such as roots or rocks—protrudes more than 4 inches above ground level. On steep sidehill traverses, create a bench that will hold snow and provide a level tread. The placement of logs, rocks, and brush on the downhill side of a slope can sometimes do the same job by collecting and holding snow to form a terrace.

Log corduroy (logs laid perpendicular on the trail), hay, and conifer boughs, or the combination of these materials (see figure 10.4), can be a temporary solution

10

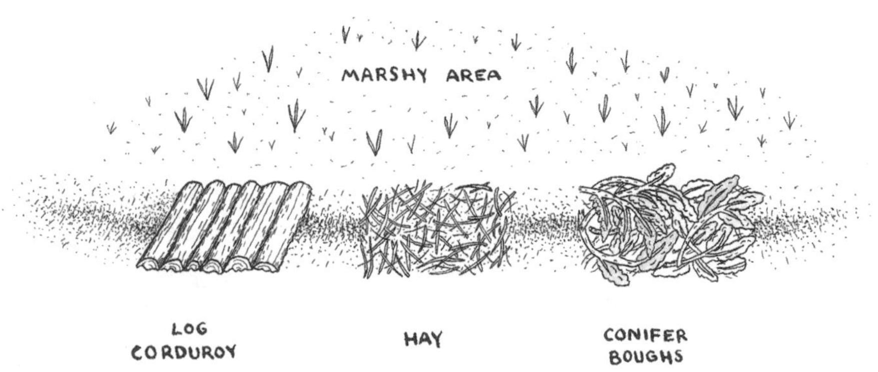

Figure 10.4. Options to firm up wet spots on ski trails.

to traverse short wet or boggy areas, but ditching and filling is more effective and permanent. Most wet areas will continue to melt snow or develop ice until more permanent solutions are employed. Adding mineral soil on top of a geotextile fabric helps disperse loads and minimizes erosion. Open ditches that cross trails often require a small bridge. Culverts can resolve this situation. However, culverts can result in large washouts if installed improperly or not maintained regularly, and they do occasionally freeze and clog. Be certain the culvert size is appropriate for the width of the treadway and the volume of water or snowmelt expected. Plan culvert sizing in larger diameters for good measure. Smooth-interior plastic culverts are more resistant to clogging than corrugated metal and are light enough to drag across a rough corridor when transporting them to the site. (*Note*: Consider using alternatives to culverts, such as short-span bridges, to allow for aquatic organism passage because culverts present a barrier to most aquatic organisms.)

GRADIENT

Variety and challenge should be objectives for any ski trail. Avoid long flats, and intersperse long climbing grades with level sections or short downhills. A good mix of terrain should include approximately one-third flat rolling ground, one-third uphill, and one-third downhill.

Sustained grades (about 200 feet) of 8 percent or less are recommended for novice trails, but maximum grades of 10 percent are acceptable for short distances (100 feet). Intermediate trails should have extended grades (about 300 feet) held at no more than 10 percent and keep maximum grades of 20 percent to 300 feet or less. Expert trails can and should have long, challenging grades, but grades greater than 15 percent generally get exhausting after about 400 feet. A 40 percent grade is the maximum for even expert skiers. Short sections of higher-than-average grade are acceptable at all levels of difficulty. Steeper grades require a wider trail that allows skiers to snowplow, sidestep, or herringbone. On curves, widening alone is not always sufficient. Provide appropriate runouts on curves with slopes by clearing the outside of the curve from the top and continuing along the width well past the curve exit. In addition, the turning radius of curves should match the slope and the skiers' expected speed.

The table below shows the approximate distances a skier will travel before attaining speed on slopes of varying degrees of steepness. These estimates are useful for gauging suitable grades in combination with length of runout, angles of turns, and trail width.

GRADIENT		
Grade in percentages	Grade in degrees	Maximum Length in Feet to Reach 20 MPH
10	6	250–300
12	7	100–125
15	9	80
20	12	60
25	14	40
30	17	30

LENGTH

The lengths of trails depend on the types of skiers who are expected to use them. It is helpful to look at statistics. Skiers usually travel between 2 and 8 miles per hour, with most averaging a little faster than 3 miles per hour. The majority of trails range in length from 4 to 8 miles, and skiers usually plan outings of two to four hours. An integrated system of novice, intermediate, and expert trails provides opportunities for excursions of varied lengths and can accommodate the afternoon, evening, and full-day skier. Generally, novice trails are 3 to 5 miles long and may be shorter when geared toward young children or new skiers. Intermediate trails, usually 5 to 8 miles long, incorporate a combination of easier and more difficult terrain. Expert trails can be longer, but carefully consider the terrain; a trail that climbs for 6 miles may take longer to ski than a rolling trail of equal mileage. Remember that long descents, especially after long climbs, can lead to very cold skiers.

➔ STREAM CROSSINGS AND BRIDGES

Natural stream crossings are inexpensive and can be easy to maintain if the bank has a suitable approach. Choose natural crossings only if the stream is slow and shallow; water needs to freeze early in winter and remain frozen for the crossing to be safe and useful. Even when there is sufficient snow to cover a ski trail, stream crossings—even small ones—may not freeze or may reopen during a thaw and prevent passage. However, after several years of warm winter temperatures and low snow cover, many trail maintainers are no longer able to rely on ice and snow depth for crossings. They have responded by building bridges. Generally, if the trail is dependent on a stream crossing, it is safest to bridge the stream. This can also lengthen the ski season.

The same basic construction principles apply to ski trail bridges as they do to footbridges. The major differences between the two are width, approach configuration, and grades onto and off the bridges. Ski touring bridges should be built 8 to 12 feet wide, if possible, to hold snow and to compensate for crowning (see figure

Figure 10.5. This ski trail bridge accommodates users, snowpack, and equipment.

10.5). If planning to groom the trail with machinery, make the bridge at least as wide as the widest grooming implement—preferably as wide as the trail tread.

Align the ski trail to cross the bridge in a straight line. Do not build a bridge as part of a curve in the trail. If the trail must curve at a stream, plan to have the turn completed before or after the bridge crossing. Consider the expected speed of skiers when approaching a bridge. It is best to have skiers cross a bridge in full control even if it means altering a trail design to slow their approach.

Ideally, a bridge approach grade should be level with trail grade or slightly elevated between 0 and 5 percent. If needed, raise the trail with a ramp or fill in a low spot with rocks and soil. Be sure that skiers cannot catch ski tips under the exposed edge of bridge decking. Placing a face board—typically a piece of decking that caps the end of the log stringers—keeps this from occurring, and the board will also cover the end grain of the stringers, keeping snow from slipping between the stringers and decking.

Bridge projects can get very complex, especially if they involve long or multiple spans, very steep or unstable banks, or the need to support heavy grooming and trail-building equipment. Consider contacting a trail professional or civil engineer if bridge requirements become complicated and/or need to be built to certain load specifications.

Since ski bridges are used when covered with snow, decking can also be made from rawer materials, such as rough-cut decking. Decking laid perpendicular to the direction of skier travel allows skis to slide over the board spaces if snow cover is minimal. Parallel stringers without decking can be used, but the stringers must fit tightly together. Install curbing along the outside edge of the bridge to prevent snow from sloughing off.

If railings are needed, construct them at least 42 inches high. Allow for snow depth when determining railing height, and do not leave railing ends protruding, especially if skiers are expected to cross at fast speeds. If the approach to a bridge is immediately after a steep hill in which skiers may gain significant speed, avoid railings unless the bridge is very high.

Shovel and pack snow onto the deck after the first snowfall to develop and maintain a better base. Since bridge snow tends to develop a distinct crown as winter progresses, it may be necessary to knock this crown down from time to time and spread it across the bridge. If the crown is thin, add more snow. Some maintainers leave a snow shovel hanging on the bridge or on a nearby tree for this work.

➔ TRAIL SIGNS AND MARKING

Post trail difficulty rating signs and information about distances, current conditions, trail closures, and waxing at the trailheads (see figure 10.6). A large map of the entire area is always useful. Also post difficulty ratings at each trail junction. If the trail system has a large number of intersections, adding intersection numbers or letters that correlate with a map is helpful.

Figure 10.6. Ski trail signs.

10

Four-inch plastic cerulean blue diamonds are the standard markers for most ski trails. Plastic diamond markers are available in a variety of colors if needed to distinguish multiple trails. The standard difficulty rating and hazard markers used by most ski touring organizations are often printed on heavy plastic at trail junctions and along the route. A red exclamation point on a yellow plastic triangle is used to mark the beginning of a steep descent or a sharp corner. All plastic signs and markers can be purchased through the Cross Country Ski Areas Association (see appendix A, page 235).

Place signs and markers approximately 5 feet above the highest expected level of snow cover. When attaching signs to trees, use self-drilling Torx screws, and leave the heads sticking out about an inch to allow for tree growth. The Torx head allows the user to apply enough torque to back the screw out even if the tree grows around the exposed length of the screw. Ski trail markings can also be painted to avoid importing bits of plastic into the environment. Areas that are treeless or experience extremely deep snow conditions are marked using poles set in the snow or ground.

CHAPTER 11

KIOSKS AND USER EDUCATION

AT-A-GLANCE

Before hikers begin a trip, they should receive the most recent and accurate information about the trail, as well as safety tips and conservation messages.

- ➔ **Kiosks:** Convey information via a kiosk at the trailhead. Choose a design based on expected traffic and user needs.
- ➔ **Construction and Installation:** Build the bulk of the kiosk off-site. Construction can be time-consuming and expensive.
- ➔ **Education and Information:** Visitors should have access to maps, as well as a description of the trail and any unique features, regulations, and safety information.

Kiosks, or information boards, play an essential role in introducing the visitor to a trail and its environs. Signs, maps, Leave No Trace guidelines, and other information are valuable to both the inexperienced and experienced outdoor traveler. Warning visitors of safety concerns and encouraging responsible use of the outdoors helps to set a precedent and to develop land ethics for future generations using our public lands. There are many different designs for kiosks, but all kiosks serve a similar purpose: to educate and inform.

In recent years, there has been a notable shift in trail use: day hiking has increased, and backpacking has steadily declined. With a growing population taking interest in outdoor activities and with recreational areas becoming more accessible, the potential that a less experienced visitor will use a trail is relatively high. As a result, land managers and trail maintainers need to reach out to all experience levels. Well-designed information kiosks that assist all visitors are a critical factor in the continued stewardship and enjoyment of our public lands and outdoor recreation areas.

➔ KIOSK DESIGNS

Kiosks can range from a single panel containing a few facts to three or more panels with detailed information. They can be constructed in a linear fashion or angled in to surround the user with cover. The size of the kiosk is determined by the type of use in that area, the number of visitors, and the amount of information that needs to be conveyed.

Many kiosks, such as those used in the White Mountain National Forest in New Hampshire, are three-sided with a roof to protect the panels (see figure 11.1). These are at prominent trailheads throughout the forest. Only single-paneled kiosks are needed to relay key information at less visited trailheads in the White Mountains (see figure 11.2).

Figure 11.1, left. Three-sided kiosk.
Figure 11.2, right. Single-paneled kiosk.

Like a trail or bridge, a kiosk should complement the location, the needs of user groups, and the character of the trail. Kiosks should blend into the immediate environment. For example, in a remote area, a rustic and simple design with basic information would be appropriate. However, a residential park or highly populated and easily accessible site might require a larger, more elaborate kiosk to reach a broader audience. Other styles of kiosks, including those that use custom design work, can be chosen for aesthetics and allure. You can see an example of this at the Falling Waters/Old Bridle Path trailhead kiosk in New Hampshire's Franconia Notch State Park: the top is shaped like the profile of a mountain range (see figure 11.3).

Figure 11.3. A kiosk with the profile of a mountain range.

The materials for the construction of the kiosk are as important as its design. Use materials that fit the character of the landscape and are able to convey all necessary information. In remote locations, use round logs or hand-hewn lumber to provide a rustic sense. Milled lumber, metal, or cement are appropriate in a town park or road-accessible area. Many kiosks have hinged panes of Plexiglas secured with a lock so that maintainers can easily and regularly rotate information. Consider the possibilities of theft and vandalism when designing a kiosk. Selecting durable construction materials and anchoring the kiosk firmly in the ground can help prevent damage. Vandal-proof bolts and screws are widely available (as discussed in the "Making Trail Signs" section on page 173 in Chapter 8) and can help protect the structure and information panels.

➔ CONSTRUCTION AND INSTALLATION

First, select the kiosk's general location. In most cases, addressing visitors as they begin their trip is best. Kiosks at trailheads, parking areas, or campgrounds draw users before they head down a trail. Once a general location is selected, locate a specific site. Because many people will walk right up to the panels of the kiosk, the ground around it will be trampled significantly. Consider placing gravel or bark chips around the kiosk to harden and protect the area.

Create detailed plans for construction. Kiosks provide information that land managers and trail maintainers want to convey to the user population. Local history, regulations, safety information, and maps are common components. Illustrated plans will help determine material choices, styles, and colors that will work best for the kiosk's purpose and location. In many cases, land managers will need to review and approve comprehensive procedures and drawings before construction can begin.

Construction can be time-consuming and expensive. Due to the lack of electricity (for power tools) at most trailhead sites, not to mention working space that is level and sufficiently spacious for efficient and high-quality construction, it is recommended that kiosks are pre-built from plans.With this step completed, a group can install the final product by piecing it together on-site.

➔ EDUCATION AND INFORMATION

Since the trailhead is the introduction to a trail and the area, carefully consider the information to be posted before finalizing the size and style of a trailhead kiosk. Introduce visitors to the unique aspects of the location, convey safety information, and stress the importance of stewardship (see figure 11.4). Be selective. If the kiosk is crowded with information, visitors may lose interest or miss important messages.

Concise and inviting signs attract attention. If signs contain long notices with several "don't" phrases, visitors will likely move on without learning the intended information. Incorporating artwork, maps, or photos can be an effective way to keep kiosks interesting and attractive.

Figure 11.4. A kiosk with regulations and information about safety and stewardship.

Think about which messages are most significant for visitors to understand. Resource conservation and stewardship? Dangers? It is often important to highlight a description of how the area is unique. All of this potential information is meaningful in some way, so the real challenge is to keep the communication interesting, simple, and relevant. The possibilities for kiosks are limitless, but here are the basics to include:

- A map or layout of the land. Include trail descriptions if appropriate.
- A brief description of the unique features of the area. Drawings or illustrations of local plants or wildlife can spark readers' interest. Perhaps an important connection to local or national history is worth highlighting.
- Safety information. It is impossible to ensure the complete safety of each visitor, but users can be warned about the known dangers. These may include potential avalanches, stream crossings in high water, quickly changing weather, potable water, wildlife, and poisonous plants or snakes. The information should be clearly posted with suggestions for safe travel.
- Hike Safe principles. These will encourage users to take responsibility for their trip.
- Stewardship information. An understanding of and respect for stewardship can inspire users to cooperate in caring for the local environment and can offer options for visitors to get involved.
- Carry in/carry out message and the Leave No Trace principles. The message and principles focus on taking steps to minimize human impacts on resources, which is an important philosophy that all visitors should take to heart.
- Contact information for the trail organization and land manager.

Once complete, the kiosk can help in outreach and in the education of countless users. However, the materials in the kiosk must be regularly reviewed and updated when necessary. Outdated information can lead to confusion, frustration, or even unsafe conditions.

With some time and thought during the planning and installation of the kiosk, it can serve as a valuable source of information and education for all visitors for many years to come.

CHAPTER 12

ACCESSIBILITY AND UNIVERSAL DESIGN TRAILS

AT-A-GLANCE

Meticulous planning and design with attention to detail will ensure a professionally engineered trail. Navigate accessibility standards and guidelines and select the best materials to achieve the desired specifications.

➔ **Planning and design.** When constructing trails to accessibility and universal design standards, pay extra attention to planning and design.

➔ **Tread surfaces.** A variety of trail surfaces need to be considered with the trail's intended use and users.

➔ **Other design features.** Incorporate specialized design and constitution features for accessible accommodation.

"Accessible" can refer to many trail designs, ranging from universal access trails that can accommodate wheelchairs and are compliant with the Americans with Disabilities Act (ADA) to interpretive trails that are available to most physical abilities. Recently, trails are also being designed for neurodivergent users, such as people with autism. Such trails not only make their way through the wild, but include sensory-friendly activity stations and additional markers alerting hikers to what's coming up next on the route.

Although "accessible" has been a catch-all term referring to a variety of highly engineered trails, a better description would be a "trail that complies with trail accessibility guidelines." Regardless of the extent of accessibility, a few attributes of this type of trail are certain: planning and design are extremely important, materials must be chosen carefully, and construction costs are generally greater than those of less engineered trails (see figure 12.1).

The following sources contain laws, specifications, and guidelines regarding accessible trails:

- Architectural Barriers Act Accessibility Standards
- Forest Service Outdoor Recreation Accessibility Guidelines (FSORAG)
- Forest Service Trail Accessibility Guidelines (FSTAG)
- Outdoor Developed Areas Accessibility Guidelines (ODAAG), developed by the Architectural and Transportation Barriers Compliance Board (United States Access Board)

Find standards and guidelines at the United States Access Board (access-board.gov) or through the specific land management agency resources. Be aware that state, local, or municipal guidelines also may be applicable to components of the project.

Figure 12.1, above. Universal trail designs yield the greatest accessibility.

Figure 12.2, below. Universal trails can have a variety of surfaces.

➔ PLANNING AND DESIGN

When constructing an accessible trail, planning and design of unique elements must take top priority. For example, if designing an ADA-accessible trail, grade and surface material are paramount to be ADA compliant. The trail's purpose and level of accessibility will determine the design and the required features, as well as the costs that differ from a standard trail. Decide if the trail is for recreation, transportation, or a combination of the two. In the context of an urban or suburban environment, a trail could serve both purposes by using a hard surface tread material or finely crushed packed gravel. Therefore, it is important to determine if the specifications for the desired use fit the project area. These trails require intensive planning, design, and layout. They also generally need a larger dedicated trail corridor than standard hiking trails.

➔ TREAD SURFACE CONSIDERATIONS

Level of accessibility, projected user types, and weight considerations determine the tread surface requirements. In general, surfaces can be divided into impermeable, semipermeable, and permeable in regard to drainage and finish. For example, for wheelchair compliance, a hard surface tread (typically asphalt or another aggregate or finely crushed packed gravel) is needed (see figure 12.2). Regardless of the surface material, meticulous maintenance is necessary to maintain accessibility standards.

Hard-surfaced trails tend to be in urban or suburban communities to accommodate a potentially high volume of multiple user types. Often, this type of trail may also serve as a route for local transportation. The best example of this level of trail construction are the rail-trail networks on abandoned railroad grades. These trails are frequently paved or use the existing packed gravel of the grade and can accommodate vehicles and pedestrians.

Finely crushed packed gravel surfaces offer an alternative to asphalt or other impermeable surfaces in areas that have moderate use (see figure 12.3). Depending on the exact makeup of the material and the maintenance performed, these trails can also meet a variety of objectives, including ADA accessibility. This semipermeable material is a good blend of durability and aesthetics.

Figure 12.3. Universal trail with crushed stone.

Figure 12.4. Natural surface trails are common in universal design.

Natural tread surfacing uses native or locally sourced gravel but has been constructed and manipulated with a focus on greater accessibility and clearance (see figure 12.4). This type of surface is suitable for low to moderate use; it is not designed to any specific accessibility guidelines but provides the least number of barriers without extensive engineering. To accommodate users and drainage, these trails should generally be built at less than 15 percent grade and should not cross slopes that are more than 15 percent grade.

➔ TRAIL GRADE

Grade is an extremely important component in the design of an accessible trail. If designing to be ADA compliant, refer to the latest ADA or federal agency specifications. In general, it is best practice to limit grade to less than 10 percent, with a cross slope of no more than 5 percent. Due to slope restrictions, it may be necessary to include long sweeping turns to reach desired features such as overlooks or rest spots. Measure grade with more precise devices and tools, in some cases using survey equipment. (See Chapter 4, page 57, regarding measuring grade for new trail design and layout.)

TREAD SURFACES AND POTENTIAL USERS		
Hard	**Finely Crushed Gravel**	**Natural**
Wheelchair users	Wheelchair users	Bicyclists
Bicyclists	Bicyclists	Walkers
Walkers	Walkers	Equestrians
Runners	Runners	Runners
Skaters	Nordic Skiers	Nordic Skiers
Nordic Skiers		

GENERAL TREAD REQUIREMENTS	
Tread width	36 inches
Tread openings	½ inch
Tread obstacles	2 inches high maximum
Exceptions for tread obstacles	3 inches high when running and cross slope is less than 5 percent

GENERAL SLOPE SPECIFICATIONS	
Percent Slope	**Maximum Distance between Level Landings**
0–5 percent	200 feet
6–8 percent	30 feet
9–10 percent	10 feet
11–14 percent	5 feet

CROSS SLOPE SPECIFICATIONS	
Maximum Cross Slope	**Maximum Distance**
0–2 percent recommended	Any distance
3–5 percent	Any distance
6–8 percent	10 feet
9–12 percent	5 feet

➔ OTHER DESIGN FEATURES

Accessible trails create a highly manipulated experience due to the demanding nature of their specifications. The design and layout will directly influence the user's experience more than that of a standard hiking trail. Take advantage of the opportunity to highlight the topography, cultural resources, and changes in

Figure 12.5, top. Accessible design boardwalk with pull-off.
Figure 12.6, bottom. Accesssible design bridge and boardwalk with railings and curbing.

the environment to offer a more unstructured experience. Intermittently provide pull-offs and areas to get off the main treadway to observe the local ecosystem (see figure 12.5).

By extension, bridges must be designed and constructed to a more finished manner. Regardless of bridge height and accessibility standards, bridges should have railings and curbing (see figure 12.6).

➔ MAINTENANCE

Maintenance of accessible trails requires frequent and intensive attention. The treadway must be kept smooth and unencumbered for easy travel. It is good practice to store extra tread material on-site or nearby for future needs. The tread's shoulder should be maintained like that of a road shoulder and brushed annually or biannually.

CHAPTER 13

TRAIL CREW LEADERSHIP

AT-A-GLANCE

Good leadership, communication, and attentiveness to creating inclusive and equitable spaces will ensure positive project outcomes, crew cohesiveness, and safety.

- ➔ **Leadership.** Good leadership is vital to crew safety, successful work, and camaraderie.
- ➔ **Communication.** Clear instructions and open communication are essential when leading a crew.
- ➔ **Equity and Inclusion.** In order to foster a positive experience for participants, leaders must seek to create equitable and inclusive group culture.
- ➔ **Safe Work Environment.** Physical and emotional safety needs must be met for all crew members.

Leadership is a quality that cannot be purely taught but must be learned, practiced, and refined. Leadership style in the context of a trail crew can shape the work atmosphere and the quality of the project. Good leadership is essential for a safe, productive, and healthy working environment. A leader doesn't necessarily have expertise in all disciplines but is proficient in most and can learn and refine skills while simultaneously guiding others. Generally, there are three main components to good crew leadership:

1. **Technical skills**. A good leader has extensive knowledge of the technical skills required for trail work, as well as training and experience on the related safety components.
2. **Leadership skills.** A good leader exhibits strong work ethics and promotes a culture of safety and a positive work environment.
3. **Management skills.** A good leader possesses the ability to efficiently coordinate and smoothly manage a crew, materials, and scheduling.

A crew leader's credibility hinges on technical skills and experience. The stronger the skills, the easier crew leadership can be. This doesn't mean that crew leaders must be experienced in every discipline. Rather they possess the appropriate skills for a particular project and are able to learn new skills and to adapt to changing conditions while simultaneously leading a crew. In fact, mastering a discipline doesn't necessarily make one a good leader. Some people are more naturally leaders, and others may have strong skills but are not interested in leadership responsibilities.

AMC and other outdoor organizations offer leadership training courses in which the skills taught can be carried over to leading trail crews, including courses in diversity, equity, and inclusion. Another resource for leadership training is the book *AMC Guide to Outdoor Leadership*.

➔ EQUITY, INCLUSION, AND DIVERSITY

When leading trail crews and when training future leaders, it is imperative to foster a culture of equity and inclusion that values and celebrates diversity. Diversity in this context means that intentionally and proactively building teams whose makeup includes people from historically and systemically marginalized populations. These groups include women, racial and ethnic minorities, LGBTQIA+ individuals, people living with disabilities, and more. Equity means that all people will have equal access to resources. It also accounts for systemic barriers and oppression that exist. Last, inclusion goes beyond just welcoming folx (including queer, trans, non-binary people of color), but rather seeks to celebrate and amplify those who have been historically marginalized. (Definitions adapted from the Avarna Group.) All trail crew leaders, crew members, and volunteers have the responsibility to be active in equity, inclusion, and diversity work and to help create a culture free of bias.

The work of equity, inclusion, and diversity is constantly evolving and is a lifelong learning endeavor. The act of fostering inclusive and equitable group spaces begins with a leader understanding their own biases and reflecting on the ways in which they show up in the world. Once with a group, leaders are responsible for modeling this behavior and setting up structures that support equity and inclusion such as group norms, open communication, and respect for all participants and their lived experience.

➔ COMMUNICATION

Good leadership begins with good communication. Clear and open communication is essential to safety, productivity, and overall morale. A leader's style of communication and expression sets the tone and expectations of communication within the crew. Listening is imperative and will ensure trust and better understanding. There are many ways to develop good communication skills. The following are some basic points to remember.

- Identify: Establish a position to give instructions or make requests
- Request: Clearly state request or instructions
- Probe: Ask listener if there are any questions
- Clarify: Answer listener's questions
- Seal: Reiterate request or instructions

It may not be necessary to use this entire list every time you communicate with someone, but it provides a good base from which to work. It ensures that instructions are clear, questions are answered, and expectations are understood.

➔ EXPECTATIONS

It is important to establish clear expectations for a project regarding the timeline, desired results, and daily goals. Get to know the motivations and aspirations of individuals and the crew as a whole, as well as their own expectations. This helps in identifying skills that need to be learned and in assigning workers to specific work projects or teams. The clearer the expectations of the leader, the better the experience, work quality, and sense of responsibility of the crew. In addition, forming a goal-oriented culture will foster camaraderie and fulfillment with the project.

➔ CREATING A SAFE WORK ENVIRONMENT

The first and foremost responsibility of the crew leader is the safety of the crew. A safety culture needs to be established early on in crew development. The leader must set pacing and provide adequate breaks during workdays. This is important because it will affect the functioning of the crew.

Another essential aspect of leadership is fostering a work environment that engenders trust and is open to grievances and issues being brought forward and addressed in confidence. There are two main issues that crew leaders commonly need to manage: violations of technical and safety issues, and interpersonal concerns that are disruptive to the crew. Even though it is important to foster an open environment, it is also paramount to establish authority in this context. It must be made absolutely clear that physically and verbally abusive actions and sexual harassment will not be tolerated. Incidents that involve these kinds of behaviors need to be dealt with swiftly and firmly.

It is vital for a crew leader to be proactive and not reactive. Good leaders anticipate problems before they arise and take preventive actions.

Conflict is inevitable. However, conflict handled well can lead to positive outcomes by promoting change and increasing cohesiveness. Ultimately, effective handling of conflict instills confidence and trust among the crew and between the crew and leader.

In conflict resolution, be aware that the real issues may not always be apparent. Separate the people involved in the conflict from the rest of the crew to provide privacy and confidentiality. Remember to listen and avoid prejudgments. Clarify the issues and find common ground between those involved in the dispute. Cultivate open dialogue and build trust. Identify resolution as the ultimate goal.

➔ TRAINING

Good leaders provide further training opportunities for the crew. This encourages continued learning, leadership, and problem solving. Offer increased responsibility to individuals who are proficient in their technical skills and welcome a challenge.

➔ TRAIL CREW DYNAMICS

Trail crew culture varies depending on region, agency, experience, and personalities. It is important to understand background, gender, race, ethnicity, and other factors within the crew. Foster a work environment of acceptance and inclusivity. Be aware of bias and stay observant of crew behavior.

A successful crew is typically a mix of personality types. Diverse crews benefit from the perspectives brought to the collective. It is helpful to understand the personality, strengths, and motivations of each crew member to determine the supervision style that is most effective.

It is imperative to praise work well done. This contributes to the camaraderie, motivation, and morale of the overall crew. Praise individuals and the crew as often as reasonably justified, especially if working with volunteers. Feedback is also important, especially constructive feedback. For example, compliment what worked well on the project, mention something that could be improved, and then weigh the positive over the negative attributes. The goal is to foster good work and to encourage that activity into the future; do not dwell on what didn't work.

➔ LEAVE NO TRACE AND TRAIL WORK

Leave No Trace™
Center for Outdoor Ethics | LNT.org

To help preserve the quality of the sites that we visit, AMC's Trails Programs promote a minimal impact camping ethic specific to the type of sites we use. These are guidelines, not rules, and must be accompanied by an underlying respect for the wilderness.

SEVEN PRINCIPLES OF LEAVE NO TRACE:

- Plan ahead and prepare
- Travel and camp on durable surfaces
- Dispose of waste properly
- Leave what you find
- Minimize use and impact of fires
- Respect wildlife
- Be considerate of other visitors

These principles are specific to the mountains and forests of the Northeast. Consider also site-specific variables of soils, vegetation, wildlife, moisture level, and the amount and type of use that the area receives.

These principles are important for hikers and backcountry travelers but also apply to trail work. Everything is related to minimizing and concentrating impact.

1. Plan ahead and prepare

Carefully designing your trip to match your expectations and outdoor skill level is the first step in being prepared.

- Know the area and what to expect. Many resources are available effective planning—guidebooks, local land managers (USFS), maps, other guides, and instructors.
- Keep group size to ten. The Appalachian Trail and Wilderness Areas in the White Mountains (that is, Great Gulf, Pemigewasset, Dry River, Caribou-Speckled, Sandwich Range) are limited to groups of ten.
- Select appropriate equipment. Be prepared to set up a low-impact campsite with stoves, tents, and bear line. Carry a trowel for digging cat holes.
- Repackage food. Repackaging food eliminates extra weight and minimizes potential litter in the backcountry.

2. Travel and camp on durable surfaces

In high use areas, some impact may be unavoidable. Concentrating impact on durable surfaces (rock, sand, gravel, snow, pine needles, or leaf litter) or established trails, tent sites, or shelters minimizes impact on more vulnerable sites.

- In popular areas, find sites that have already been affected or "hardened" and will not be affected much by additional use.
- Stay on trails. Avoid stepping off the trail and trampling vegetation. Encourage participants to wear gaiters to protect them from mud and water on wet sections of trail. Do not shortcut switchbacks.

- In alpine areas walk only on the trail or on exposed rock. Alpine vegetation faces the challenges of thin soils and harsh conditions, and these plants are especially sensitive to the impact of careless hikers/campers.
- Choose an established campsite away from trails and water. The site should be at least 200 feet from trails and water and at least ¼ mile from huts, shelters, and trailheads.
- Select appropriate and durable campsites. Good campsites are found, not made. Camp on durable surfaces and do not stay in the same location for more than one or two nights. Make your site visually unobtrusive—it should not be visible from the trail.
- Leave your site clean. Allow affected sites to remain appealing. Try to leave the site better off than you found it.
- When breaking camp, naturalize the site. Replace rocks, logs, and twigs that you have moved. Survey the site for any impacts, such as spilled food that you may have left behind. Make sure that the site does not invite others to camp there after you.

  Trail camps. In choosing a new campsite, recognize that this site will get used much more than the typical camp. A camp should be durable and well hidden so as not to attract other users. Limit designated trails within the site to concentrate impact. Brush in the beginning of the access trail at the end of each week to keep the site low-key. Always keep the site clean to avoid attracting animals and for the benefit of the next crew that comes in.

  Trail work. When quarrying, use designated trails to concentrate impact. In alpine areas, rock-hop when quarrying and always use the "bucket brigade" technique to pass rocks as opposed to individuals traveling through vegetation to get rocks. Never pull rocks out of soil in alpine zones.

3. Dispose of waste properly

- Reduce litter at the source. Repackaging food before entering the backcountry reduces the amount of trash to be packed out and eliminates unnecessary weight. Leave bulky packaging and easily lost items (such as twist ties) at home.
- Dispose of trash and garbage properly. Any trash you generate is your responsibility to pack out—this includes paper or cardboard, leftover food (even orange peels and apple cores!), toilet paper, and similar items. Burning waste or throwing trash into outhouses is not an acceptable disposal practice.
- Dispose of human waste responsibly. Correctly disposing of human waste protects water sources, prevents spread of illnesses, and eliminates unaesthetic impact on other visitors. When possible, use outhouses.

- Cat holes: Cat holes should be at least 200 feet from water, trails, and campsites. Holes should be dug 6 to 8 inches into deep, dry, organic soil. This depth is suggested so that animals will not dig up the holes but they are still in the layer of soil where most of the microorganisms live and can therefore help with decomposition. After use, mix in some soil with a stick and then fill in and disguise the hole.
- Urination: Urine poses very little threat to human health, but you may want to urinate away from camp simply to avoid odors and the animals they may attract. Urine on snow is also unsightly but can easily be covered.

- Toilet paper and personal hygiene products: Both toilet paper and hygiene products must be packed out in Ziploc bags—burying is not an effective means of disposal because animals may dig them up. Used hygiene products should be hung up in a bear bag while the campsite is still in use so as not to attract animals. Encourage experimentation with alternative forms of toilet paper (for example, smooth rocks, leaves, snow).
- Minimize soap and food residues in wastewater. Soap is unnecessary in dish washing; hot water, sand, and duff from the forest floor work well for scrubbing and sanitizing. Remove all food scraps and floaters from dishwater by straining the used water through a screen or green dish scrubber. Scatter the water away from camp. Do not sump wastewater.
- Be careful with food and odors in bear country. Read local postings about bear activity, and make your camp bear-proof by hanging all food and toiletries (including used personal hygiene products) on a bear line 10 feet off the ground, 4 feet from nearby trees, and 100 feet from tents.

4. Leave what you find

- Minimize campsite alterations. Choose a campsite that you can enjoy in its natural state without building lean-tos, benches, or fire rings. If you find a site where these already exist, help return the site to its original state by dismantling them (leave fire rings in areas where they are legal and properly located because they prevent further impact).
- Avoid damaging trees and plants. Place tents on durable surfaces. Although flowers, wild edibles, and tree barks are tempting to collect, think about how much impact visitors can have if every person takes a few flowers or other plants.
- Do not disturb natural and cultural artifacts. In addition to leaving growing plants for future animal and human visitors to enjoy, leave artifacts—such as rocks, antlers, and remains of old logging camps—where they are found.
- Respect private land. Many trails pass through privately owned property. Park in designated areas and enjoy the privilege of using the land without negatively affecting it.

Trail work. Avoid cutting out vegetation, dead or alive, for quarry trails. When finished with a quarry trail, brush it in well and as naturally as possible.

5. Minimize Use and Impact of Fires

- Know and follow fire restrictions. Some sections of the Appalachian Trail and other trails prohibit fires. Be properly prepared by always carrying a lightweight stove for cooking.
- Make your fire small and safe. Where fires are permitted, build them in a responsible manner that will not leave a lasting impact. Gather dead and downed wood from a wide area rather than just around your site. Use small-diameter wood and keep your fire controlled.
- Select a fire site carefully. Only burn where it will not leave lasting impact in the form of scars and damaged organic soil. Fire pans (which you can carry in and out with you), mound fires (controlled fires built on 6 to 8 inches of mounded mineral soil as an insulating layer), and twiggy fires (built on top of frying-baking pans for baking) are all acceptable ways to enjoy a fire in the wilderness without leaving permanent damage.

6. Respect Wildlife

- Observe from a distance. Always watch or photograph animals from far away so as not to startle them or force them to flee. Avoid quick movements and direct eye contact, which may be interpreted as aggressive.
- Be aware of sensitive times and habitats. Consider the seasonal stresses that wildlife face. In some situations, stay clear of animal habitats for your safety as well as that of the animals.
- Never feed animals. Feeding wild animals damages their health, alters natural behaviors, and exposes them to predators and other dangers.
- Store food and trash securely. "Food" includes garbage, canned food, stock feed, pet food, fuel, and scented or flavored toiletries. In bear country, hang food and the items listed here from tree limbs 12 feet off the ground, 6 feet from the tree's trunk, and 6 feet below the supporting limb, or store them in specially designed bear-resistant canisters or on-site lockers.
- Control your pet. Wildlife and pets are not a good mix. Even on a leash, dogs harass wildlife and disturb other visitors.

Trail camps. Food storage must be neat and clean all the time! Prevent odors by cleaning recyclables with dishes after meals; separating trash, recycling, and compost and keeping compost in a tight container; picking up food scraps after every meal; and cleaning stoves nightly.

7. Be considerate of other visitors

- Respect other visitors and protect the quality of their experience. Choose and maintain a cooperative spirit in wild lands. Although our motivations and sense of adventure vary, there's always room on the trail for people with open minds and generous hearts.
- Yield to others. Simple courtesies, such as offering a friendly greeting on the trail, wearing earth-toned clothing to blend in with the scenery, stepping aside to let someone pass, waiting patiently for a turn, or preserving the quiet, all make a difference.
- Let nature's sounds prevail. As much as possible, keep noise down, especially at night or in remote areas.

  Trail work. Keep your crew's volume down as much as possible while working. When taking breaks, leave the trail clear for hikers to pass by.

For Leave No Trace information and materials, contact the Leave No Trace Center for Outdoor Ethics, P.O. Box 997, Boulder, CO 80306; 800-332-4100 or 302-442-8222; lnt.org. For a schedule of AMC Leave No Trace courses, see outdoors.org/education/lnt.

GLOSSARY

adze A cutting tool with a blade set at a right angle to its handle, used for hewing timber by hand.

backfill Mineral soil used to support a drainage structure. Backfill is used behind a rock or log water bar or to reinforce a drainage dip.

basic maintenance (annual maintenance) Involves four tasks, listed in order of priority: cleaning drainage, clearing blowdowns, brushing, and blazing or marking. All should be done annually or more often if needed.

bevel An angle less than 90 degrees. In trail work it pertains to the angle of a tool's blade.

bog bridge A low wood bridge that helps hikers cross muddy or wet sections of trail. Bog bridges are made of two base logs and one to three stringers.

bucking saw A crosscut saw used for applications other than felling. It is wider, stiffer, and heavier than a felling crosscut saw. It also has a straight back, unlike the concave back of the felling saw.

buffer zone The land on each side of the trail treadway. Buffer zones shield the hiker from activities that are detrimental to the hiking experience, such as housing development, mining, or logging. Also known as *protective zone.*

bull rail Curbing that is installed on either edge of bridge decking for safety or to retain snow for winter use.

check dams Steplike structures perpendicular to the trail that aid in soil retention. They can be made of either rock or wood.

circle of danger The area surrounding a worker that is unsafe due to tool use. The inner (or primary) circle of danger is the area the tool can reach while the worker is using it. The outer (or secondary) circle of danger is the area the tool could reach if the worker lost control or let go of the tool.

crib stairs These are used where livestock lives or where the terrain is not steep enough to warrant rock stairs. They consist of a frame of either rock or wood, which is then filled with rock of graduating sizes down to the stepping surface of gravel or mineral soil. Crib stairs retain existing soil and prevent further erosion on a slope while creating flat platforms that are pleasing to both hikers and pack stock. Also referred to as *check stairs* or *terrace stairs.*

cribbing or crib box A vertical support column for a bridge or pier that is typically made from short logs placed in an overlapping manner, similar to that of a log cabin.

definers Structures that channel or focus foot traffic onto a hardened or harder tread, thus protecting soils that may be wet, thin, or supporting fragile plant life. Scree and rock steps are examples of definers.

drainage Devices or structures, such as water bars, drainage dips, and ditches, that remove water from the trail tread or prevent water from entering the tread and thus limit or eliminate the effects of erosion.

duffing The process of scraping off leaf litter, pine needles, roots, bark, and the dark, organic, decomposed layer of soil below. It is the first stage in tread construction.

easement Grants a nonowner the right to use a specific portion of land for a specific purpose. Easements may be limited to a certain period of time or may be granted in perpetuity; in some cases, termination may be predicated upon the occurrence of a particular event. An easement agreement survives transfer of land ownership and is generally binding upon future owners until it expires on its own terms.

erosion control Includes work or devices designed to control surface erosion (drainages, hardeners, definers, and stabilizers).

fee simple A complete transfer of land ownership from one landowner to another party, usually by purchase. Also known as *fee purchase* or *ownership-in-fee.*

felling saw A crosscut saw used for felling trees. A felling crosscut saw is narrower and more flexible than a bucking crosscut saw and has a slightly concave back. The increased flexibility and lightness make it easier to wield during the felling process.

grade A measurement of the rate of rise of a trail, road, or slope. Expressed as a percentage. A trail that rises 9 vertical feet in 100 horizontal feet has a 9 percent grade. Grade is different from angle; angle is measured with a straight vertical as 90 degrees and straight horizontal as 0 degrees. A grade of 100 percent has an angle of 45 degrees.

gravel An assortment of small stones, often between ¼ inch and 1 inch each.

hardeners Objects used to eliminate the impact of foot travel through wet areas. Hardeners include bog bridges, stepping-stones, and turnpikes (a raised tread).

hew see *adze.*

lease The grant of an interest in land upon payment of a determined fee. The fee does not have to be monetary, but some consideration must be given for the right to use the land or the lease will not be legally binding.

license In trail work, this is a document that allows the licensed party to enter the land of the licensor without being deemed a trespasser.

mineral soil Found below the organic horizon, mineral soil comprises clays, silts, sands, and other inorganic materials. Mineral soil can provide a stable and durable treadway when properly drained.

oral agreement Generally, a contract involving the sale of real estate is not binding unless it is in writing. Therefore, an oral agreement that transfers ownership of land is not legally binding. Although some types of agreements for the use of land need not be written, an oral agreement will always be difficult to enforce because the parties may disagree over the original terms of their contract. An oral agreement is therefore inappropriate for use in a trail project except possibly during the preliminary planning stages.

outflow The off-treadway ditch portion of a drainage structure, intended to remove all water from the trail.

pin rock A medium-sized rock, usually 150 to 250 pounds, whose mass is used to anchor a log step or water bar.

pinned stairs Steps of wood or rock, or an entire wood ladder, secured to a slab rock surface with rebar.

rock treadway A trail surface hardened by using well-placed flat rocks, much like a backyard patio. Also called *rock patio.*

rubble Small- to medium-sized rocks scattered around the trail to prevent hiker traffic, particularly in alpine zones.

rubble wall A simplified version of a retaining wall, consisting of rocks that are not neatly placed together. Helps retain a slope or prevent hiker travel.

scree Material used to define a trail and/or to channel hiker traffic. Made of medium to large rocks, scree is set along rock staircases to stabilize soils and to direct hikers onto the staircases. Scree is also built into walls in alpine areas to define the treadway and keep hikers off fragile vegetation.

sheave The groove wheel for holding a wire rope within a pulley or block. The wheel spins on an axle, reducing friction and wear on the rope.

sidehill trail A type of trail, often literally cut out of the side of a hill, that gains elevation by moving up a slope, gradually following the contour. Sidehill trails are well suited for accessible trails, routes used by pack animals, or other applications where grade must be limited.

stabilizers Structures to hold soil in place and prevent erosion from water, hiking traffic, gravity, or other forces. Stabilizers include rock stairs (for steep-gullied or eroding slopes) and crib stairs (to anchor soil above or below a trail on a slope).

stepping-stones Large stones carefully placed in the tread to allow hikers to step from one to another to cross a small stream or long muddy section of trail.

stringer A horizontal piece (often a log) in a bridge or wood turnpike that runs parallel to the trail and gives support to the structure.

switchback Used to gain elevation on sidehill trails, a switchback is a zigzagging section of trail that turns in one direction and then makes a sharp turn in the opposite direction.

terminus Term applied to both the trailhead (the start of the trail, usually at roadside) and the destination (a mountain summit, waterfall, mill site, or similar feature).

trail *Webster's New World Dictionary* defines a trail as "a blazed or trodden path through a wild region," but it's more than that; a good trail also protects the region it passes through from damage.

trail corridor Includes the treadway, right of way, buffer zone, and all the lands that make up the environment of the trail as experienced by the hiker. The U.S. Forest Service has called it the "zone of travel influence."

trail right of way The area around the treadway that is cleared for the passage of the hiker. It is usually 4 to 6 feet wide, depending on vegetation density. If a trail has other uses besides hiking, such as cross-country skiing or mountain biking, the right of way will likely be wider. The term "right of way" also refers to legal right of passage, as would be the case with a protected trail on private land.

trailhead The beginning of a trail.

tread or treadway The surface on which the hiker makes direct contact with the ground. It is the location for virtually all improvements intended to conserve soil resources.

turnpike A box made of log stringers or rocks and filled with smaller rocks and mineral soil. It is used to both harden and elevate the trail in a muddy or wet section.

visioning The first phase in the trail project planning process, which involves conceptualizing the trail project.

APPENDIX A

➔ SUPPLIERS OF TOOLS, EQUIPMENT, AND MATERIALS FOR TRAIL WORK

This list is not complete. The companies listed are some of the ones that AMC purchases tools and other supplies from most frequently. Many of the more common tools can be purchased from hardware stores, home supply centers, or other specialty stores. Most of these companies are wholesalers and/or manufacturers and may sell direct, but only in bulk. These brands can be found or ordered at many hardware stores, or call the company for the name of a local dealer.

Cross Country Ski Areas Association (CCSAA)
xcski.org
P.O. Box 818, Woodstock, VT 05091
802-236-3021
Provides nordic industry support via membership.

E.T. Techtonics
ettechtonics.com
214 Industrial Ln., Alum Bank, PA 15521
888-274-7855
contact@ettechtonics.com
Supplier of engineered fiberglass bridges and building systems.

Forestry Suppliers, Inc.
forestry-suppliers.com
205 West Rankin St., P.O. Box 8397, Jackson, MS 39284
800-647-5368 (orders), 800-543-4203 (fax)
Forestry Suppliers, Inc. sells many of the tools and supplies a trail worker might need. For a catalog, call 800-360-7788.

Griphoist Division of Tractel, Inc.
tractel.com
51 Morgan Dr., Norwood, MA 02062
800-421-0246, 781-828-3642 (fax)
AMC uses the Griphoist most often with rock work, but recognizes it as an extremely durable and useful tool all around.

Labonville, Inc.
labonville.com
504 Main St., Gorham, NH 03581
800-764-9969, 603-752-7621 (fax)

Labonville is an honest-to-goodness North Woods logging supply company, with a long history of selling top-quality safety gear and clothing for the logger, as well as a full line of work and outdoor clothing, boots, tools, and other gear.

Lansing Forge Inc.
lansingforge.com
142 Main St., Leetonia, OH 44431
330-427-6242, 330-427-6128 (fax)

Lansing Forge (Leetonia division) makes many "high-grade construction, hardware, and marine tools." For the trail worker, Lansing Forge makes pick mattocks, picks, cutter mattocks, rock bars (which they call wedge point or pinch point crow bars), tampers, and other specialty tools. Their tools are very rugged and will hold up to many years of hard use.

Seymour Tools
5790 Walnut Wood Way, Dayton, OH 45415
888-274-2451, 937-535-2750 (fax)

Parent company of O.P. Link Handle Company. Wooden tool handle manufacturer.

Snow & Nealley Co.
theworkingaxes.com
Smyrna, ME 04763

Snow & Nealley makes what we believe to be the best single-bit ax on the market today. In fact, new trails department employees are issued new Snow & Nealley 3½-pound axes as part of their orientation. S&N also makes draw shaves, bark spuds, broad axes, mauls, cant dogs and hooks, timber tongs, pulp hooks, and pickeroons. Their tools are American made and carry a lifetime warranty.

Trail Services
trailservices.com
P.O. Box 8057, Bangor, ME 04402
207-947-2723, 207-945-6050 (fax)

Trail Services provides any trail tool, Griphoists, rock drills, hand tools, lightweight generators, stone tools, and lots of good technical info in the yearly catalogs.

Trow and Holden Inc.

trowandholden.com
45 South Main St., Barre, VT 05641
802-476-7221, 802-476-7825 (fax)
info@trowandholden.com

Trow and Holden has been manufacturing stone-cutting tools for 130 years. It produces stone-cutting, carving, and shaping hand and mechanized tools and equipment.

Voss Signs LLC

vosssigns.com
P.O. Box 553, Manlius, NY 13104-0553
800-473-0698, 315-682-7335 (fax)
sales@VossSigns.com

Voss manufactures stock and custom aluminum and plastic signs and markers for forests, parks, wildlife preserves, private property, and other applications. They specialize in custom signs and have complete typesetting and art facilities.

APPENDIX B

➔ RECOMMENDED READING

Birchard, William, Jr. and Robert D. Proudman. *Appalachian Trail Design, Construction, and Maintenance, 2nd ed.* (Harpers Ferry, WV: Appalachian Trail Conservancy, 2000). 237 pp. Available at 888-287-8673 or atctrailstore.org.

Birkby, Robert C. *Lightly on the Land: The SCA Trail Building and Maintenance Manual, 2nd ed.* (Seattle, WA: The Mountaineers, 2005). 344 pp. Available at 800-553-4453 or mountaineers.org.

Doucette, Joseph E. and Kenneth D. Kimball. "Passive Trail Management in Northeastern Alpine Zones: A Case Study." In: More, Thomas A., et al., eds. *Proceedings of the 1990 Northeastern Recreation Research Symposium*, Saratoga Springs, NY, Feb. 25–28, 1990. U.S. Forest Service, General Tech. Report NE-145:195–201.

Griswold, Stephen. Trail Handbook: Sequoia and Kings Canyon National Parks. (Three Rivers, CA: U.S. Department of Interior, National Park Service, 1991). 86 pp.

Hallman, Richard G. "Handtools for Trail Work: 2005 Edition." 0523-2310-MTDC. (Missoula, MT: U.S. Department of Agriculture, Forest Service, Missoula Technology and Development Center, 2005). 54 pp. Available at www.fhwa.dot.gov/environment/recreational_trails/publications/fs_publications/05232810/.

Hesselbarth, Woody; Vachowski, Brian; and Davies, Mary Ann. "Trail Construction and Maintenance Notebook: 2007 Edition." 0723-2806-MTDC. (Missoula, MT: U.S. Department of Agriculture, Forest Service, Missoula Technology and Development Center, 2007). 178 pp. Available at www.fhwa.dot.gov/environment/recreational_trails/publications/fs_publications/07232806/.

Michael, David and Brian Vachowski. "Saws That Sing: A Guide to Using Crosscut Saws." 0423 2822. (Missoula, MT: U.S. Department of Agriculture, Forest Service, Missoula Technology and Development Center, 2004). 64 pp. Available at www.fhwa.dot.gov/environment/recreational_trails/publications/fs_publications/04232822/.

Miller, Warren. "Crosscut Saw Manual." Gen. Tech. Rep. 7771-2508-MTDC. (Missoula, MT: U.S. Department of Agriculture, Forest Service, Missoula Technology and Development Center, 1988). 28 pp. Available at www.fhwa.dot.gov/environment/recreational_trails/publications/fs_publications/77712508/.

Mrkich, Dale and Jerry Oltman. "Hand Drilling and Breaking Rock for Wilderness Trail Maintenance." 8423 2602. (Missoula, MT: U.S. Department of Agriculture, Forest Service, Missoula Technology and Development Center, 1984). 27 pp. Available at www.fhwa.dot.gov/environment/recreational_trails/publications/fs_publications/84232602/.

Parker, Troy Scott. *Natural Surface Trails by Design: Physical and Human Design Essentials of Sustainable, Enjoyable Trails.* (Boulder, CO: Natureshape, 2004). 80 pp. Available at natureshape.com.

Snodgrass, Kathleen. "Forest Service Trail Accessibility Guidelines (FSTAG) Pocket Version." 1523-2812-MTDC. (Missoula, MT: U.S. Department of Agriculture, Forest Service, Missoula Technology and Development Center, 2015.) Available at www.fhwa.dot.gov/environment/recreational_trails/publications/fs_publications/.

Steinholz, Robert T. and Brian Vachowski. "Wetland Trail Design and Construction 2007 Edition." 0723 2804. (Missoula, MT: U.S. Department of Agriculture, Forest Service, Missoula Technology and Development Center, 2007). 90 pp. Available at www.fhwa.dot.gov/environment/recreational_trails/publications/fs_publications/07232804/.

Webber, Peter, ed. *Trail Solutions: IMBA's Guide to Building Sweet Singletrack.* (Boulder, CO: International Mountain Bicycling Association, 2004). 272 pp. Available at imba.com.

———. *Managing Mountain Biking: IMBA's Guide to Providing Great Riding.* (Boulder, CO: International Mountain Bicycling Association, 2007). 256 pp. Available at imba.com.

Weisgerber, Bernie and Brian Vachowski. "An Ax to Grind: A Practical Ax Manual." 9923 2823P. (Missoula, MT: U.S. Department of Agriculture, Forest Service, Missoula Technology and Development Center, 1999). Available at www.fhwa.dot.gov/environment/recreational_trails/publications/fs_publications/99232823/.

Zeller, Janet; Doyle, Ruth; and Snodgrass, Kathleen. "Accessibility Guidebook for Outdoor Recreation and Trails." 1223-2806P-MTDC. (Missoula, MT: U.S. Department of Agriculture, Forest Service, National Technology and Development Program, 2012.) Available at www.fhwa.dot.gov/environment/recreational_trails/publications/fs_publications/.

"North Country Trail Handbook." (Lowell, MI: North Country Trail Association, 2019). Available at northcountrytrail.org/volunteer/volunteer-resource-center/trail-management/.

➔ INTERNET LINKS AND RESOURCES

americanhiking.org American Hiking Society. Hosts National Trails Day annually.

americantrails.org American Trails. Provides information on all types of trails, trainings, resources, library, calendar of events, online bookstore.

www.fhwa.dot.gov/environment/recreational_trails/publications/fs_publications Forest Service Publications.

lnt.org Leave No Trace. Educational resources promoting minimum-impact practices in the outdoors.

pcta.org Pacific Crest Trail Association. Online curricula for Trail Skills College courses.

pnts.org Partnership for the National Trails System. Online resources focused on the member not-for-profit trail organizations and federal agency partners that are part of the 30 national scenic and historic trails within the National Trails System.

railstotrails.org Rails to Trails Conservancy. Information on trail project planning, funding, and so on.

trailbuilders.org The Professional Trailbuilders Association. A source for information on professional trail builders and contractors, resource links, equipment information, project solutions, employment opportunities, and training.

worldtrailsnetwork.org World Trails Network. A consortium of trails organizations worldwide.

APPENDIX C

➔ LIST OF TABLES, SIDEBARS, FIGURES, AND PHOTOS

TABLES

SIDEBARS

FIGURES AND PHOTOS

Chapter 1: Trail Formats and Anatomy

Chapter 2: Planning a Trail Project

Chapter 4: Trail Layout and Design

Chapter 6: Safety, Preparation, and Tools

Chapter 7: Building Materials for Trail Construction

Chapter 8: Trail Construction and Maintenance

Chapter 9: Bridges

Chapter 10: Ski Trails

Chapter 11: Kiosks and User Education

Chapter 12: Accessibility and Universal Design Trails

INDEX

➔ N

➔ O

➔ P

➔ R

➔ S

➔ T

➔ U

➔ V

➔ W

ABOUT THE AUTHOR

Ryan Harvey is a licensed professional forester, land manager, and trails consultant. He has held various backcountry stewardship positions in the White Mountains, Adirondacks, and Berkshires, including nine years serving in the Pemigewasset district of the White Mountain National Forest. Now working as a forester, he oversees land management of both private and public lands. As a trail consultant, he continues to work with New Hampshire towns and residents to build and maintain recreational trails.

AMC BOOK UPDATES

AMC Books strives to keep our guidebooks as up-to-date as possible to help you plan safe and enjoyable adventures. If we learn after publishing a book that relevant trails have been relocated or route or contact information has changed, we will post the updated information online. Before you hit the trail, visit outdoors.org/books-maps and click the "Book Updates" tab.

While hiking, if you notice discrepancies with the trip descriptions or maps, or if you find any other errors in this book, please let us know by submitting them to amcbookupdates@outdoors.org or to Books Editor, c/o AMC, 10 City Square, Boston, MA 02129. We will verify all submissions and post key updates each month.

AMC Books is dedicated to being a recognized leader in outdoor publishing. Thank you for your participation.